VOICES ONE
FORGIVENESS

FORGIVENESS

Ireland's Best Contemporary Short Stories.

Edited by Augustine Martin

VOICES ONE

Four Walls Eight Windows, New York

First U.S. edition published by:
Four Walls Eight Windows
PO Box 548
Village Station
New York, N.Y. 10014

Published in association with Ryan Publishing Co. Ltd.

First printing November 1989.

Library of Congress Cataloging-in-Publication Data:

1. Short Stories, English - Irish authors.
2. English fiction - 20th century.
3. Ireland - Fiction. I. Martin, Augustine.

PR8876.F67 1989   823'.01089415'09045   CIP
89-17014

ISBN: 0-941423-32-8 (cloth)
ISBN: 0-941423-33-6 (paper)

For Sandra
Faith is everything

For Kevin
I have faith in you
Maj · Christmas · 90

Contents

Introduction

The Irish short story, approaching its hundredth birthday just now, has lost none of its valiancy. Even more than the novel, the play or the poem the short story has hacked at the quarry-face of Irish social and political conditions and produced its masterpieces: some appearing to take the shape that nature had given them in the earth, others smooth with the polish of both conscious and self-conscious artistry. The founder of the Irish short story was, of course, George Moore whose 'Untilled Field' appeared in 1903 when Joyce was beginning to write the 'epicleti' which went to make up 'Dubliners' (1914), the second great landmark in the genre. These two books, one based on rural the other on urban Irish reality, contain the seeds of this 'modest form' as it developed through newspaper and journal publication, collection and anthology, down to the urgently contemporary body of fiction we introduce between these covers. Like the early work of Moore and Joyce many of a these stories appeared first in Irish newspapers - 'The Irish Press', 'The Irish Times' and 'The Sunday Tribune' - some of them as recently as 1988. They are faithful to their ancestry both in technical innovation, and their uncompromising engagement with the realities of life as it is lived in contemporary Ireland.

'The Untilled Field' had the most selfconscious of origins. Moore, having brought to English fiction, in 'Esther Waters', the realism of Zola and the French, came to Dublin to help found a theatre in 1899, and remained to write the history of that adventure in 'Hail and Farewell' twelve years later. The Irish language movement was in full spate, so Moore was invited to write a series of short stories which might be translated into Irish and published in a Jesuit magazine called 'The New Ireland Review'. Remembering his Russian friend, Turgenev, from his Paris days Moore found himself composing what amounted to 'a portrait of my people' along the lines of 'A Sportsman's Sketchbook'. Moore, like the great Russian, was a landlord at a time when the old order was changing in both their countries. He was therefore closely attuned to the rural scene, the tensions in the social structure.

His short story was the instrument with which to lay bare the sociological realities he observed; his themes and settings proved central and recurrent in a literary tradition he helped to found.

A glance at these themes and at the titles in the present volume proves either the power of a writing tradition or the persistence of certain human issues on this island, or both: emigration, sexual hunger, rural depopulation and poverty, religious anxiety, the tyranny of routine, political compromise, as well as the universal concerns of greed, power, loneliness, social injustice -

The holiness of monks and after
Porter-drinker's randy laughter'.

Joyce whose first efforts were published in George Russell's paper, 'The Irish Homestead' (1904), completes the thematic picture with his haunting, damp vistas of city streets and garrulous pubs, while bringing into play a new range of technique to reveal the inner reality of Dublin's quotidian life. Joyce's skill with interior reverie, the ventriloquial precision of his dialogue, the suggestiveness of his symbolic devices, his vivid feeling for scene and atmosphere, his subtle exposure of a city's 'moral' paralysis' - caught at a time when Yeats was declaring Romantic Ireland dead and gone - made the short story a magnetic challenge for the writers who followed him. What vehicle of comparable length could embody at once the beauty of poise of a lyric poem and the force of a social diatribe?

James Stephens, whose first volume 'Here Are Ladies' (1913) forms part of the tradition, learned from the example of Oscar Wilde that a story did not require a murder or a philosophy to justify it. It was a blessing that these first seminal Irish collections were so free from the violent action or the old mechanical sense of plot that had marked the collections of 'tales' which had preceded the short story in the nineteenth century, or later in such writers as O. Henry. As a result this modest form could become the perfect vehicle for private experience, for what Thoreau called the life of 'quiet desperation' and John Montague called the 'drama of non-event'. In time Frank O'Connor was to declare this quality the hallmark of the modern short story - its ability to register the experience of 'lonely men', of those 'submerged population groups' whose life-pattern found no expression in the larger mimetic forms, the novel and the play. Seumas O'Kelly's study in origins, 'The Weaver's Grave', and Stephen's unadorned narrative of survival in 'Hunger' are monuments to that aesthetic proposition.

This exploration of the unremarkable lasted down to Daniel Corkey's collection, 'A Munster Twilight' (1916) only to be shattered with that gunfire that has been a sporadic concomitant of Irish literature ever since. Corkery devoted a full volume, 'The Hounds of Banba' 1920, to the War of Independence; and it's tragic violence formed, together with that of the Civil War, a major theme in the work of a new generation - Liam O'Flaherty, Frank O'Connor and Sean O'Faolain. In O'Flaherty's 'The Mountain Tavern', O'Connor's 'Guest of the Nation' and O'Faolain's 'Midsummer Night Madness' the myths and fantasies of the armed struggle were analysed in the dreary daylight of the new state. The witness of Yeats again informs the mood of the Twenties and Thirties:

We have fed the heart of fantasies;
The heart's grown brutal with the fare;
More substance in our enmities than in our love.

The irony and occasional bitterness that tinged their account of the new social realities, the sanctimony, obscurantism and caution that governed daily life in the cities and the provinces, are well summarised in the last line of Thomas Kinsella's great poem, 'Night Walker' in which he images the new Ireland as the 'Sea of Disappointment'.

It was Mary Lavin more than anyone, with her quiet vigilance at the centre of the ordinary, who restored the contemplative tone of Joyce to the short story. Her studies of human emotion, often thwarted by the exigencies of provincial life, recalled the story to its humbler, more domestic, responsibilities. With a unique, unfussed perceptiveness she recorded forever the humdrum, insular, complacent Ireland of the Thirties and the war years when life seemed in permanent, impoverished quarantine. A similar mood, more mordant and at the same time more romantic , found its urban expression in James Plunkett's volume, 'The Trusting and the Maimed' (1955). Thus a period of similar economic recession and low national morale conspired to produce a social vision as bleak as Joyce's but with the nerviness and impatience of a generation aware that it must have the solutions, however obscurely, in its own hands. A similar tenseness, begotten of a similar mood and situation, informs the stories of Hugo Hamilton and Dermot Bolger in the present volume. Yet the endemic loneliness that the short story seems eternally drawn to takes forms so personal in stories like, Leland Bardwell's 'The Hairdresser' and Linda Anderson's 'To Live or Die' that any dream of societal reform or political revolution appears not only remote but irrelevant. A body of stories that tingle with so many unanswered questions may therefore witness to a literature in a reasonable state of health.

The present publication, which we hope will be a biennial event concentrates chiefly on what is new and significant in the form, keeping a modest representation of more senior living writers so that a sense of tradition and continuity is kept alive. Thus Bryan MacMahon's evocation of archaic Irish custom and ritual, 'The Good Dead in the Green Hill's' provides a stately backdrop to all the varied activity that composes and discomposes the more recent scene. Sam McAughtry, a comparative newcomer to the short story, in his vivid historical genre piece, 'The Passing of Billy Condit', sets the scene for the sense of conflict that underlies, implicitly, the present condition of Ireland. The political unrest and guerilla action that had formed the thew and sinew of the early fictions of O'Connor and O'Faolain pulse uneasily beneath the droll comedy of Benedict Kiely's 'Bluebell Meadow'; the domestic realism of Terence de Vere White's 'Someone's Coming'; the meditation on love, history, obsession, Anglo-Irish relations, in the mind of the old Canon in 'Autumn Sunshine'.

It is probable that Moore's programme of building through a volume of stories 'a portrait of my people' is now impossible. Ireland no longer sits still to be painted. Its social inequalities may not be as desperate as before but the nature of modern society with its instant communications makes them more dramatic and visible. Dermot Bolger's urban derelict and rural tinker seem hardly to inhabit the same cosmos, let alone the same small nation state, as the comfortable sophisticates of Val Mulkern's 'Memory and Desire'. Present day Ireland must be one of the most uneasy and restless of modern societies. The violence and anguish of the conflict in Northern Ireland, terrible in itself, acts also as a daily symbol of divisions, social, religious material in the body politic of the Republic. That uneasiness is all over these stories, never directly stated, but present by implication and allusion. While poets seem capable of confronting the violence directly - notwithstanding Seamus Heaney's wry admonition 'whatever you say, say nothin' - the short story writers tend to release it in disturbing hints and sidelong epiphanies.

Ireland has the largest young population in western Europe and one of the most educated anywhere. Unemployment just now would be causing a violent revolution at home were it not for wholesale emigration. A great number of these young emigrants simply find the country too small for their ambitions. These exiles share the boats and planes with the poor of the urban ghettoes and the peasant west. The twain seldom meet at home or abroad - America where illegal entry makes strange bed-fellows may be an exception - but are always fiercely aware of each other. Dublin, famous in song and story for its drink and conversation, is now as corrupt and sophisticated as any other capital city, with a large delinquent population, ravaged by drugs and aids and the criminality that inevitably follows them.

It is at the same time acquiring a world reputation as a centre of pop culture with a burgeoning export trade in recording - U2, Chris de Burgh and the Hothouse Flowers sharing studios with The Chieftains, the Dubliners and the Pogues. Literary critics have joined historians and philosophers - with the usual corps of gurus without portfolio - in a search for national identity. The vast challenges of a single Europe in 1992 encounter from one faction the acid criterion: 'will we at last be able to buy a car at a reasonable price?' by another as if Yeats' Rough Beast of prophesy had been sighted in the Bog of Allen. The worst lack all conviction while the best are full of passionate intensity. On the curious economic see-saw factories close down weekly in the cities and provincial towns while others - 'more suitable to the climate of an open Europe market' - open up. There is relentless media recrimination and soul-searching. Everyone is talking and no-one is listening: we apprehend an anger in the words but not the words.

Two guarantors of the traditional Ireland seem to be on the slide - the Irish Language - flagship of traditional nationalism - and the Catholic Church. In the North the bishops raise their voices in vain against the violence, in the South they have taken up the role of the political Opposition on behalf of the poor, the homeless and the unemployed. In both cases the stick is equally cleft beneath them: the sectarian violence in the North is laid at their door while in the South their intransigence on birth control is blamed for the unmanageable young population.

The same younger generation - apart, of course, from the yuppies on their gleeful way to the bank - tends to view traditional patriotism and religion with indifference if not hostility. An eloquent symbol of this ironic climate is a theatre group called THE PASSION MACHINE functioning in a north city Jesuit premises, the St Francis Xavier Hall, who produce raunchy, scatological plays of low Dublin life which then transfer to the Olympia Theatre where they draw gales of laughter from the clergy and middle classes whose ethos they persistently scarify. Censorship, on which the writer could focus his anger in the past, no longer exists as an issue. While the zealots raged in New York and Athens at the showing of Scorsese's 'Temptation of Christ' it was shown uncut in Dublin and closed in a week. The old order changes and the new, as yet, has no discernible shape. That interim, as I hope this book shows, provides a perfect opportunity for the writer of short stories.

Augustine Martin
Dublin, 1989

The Last Of The Mohicans

Joseph O'Connor

It was about three years since I'd seen him. And here he was, sweating behind the burger bar in Euston Station, a vision in polyester and fluorescent light. Jesus Christ. So Marion was right that time. Eddie Virago, selling double cheeseburgers for a living. I spluttered his name as he smiled in puzzled recognition over the counter. Mr God, Eddie Virago. In the pub he kept saying it was great to see me. Really wild he said. I should have let him know I was coming to London. This was just unreal.

Eddie was the kind of guy I tried to hang around with in college. Suave, cynical, dressed like a Sunday supplement. He'd arrive deliberately late for lectures and swan into Theatre L, permanent pout on his lips. He sat beside me one day in the first week and asked me for a light. Then he asked me for a cigarette. From then on we were friends. After pre-revolutionary France we'd sit on the middle floor of the canteen sipping coffee and avoiding Alice the tea-trolley lady. "Where did you get that tray?" she'd whine, "no trays upstairs." And Eddie would interrupt his monologue on the role of German expressionism in the development of film noir to remove his feet from the perilous path of her brush. "Alice's Restaurant" he called it. I didn't know what he was talking about but I laughed anyway.

He was pretty smart our Eddie. He was a good looking bastard too. I never realised it at first, but gradually I noticed all the girls in the class wanted to get to know me. Should have known it wasn't really me they were interested in, "Who's your friend?" they'd simper, giggling like crazy. The rugby girls really liked him. You know the type. The ones who sit in the corridors calculating the cost of the lecturers' suits. All school scarves, dinner dances and summers in New York without a visa - more exciting that way. Eddie hated them all. He resisted every coy advance, every uncomfortable botched flirtation. They were bloody convent-school girls. All talk and no action. He said there was just one thing they needed and they weren't going to get it from him.

Professor Gough liked making risque jokes about the nocturnal activities of Napoleon and everyone in the class was shocked. Everyone except Eddie. He'd laugh out loud and drag on his cigarette and laugh again while everybody blushed and stared at him. He said that was the trouble with Ireland. He said we were all hung-up about sex. It was unhealthy. It was no wonder the mental homes were brimming over.

Eddie had lost his virginity at the age of fourteen, in a thatched cottage in Kerry. Next morning, he'd shaved with a real razor for the first time and he'd felt like a real man. As the sun dawned on his manhood he had flung his scabby old electric in the Atlantic. Then himself and his nineteen year old deflowerer ('deflorist' he called her), had strolled down the beach talking about poetry. She'd written to him from France a few times, but he'd never answered. It didn't do to get too involved. The entire Western Civilisation was hung-up on possession Eddie said. People had to live their own lives and get away from guilt-trips.

We were close, Eddie and me. I bought him drinks and cigarettes and he let me stay in his place when I got kicked out that time. His parents gave him the money to live in a flat in Donnybrook. He called them his 'old dears'. I went home after a while but I never forgot my two weeks on the southside with Eddie. We stayed up late looking at films and listening to The Doors and The Jesus and Mary Chain and talking about sex. Eddie liked to talk about sex a lot. He said I didn't know what was ahead of me. He was amazed that I hadn't done it. Absolutely amazed. He envied me actually, because if he had it all to do over again the first time was definitely the best. But that was Catholic Ireland. We were all repressed, and we had to escape. James Joyce was right. Snot green sea, what a line. It wasn't the same in India he said. Sex was divine to them. They had their priorities right.

Eddie went away that summer, to Germany, and he came back with a gaggle of new friends. They were all in Trinity, and they'd worked in the same gherkin factory as him. They were big into drugs and funny haircuts and Ford Fiestas. Eddie had the back and sides of his head shaved and he let his fringe grow down over his eyes and he dyed it. Alice the tea trolley lady would cackle at him in the canteen. "Would you look?" she'd scoff. "The last of the Mohicans." Everyone laughed but Eddie didn't care. He didn't even blush. He rubbed glue and toothpaste into his quiff to make it stand up, and even in the middle of the most crowded room you could always tell where Eddie was. His orange hair bobbed on a sea of short back and sides.

He went to parties in his new friends' houses, and they all slept with each other. No strings attached. No questions asked. He brought me to one of them once, in a big house in Dalkey. Lots of glass everywhere, that's all I remember. Lots of glass. And paintings on the walls, by Louis Le Brocquy and that other guy who's always painting his penis. You know the one. That was where I met Marion. She was in the kitchen searching the fridge while two philosophy students groped under the table. She didn't like these parties much. We sat in the garden eating cheese sandwiches and drinking beer. Eddie stumbled out and asked me if I wanted a joint. I said no, I wasn't in the mood. Marion got up to leave, with some bloke in a purple shirt who was muttering about deconstruction. Eddie said he wouldn't know the meaning of the word.

We bumped into her again at a gig in The Underground one Sunday night. It turned out the deconstructionist was her brother and he was in the band. When she asked me what I thought I said they were pretty interesting. She thought they were terrible. I bought her a drink and she asked me back to her place in Rathmines. In the Jacks I whispered to Eddie that I didn't want him tagging along. He said he got the picture. Standing on the corner of Stephen's Green he winked at us and said "Goodnight young lovers, and if you can't be good be careful."

It wasn't at all like Eddie said it would be. Afterwards I laughed when she asked me had it been my first time. Was she kidding? I'd lost it in a cottage in Kerry when I was fourteen. She smiled and said yes, she'd only been kidding. All night long I tossed and turned in her single bed listening to the police cars outside. I couldn't wait to tell Eddie about it.

We went for breakfast in Bewleys the next morning. Me and Marion I mean. She looked different without make up. I felt embarrassed as she walked around the flat in tights and underwear. It was months later that I admitted I'd been lying about my sexual experience. She laughed and said she'd known all along. She said I paid too much attention to Eddie. That was our first row. She said that for someone who wasn't hung-up he sure talked a lot of bullshit about it.

At first Eddie was alright about Marion and me. I told him we had done it and he clapped me on the back and asked me how it was. I said I knew what he'd been talking about. It had been unreal. He nodded wisely and asked me something about positions. I said I had to go to a lecture.

But as I started spending more time with Marion he got more sarcastic. He started asking me how was the little woman, and what was it like to be happily married. He got a big kick out of it and it made me squirm. He'd introduce me to another one of the endless friends. "This is Johnny" he'd say, "he's strictly monogamous." We still went for coffee after lectures, but I was more and more alone in the company of Eddie and his disciples. Marion took me to anti-amendment meetings and Eddie said I was wasting my time. He said it didn't make any difference. Irish people took their direction straight from the Catholic church. He told me we hadn't a hope. "Abortion?" he said, "Jesus Christ, we're not even ready for contraception." I tried to tell him it wasn't just about abortion but he scoffed and said he'd heard it all before.

Eddie dropped out a few months before our finals. He left a note on my locker door saying he'd had enough. He was going to London to get into film. Writing mainly, but he hoped to direct of course, in the end. London was where the action was. He was sick and tired of this place anyway. It was nothing. A glorified tax haven for rich tourists and pop stars. A cultural backwater that time forgot. He said no one who ever did anything stayed in Ireland. You had to get out to be recognised.

I was sad to see him go, specially because he couldn't even tell me to my face. But in a way it was a relief. Me and Eddie, we'd grown far apart. It wasn't that I didn't like him exactly. I just knew that secretly we embarrassed the hell out of each other. So I screwed his note into a ball and went off to the library. And as I sat staring out the window at the lake and the concrete, I tried my best to forget all about him.

Marion broke it off with me the week before the exams started. She said no hard feelings but she reckoned we'd run our course. I congratulated her on her timing. We were walking through Stephen's Green, and the children were bursting balloons and hiding behind the statues. She said she just didn't know where we were going anymore. I said I didn't know about her, but I was going to Madigan's. She said that was the kind of thing Eddie would have said, and I felt really good about that. She kissed me on the cheek, said sorry and sloped off down Grafton Street. I felt the way you do when the phone's just been slammed down on you. I thought if one of those Hare Krishnas comes near me I'll kick his bloody head in.

I got a letter from Eddie once. Just once. He said he was getting on fine, but it was taking a while to meet the right people. Still, he was glad he'd escaped 'the stifling provincialism' and he regretted nothing. He was having a wild time and there was so much to do in London. Party City. And the women! Talk about easy. I never got round to answering him. Well, I was still pretty upset about Marion for a while, and then there was all that hassle at home. I told them I'd be only too happy to get out and look for a job if there were any jobs to look for. My father said that was fine talk, and that the trouble with me was that they'd been too bloody soft on me. He'd obviously wasted his time, subsidising my idleness up in that place that was supposedly a university.

Eventually it all got too much. I moved in with Alias, into an upstairs flat on Leeson treet. My mother used to cry when I went home to do my washing on Sunday afternoons. Alias was a painter. I met him at one of Eddie's parties. The walls of the flat were plastered with paintings of naked bodies, muscles rippling, nipples like champagne corks. He said it didn't matter that they didn't look like the models. Hadn't I ever heard of imagination? I said yeah, I'd heard of it.

He was putting his portfolio together for an exhibition and living on the dole. He told everyone he had an Arts Council grant. He was alright, but he didn't have the depth of Eddie and he was a bit of a slob. He piled up his dirty clothes on the middle of his bedroom floor and he kept his empty wine bottles in the wardrobe. And the bathroom. And the kitchen. I got a job eventually, selling rubbish bags over the phone. There are thirty-seven different sizes of domestic and industrial plastic refuse sack. I bet you didn't know that! I had to ring up factories and offices and ask them if they wanted to reorder. They never seemed to want to. I wondered what they did with all their rubbish. "Shredders" said Mr Smart. "The shredders will be my undoing." It was always hard to get the right person on the line. Mr Smart said not to fool around with secretaries, go straight for the decision-makers. They always seemed to be tied up though. The pay was nearly all commission too, so I never had much cash to spare. The day I handed in my notice Mr Smart said he was disappointed in me. He thought I would have had a bit more tenacity. I told him to shag off. I said sixty-five pence basic per hour didn't buy much in the way of tenacity. "Or courtesy either" he said, tearing up my reference.

That afternoon I ran into Marion on O'Connell Bridge. We went for coffee in a small place in Abbey Street and had a bit of a laugh. I told her about chucking the job and she said I was dead right. She told me a secret. It wasn't confirmed yet, but fingers crossed. She was going off to Ethiopia. She was sick of just talking, she wanted to do something about the world. If Bob Geldof could do it, why couldn't she? I said that was great and maybe I'd do the same. Then she asked me all about Alias and the new flat and we talked about the old days. It seemed so long ago. I had almost forgotten what she looked like. She said her friend Mo had just written a postcard from London. She'd seen a guy who looked just like Eddie Virago in a burger joint in Euston Station. Except he had a short back and sides. I laughed out loud. Eddie selling hamburgers for a living? Someone of his talent? That would be the day. She said it was nice to get postcards all the same. She showed it to me. It had a guy on it with a red mohican haircut. Mo said she'd bought that one because it reminded her of how Eddie used to look in the old days. She said she'd always fancied him. Marion said that she'd send me a card from Ethiopia, if they had them. She never did.

In the pub Eddie and I didn't have much to say, except that it was great to see each other. When I told him the postcard story he said it all went to prove you couldn't trust anyone and he sipped meaningfully at his pint. After closing time we got the tube up to the West End, to a disco Eddie knew in Soho. Drunks lolled around the platforms singing and crying. The club was a tiny place, with sweat running down the walls. Eddie asked the black bouncer if Eugene was in tonight. "Who?" said the bouncer, "You know Eugene, the other doorman?" He shrugged and said "Not tonight man. I dunno no Eugene". I paid Eddie in, because it wasn't his pay day till Thursday. He was really sorry about that.

Downstairs he had to lean across the table, shaking the drinks, to shout in my ear. The writing was going alright. Of course it was all contacts, all a closed shop, but he was still trying though. In fact he'd just finished a script and although he wasn't free to reveal the details he didn't mind telling me there was quite a bit of interest in it. He only hoped it wasn't too adventurous. Thatcher had the BBC by the short and curlies, he said. They wouldn't take any risks at all. And Channel 4 wasn't the same since Isaacs left. Bloody shame that, man of his creative flair.

He'd made lots of friends though, in the business. I'd probably meet them later. They only went out clubbing late at night. Nocturnal animals he said. It was more cool to do that. They were great people, really wild. Honestly, from Neil Jordan downward the business was wonderful. Of course he'd met

Jordan. He crashed at his place once after a particularly wild party. Really decent bloke. There was a good scene in London. No he didn't listen to the old bands any more. He was all into Acid House. He said that was this year's thing. Forget The Clash. Guitar groups were out. The word was acid. I said I hadn't heard any and what was it like? He said he couldn't describe it really. It wasn't the kind of music you could put into words.

I did meet one of his friends later on in the night. He saw her standing across the dance floor and beckoned her over. She mus'n't have seen him. So he said he'd be back in a second and weaved through the gyrating bodies to where she was. They chatted for a few minutes and then she came over and sat down. Shirley was a model. From Dublin too. Well, trying to make it as a model. She knew Bono really well. He was a great bloke she said, really dead on. She'd known him and Ali for absolute yonks, and success hadn't changed them at all. Course she hadn't seen him since Wembley last year. Backstage. They were working on the new album apparently. She'd heard the rough mixes and it was a real scorcher. This friend of hers played them to her. A really good friend of hers actually, who went out with your man from The Hot House Flowers. The one with the hair. She kept forgetting his name. She said she was no good at all for Irish names. She really regretted it, specially since she moved over here, but she couldn't speak a word of Irish. She let us buy her a drink each. I paid for Eddie's. Then she had to run. Early start tomorrow, had to be in the studio by eight thirty. "Ciao" she said when she went. "Ciao Eddie."

It was after four when they kicked us out. The streets of Soho were jostling with minicabs and hot-dog sellers. A crowd filtered out of Ronnie Scott's Club, just around the corner. Sleek black women in furs and lace. Tall men in sharp suits. Eddie apologised for his friends not showing up. He said if he'd known I was coming he would have arranged a really wild session. Next time. He knew a really happening hip-hop club up in Camden Town, totally wild, but in a very cool kind of way.

In the coffee bar in Leicester Square he was quiet. The old career hadn't been going exactly to plan. He was getting there all right. But much slower than he thought. Still, that was the business. Things got a bit lonely he said. He got so frustrated, so down. It was hard being an exile. He didn't want to be pretentious or anything but he knew how Sam Beckett must have felt. If he didn't believe in himself as much as he did, he didn't know how he could go on. He would have invited me back to his place only a few people were crashing there so there wasn't the room. But next time, honest. It was a big place. But still, it was always full. People were always just dropping in unannounced. "You know how it is" he laughed. I ordered two more cappuccinos.

"I have measured out my life in coffee spoons" he said, and he sipped painfully. He always drank Nicaraguan actually, at home. Very into the cause. I said I knew nothing about it. He started to tell me all the facts but I said I really had to go. My aunt would be worried sick about me. If I didn't get home soon she'd call the police or something. He nodded and said fair enough. He had to split as well.

We stood in the rain on Charing Cross Road while he scribbled his address on a soggy beermat. He told me it was good to see me again. I told him I nearly didn't recognise him with the new haircut. Oh that, he'd had to get rid of that, for work. Anyway punk was dead. It was all history now. "You should come over here for good", he said, "It's a great city." I shook his hand and said I'd think about it. He told me not to let the opportunity pass me by.

The taxi driver asked me where I wanted to go. He loved Ireland. The wife was half Irish and they'd been over a few times now. Lovely country. Terrible what was going on over there though. He said they were bloody savages, bloody cowboys and Indians. No offence, but he just couldn't understand it. I said I couldn't either. In his opinion it was all to do with religion.

By the time we got to Greenwich the sun was painting the sky over the river. He said he hoped I enjoyed the rest of my holiday. I hadn't any money left to give him a tip.

Disappearance

Mary Costello

Last night I burned the crow in the back garden. Its ugly black feathers singed and smelled as the flames sucked deeper into its flesh until the bones started to crackle. I knew I was doing the right thing; I had to burn away the past two months.

It was the last day of May. We parked the car at a clearing near the forest. I had driven so I pocketed the keys - a strange irony which seemed to hint at my guilt later on. We had come from a Greek restaurant in the city. Mrs Thorpe was minding Jessie that evening so we walked at our ease where we could have the finest view of the city. This was a mountain we had returned to again and again and, in the late summer evening with the pink streaks of setting sun stretched across the horizon, it had an ethereal feel, a feeling of being suspended high above; we were alone except for the courting couples in cars below. The wide path was flanked by evergreens for most of the walk to the summit. Here the trees gave way to an impressive view of the city - the sprawling metropolis lay under a greyish haze by this time.

We walked in silence and I believed we were perfectly at one, in complete harmony with each other - 'bonded' I called it. We didn't have to speak, our mutual oneness transcended all words. Words would have spoiled the landscape of our bond, would have intruded upon that perfect unity which was us. We reached the summit and stopped. John stood at my back and rested his chin on my head. For a moment I felt incredibly light, unbearably flimsy, so totally unimportant in the general scheme of things. There are times when one feels so insignificant, one's existence so minute that only the routine of domestic chores will have any true meaning. One magnifies these chores until they alone are the importance, they alone hold our lives together.

I didn't feel John move away from me. It was only when the chill of the evening brushed against my bare arms that I turned and saw him wander off towards the rocks. The path continued past the summit over to these rocks which looked like dolmens and then round a bend where it descended gradually down the other side of the mountain. The summit was fine for me. Below me the lighting city glowed.

Sometime later I glanced towards the rocks. It was dusk and I could not be sure if the jagged shapes moved or not. John was probably climbing them. I turned and walked swiftly towards them, squinting in the poor evening light. He must have walked further on. I hurried, my feet stumbling on the jagged path. The rocks were bare and I rounded the bend. The path sloped downwards and round another bend in the distance where the forest resumed. He was not there. I turned around looking towards the summit. I think I saw him there then, smiling, laughing at his joke, his high forehead creased with lines. I walked back up and it was almost dark now. I called his name but the shrillness of my own voice frightened me and the silence of the mountain unnerved me. There was a deadening deafening finality about that silence. I waited for an hour and then my own presence frightened me.

I drove down the mountain side and the car skirted close to the verge sweeping great blades of grass with it. My descent had a fantastical sense of unreality about it. The past came to me in broken images: the night we drove from Sligo as a violent hurricane began and the roadside trees and bushes swayed dangerously. The Sunday he had gone swimming in Dun Laoghaire and seaweed had trapped his legs until he had panicked. And there was the dream he had had before Jessie's birth. He dreamt this dream so vividly and so intensely, that I had had difficulty in calming him when he awoke. He had come in from work one evening and, as usual, had called my name in the hall. I had a mischievous habit of not answering his calls and letting him find me. He searched throughout the house continuously calling. In the bathroom my arm protruded from beneath the white shower curtain. He found me dead and cold and naked, crumpled up at the bottom of the shower, my head leaning against the wall, my eyes wide open, glassy, staring at him when he drew open the curtain. He had screamed and screamed when he awoke. Now that dream screamed vividly at me as I careered down the mountainside.

The orange-pink streaks of sun had stretched and faded into the darkening sky and now, even inside the car was chill. I drove faster and faster, swerving widely around bends. I pictured John's face again at the summit, laughing at his own joke. Then I remembered another man, Ian, whom I had loved once.

He was unbearably like me, but stronger and I had loved him intensely, believing no other mind but his could ever be joined to mine. Just months after the break, I could barely reconstruct his face - I had to try hard to remember the colour of his eyes, though I liked to believe they were hazel. I had tried often to recollect the shape of his face, the line of his jaw, but I had found it impossible. How could two people so intensely bound together ever forget the minisculest detail of each other?

Perhaps I had tried too hard. I wondered for how long I would remember John's face.

I was descending faster now, possessing no sense of danger, only of movement and the chill of the night. A stream of cold air moved up and through me, a great chilling tunnel cut through my upper body, piercing its way deeper and faster as I descended, creating a hollow, a widening hole in my heart until something prompted me, and I knew I must stop or this torrential flow of night would erode my flesh through to the bone. At the base of the mountain I pulled over and shook.

My mother came to stay with Jessie and me. It was a kind gesture, but unhelpful. I think that even she held me responsible but I can never tell. She, and the police and the neighbours.

They all regarded me warily and no-one would meet my eye. I gave up telling them what had happened. How does one explain that a perfectly normal man disappears off the face of the earth? What difference did it make, so few people missed him? He was just one speck of mankind. It was nothing really in the general order of things, a tiny soul lost on the mountainside.

They found his handkerchief by one of the dolmen rocks, a white linen one with the letter J embroidered on it. My mother had bought him three, boxed, in the big Brown Thomas' sale in January. He took a freshly laundered handkerchief each morning.

I would sit and wonder what had happened to him - for the first two weeks I wondered all the time. And I thought about him so hard that I willed him back into existence, and he sat with me at our kitchen table and he threw back his head and laughed his warm sensual laugh, his fine white teeth showing. And I heard his key in the door as he came home from work each evening, and once, when I was hanging clothes out on the clothes line, I saw him stand at our bedroom window. He raised his hand to wave and I smiled. I knew then that we were irrevocably bonded and that I would never forget his face, his jawbone, his eyes. He was me too.

In July I was not so content anymore. I worked late at my play and Mrs Thorpe sat with Jessie. She was a round cheerful woman who loved Jessie but she would leave when I got home. I longed to ask her to stay, I hated the stillness of the house after the bustle of the theatre but she would always have her coat on, and I didn't have the heart to delay her. Worse still, the play was nearing the end of its run and soon there would be nothing for me but to stay home all the time. It must have been about then that I heard the purring that sounded like breathing. I had thought that it was Jessie sleeping loudly and I had rushed to check on her. Back in the kitchen I strained my ears. It was a low sound, it would subside then increase gently, like the breathing of someone sleeping. I tried to wake Jessie for reassurance but she cried.

The weather became hot and sour. My play ended. The garden overflowed with growth and Jessie cried a lot. Tiny pink blotches had broken out through her skin and she scratched at them. Every night I was awoken by her cries. I would soothe her in my arms and lift her back into her cot again. But I did not sleep. The breathing persisted, yet it did not wake Jessie. I would get up and it would seem fainter. I knew then that I magnified it in my sleep. The doctor came to see Jessie and he frowned over her pink puffy skin. She kicked her legs and flayed about, scratching frantically while he touched her.

"It's an unusual strain of diptheria - very uncomfortable. Try and stop her scratching," he said and he gave me a bottle of yellow liquid. That night I woke up sweating and heard Jessie cry. I went to her, her tiny body writhed in pain. I longed to hold her to my breast and let both of us rest in the others presence. But I had weaned her some months before John's disappearance and I knew my body was dry, dry and parched of all its moisture. We did not reassure one another. She kicked and scratched furiously, drawing blood from her tender skin, writhing about like one possessed. I fetched the lotion and rolled it over her tiny impossible body. Its sulphuric stench filled the room mingling with the humid July air. I felt ill, weak, unbearably vulnerable to my own child. She screamed as the lotion burned into the itch. Her throaty cries filled the room, the house, me. I stood over her cradle and watched her. I could tie up her hands and legs to stop her scratching.

Soon the cries ceased and her body stilled. I felt old then, and my body too leaden to drag to bed. I slept upright on a chair that night.

One hazy day in mid-July I stole into my bedroom where Jessie slept. John had been gone for nearly two months and my efforts to forget him or to continue without him were not succeeding. There was a dreariness within me. My body was changing too. I knew that it could be a reaction to the intense heat and my troubled mind, or its way of adjusting to loss. There was a third possibility and I would hug myself with hope at the thought, a hope too flimsy to mean anything yet.

I lay on the bed staring at a square of sky through the open window. A dull peace drifted about me and the faint sound of the breathing below floated up to me. A pale shaft of sunlight fell on the wall above my head. I could have drifted to sleep then but something held me back, a slight fear that was unidentifiable

- maybe an unease about sleeping in this intense heat in the middle of the afternoon. I was aware too of Jessie in her cradle, afraid that even my near-silent sleep would disturb her own tentative slumber.

Some flies buzzed about a corner of the room. Somewhere in the distance a dog barked. It was the shrill whine of a troublesome pup. It stopped and I drifted half waking, half sleeping, facing the open window.

Suddenly and violently I was disturbed by the hideous cry of a crow as it hovered by my window. Startled, I bolted up. It was large and black and ugly peering in at my private sleep, cawing out its vulgar whinge. Crows frightened me, they always creep up on me and scream at me just like now. As a child I had been cornered once by a crow and I had screamed and screamed until I was hysterical. My screaming had angered the crow more and he hopped and flew at me viciously until finally someone shunted him away with a brush. Often those days I had seen a thrush or a coal-tit in my back garden. They came and fed on the overgrown berry bushes and luscious slugs of the garden, untended now since John's disappearance. Thrushes, coal-tits, even blackbirds - gracious, inoffensive little creatures with their own endearing little tunes. Yet when I am vulnerable a hideous crow assaults my mind.

Jessie stirred and when I lifted her to me and turned towards the window the crow had gone. The stillness of the afternoon returned and resided. Flies flew about Jessie, attracted by the scent of her lotion. I thought Jessie was crying with weariness sometimes and once I heard her sigh.

I escaped into the evening pushing Jessie in her car and we walked towards the canal. Once out in the living city all would be well. But the rhythm of the traffic and the screams of brakes became as unbearable as the stillness of the house. We returned, walking quickly past the people on the footpaths, I keeping my head down for each time I looked up at the passers-by all the faces were the same. The pale puny features of a girl with reddish hair were superimposed on all the people - on a man in a white boiler suit, on children on skate boards, on an old lady walking a dog. I walked quicker, pushing Jessie. I was worried and sick and defeated.

For how long can one hover on the verge of sanity? Eventually some deity or devil will assert its presence and will push the victim over to one side or the other. My deity came to me one night in the kitchen when I discovered the source of the breathing sound that had haunted me. Jessie sat in her high chair bruising orange segments into her pink mouth. I watched her from across the table, half aware as usual of the background sound. Jessie tilted her head back and laughed at me. Suddenly the sound stopped. I strained my ears. "Shhh," I said to Jessie. I held my breath.

I glanced at the kitchen cupboards. It had stopped. Jessie banged her spoon begging my attention. I scooped her out of her chair. I knew then that it was something in my own kitchen which could be explained logically. I tested the fridge and the cooker, switching the power on and off. Then I stood before the extractor fan. John had installed it before he left - I never think of John as dead. He left us. There was no power now.

Too anxious to be excited I lifted the protective covering and there a pipe had become undone. I secured the pipe into its fitting and, quietly and as suddenly as it had ceased, the breathing sound resumed. I tested it again making sure, always making sure. The suction of air to a vent in the outer wall had caused the rising and falling drone which I had mistaken for breathing. In those few moments much of the tension of the previous two months dissipated. For a brief moment I hesitated.

Finally, triumphantly, I secured the pipe into its fitting.

The sound resumed now but it was welcome, safe. In some strange illogical way it was John's presence still with me. For the first night in weeks Jessie slept through.

Yesterday a slight wind rose, the first wind of this hot summer. I arose early and opened all the windows of the house.

The soft morning breeze lifted the lace curtains lightly. I tiptoed about the house but there was no need for Jessie had slept through now for the past four of five nights. The glow of health had returned to her cheeks and her illness had cleared up as quickly as it had come to afflict her. Throughout the day the wind strengthened and gusted about lifting petals from the rose bushes and carrying some parched leaves across the garden. The hazy willowy sun dulled as the dark clouds rolled over us. By dusk the heat debris was clearing. I walked through the garden to the end where the briars from the field beyond protrude through. I moved the long grass aside, uncertain of what to seek. I found the crow then, stiff and inanimate almost hidden in the tall grass. I picked it up by one of its legs, poised to throw it over the fence when I hesitated. I returned to the house, found some newspapers and matches and set the bird alight at the end of the garden. I smelt its flesh and listened to its bones crackle for a time.

Last night it rained. This morning I had my first bout of morning sickness, my earlier hopes realised. Now the garden smells differently, scenty, musky, heavy with moisture and fertile sap. The tall lupins and the roses still hold the droplets of last nights rain in their petals. The rhododendrons are leaning now, heavy with drops too. I walk through the long grass and the wet seeds stick to my shoes. Already I can smell the sweet wet scent of mown meadow. The birds are reappearing again after last night's torrents. Jessie comes trotting down the garden calling my name and she runs to me, gurgling and babbling in her baby talk. I lift her high in my arms and slowly in the sweet wet scent of morning we walk back to the house.

Swans

Aisling Maguire

The sound of her clapping ricochetted on the flat water.

"Don't do that," said a voice from the mesh of sedge and reeds.

She moved forward detaching herself from the shelter of the trees. A boy, sheathed in blue oilskins lay on his stomach at the lip of the inlet, a pair of binoculars propped in his hand. As Kathleen approached he curled into a kneeling position.

"They're making a nest, you'll frighten them," he explained.

"I just wanted to see them again. They disappeared as soon as I got here."

"Well, you have to be patient."

Kathleen stepped back a few paces onto the hard ground, turned her collar against the slow drifts of rain and dug her hands into her pockets. She was prepared to wait, as much, stupidly, to show the boy, that she could be patient, as to watch the swans re-emerge from the bulrushes.

When they did appear the sight of their dark flippers, paddling the drown water started an involuntary shiver in her. The pair slid along the narrow channel of the inlet, tracing a wide double chevron on the surface of the water. As she watched, the undeviating attenuation of those lines seemed to lure away the complex anger which had rankled her for months.

"They won't be back this evening," said the boy.

"Might as well go home then." She turned back into the field that lay between the estuary and the road. The boy fell into step beside her.

"Land mines." He pointed to the cow pats scattered like a fungus infecting the grass and thistles. Kathleen laughed. "There's enough of them anyway." He looked down at her khaki green wellington boots still emblazoned with the lozenge-shaped white label.

"Are you the new teacher?" he asked.

"That's right."

"Oops!" He pressed a hand to his mouth in mock embarrassment.

"Don't worry," she said. "I won't take it out on you."

Clearing two bars at a time he crossed the gate and sprang onto the road before her. She refused the hand he offered.

"Well, I'm for this path," he indicated a narrow lane that cleaved the facing hill.

"All right. I may see you in the school tomorrow."

"Yes," he nodded "they'll be back tomorrow evening." He jerked his head in the direction of the estuary. "Same bat-time, same bat-place."

"Good," Kathleen smiled. "I might come down again." She started towards the huddled buildings of the village.

"Good night, Miss." The boy called after her. She waved and continued into the declining sun, whose fierce dazzle blistered the edge of the skyline.

"Do none of you smoke?" She asked as the small group of students dispersed among the desks and easels. They glanced at the corner where she stood and saw her hand gesture towards a series of anti-smoking posters. One boy shrugged but the girl beside him said, "Ah yeh, I'd have the odd one."

"Which of you is Mary O'Malley?" She flicked her finger against a painting of a bus with fogged windows at the centre of which surrounded by smokers, sat a woman, her head encased in a green gas mask. In the background hung the rampant form of a mushroom cloud, and below round the caption: SMOKING DOES TO YOUR LUNGS WHAT THE ATOM BOMB DID TO HIROSHIMA.

A girl with lank brown hair replied, "I am."

"It's very good, very strong."

"Thank you."

"Do you believe it yourself?"

The girl's head drooped. One of the other girls reached over and put a hand on her shoulder. "Me da died of cancer last Christmas," Mary faltered, lifting her reddened face again.

The mood of the group solidifying around the girl afflicted Kathleen like a rebuke.

"I am sorry." That was all she could think to say and, regaining the rostrum, sifted the notes she had prepared the night before.

"Today," she began "I want you to sketch a box."

"A box?" The eyes of the small girl in front of her flared behind thick green-rimmed glasses. Kathleen nodded. "A box. Any kind of box. Just play around with the idea."

A snigger rose from the back of the room, where a tall heavy-set boy had wedged himself with an easel into a corner.

"What's your name?" Kathleen asked him.

"Tom, Miss," he replied.

"Aren't you going to share the joke, Tom?" The boy shook his head. "Ah no. It wasn't that funny."

"All right, so start on your boxes."

In the silence of her pupils concentration, Kathleen stared into the courtyard which was defined on one side by the Art Room. Coloured benches ranged against the wall and painted tractor tyres containing nests of bedding plants relieved the dull space of the tarmacadamed square. Parallel to the Art Room ran a corridor linking the main building to the prefab extension that housed the metal workshop, and formed the east side of the quadrangle. She could see the young boys, their faces shielded by masks as the blades of the metal cutters drove up shoals of bright sparks. Above their anonymous heads their master Sean Laverty waved at her. She nodded and, hearing the bell, faced her own class again. Already the kids had begun to pack their bags.., Some were even standing at the door.

"Go on," she said. "I'll see you on Thursday." Mary remained behind.

"Yes Mary?" She hesitated to meet the girl's eyes.

"I just wanted to show you, Miss White, where we put the unfinished sketches."

"That's very kind, thank you Mary."

The girl opened a cupboard under the window.

"Mrs Galvin usually leaves them in here until the next day."

"Good. I'll put them away now. I don't have another class immediately."

"O.K. See you on Thursday, Miss."

"'Bye Mary."

As soon as Mary had left the room Kathleen crossed to the opposite corner and pulled back Tom's easel. "Oh, no," she groaned. Under the heavily lettered title THE BOX he had drawn a coffin, inside which reposed the emaciated figure of a young man, arms folded over his chest, one hand clasping a revolver, the other a book. Beneath the picture in more heavy print ran the caption BOBBY SANDS R.I.P. A tremor like the touch of cold steel ran through her nerves. Without examining the other sketches she gathered them into a pile and laid them on the shelf. Dizzied, briefly, by the dark resinous air of the cupboard, she tottered as she made to stand again, seeing the room recede at uncertain angles.

"Are you alright?" Mr Laverty stooped in the doorway, his short white coat emphasising his narrow height.

"Yes. Yes. Fine." Kathleen assured him and bent to fumble shut the latch on the cupboard. "I thought you might like to come down to the staff room for a cup of coffee. I'll introduce you to the rest of the crowd."

"Thanks. I'll be right with you." She took her bag from the rostrum and joined the man at the door.

"Well, how did it go?" He asked, guiding her by the elbow through the corridor.

"All right, I think." She nodded.

"You have that Tommy Nolan in your group, don't you?"

"Tom? Yes."

"Don't give him any quarter."

She paused as they reached the staff room. "What do you

mean?"

"Just be careful. He's - " Mr Laverty's words were cut short by the ringing of the electric bell. "Blast it." He thumped his right fist into his left hand. "There goes our cuppa."

A gust of cigarette smoke cloyed with the smell of coffee and biscuits issued from the room as a short button faced woman emerged.

"We're like the poor man smelling the gravy of the rich man's dinner, Alice." Mr Laverty chafed. The woman who's orange lipstick exaggerated the line of her mouth, puckered her face and shoulders into a brief giggle.

"Have you met Miss White, Mrs Galvin's replacement?" Mr Laverty continued, and turned to Kathleen. "This is Mrs Quinn: History," he explained.

"You're welcome, I'm sure, Miss White." Shifting a bundle of copy books to the crook of her left arm, the history teacher held out her hand.

"Thank you, Kathleen is the name." She smiled as they shook hands.

Only when she had returned to the empty Art Room did Mr Laverty's incomplete warning begin to unsettle Kathleen. She would have been happier had he said nothing, for, that imprecise confidence, endorsing her own recoil, seemed to include her in an alliance of disfavour which the boy would quickly detect, when, as a stranger, she could have remained aloof, and neutral.

Along the estuary the twilight oozed in slow ripples, buoying the swans whose long necks stayed rigid as flagpoles against the mild breeze. Kathleen watched them ferry material for their nest between the bulrushes and the farther bank, and found in contemplating their remote, cool forms, the antidote to her disquietude.

"Hello." The boy's low-pitched greeting hung, disembodied, for several seconds before penetrating her thoughts. She turned to see him standing three or four paces from her, the binoculars fixed to his eyes while he adjusted their focus.

"Look," he said. "There's the nest." Dipping his head to release the leather strap, he offered her the binoculars.

As the magnification elided the expanse of water separating her from the birds, the masked eye of the male loomed in ferocious candour against her own. Quickly, she swung the glasses away to the left, where, raking the bulrushes with her eyes, she found the corner of a broad rough-woven nest.

"My God. It's huge." She exclaimed.

"Well, they're big birds."

"When will she lay her eggs?" With the glasses she tracked the movement of the smaller, female swan until she vanished behind a screen of rushes.

"In a couple of weeks. And they'll be hatched in May."

She returned the binoculars to the boy.

"Thank you."

"That's alright."

Gradually, the shade in which she stood extended itself across the water and drove the swans toward the boundary of light at the horizon. Kathleen tightened her scarf around her throat and stepped away from the trees. The boy walked parallel with her and, through the resonant stillness of the waterside, she could hear the intimate rise and fall of his breath. He did not speak until they had reached the gate.

"Well, what do you think of the place?" He pitched a grin at her.

"What place?"

"The school, of course. I saw you through the window today."

"It's fine," she said. "But I only had one class."

"I know." His grin widened. "I heard you asked them to draw a box."

"That's right." Kathleen directed at him a look that challenged his incipient mockery. "And what about you? What do you take instead of Art?"

"Chemistry." He watched the toe of his boot prise a stone from the dried mud.

"Do you like that?"

"Ah. It'll do." He lifted his head, but against the dusk his features blurred to an irregular pale outline.

"Well I'd best be away home now." He swung his leg over the gate.

Kathleen followed and dropped to the road beside him,

noticing that he did not, this evening, offer to help her down.

"Goodnight," she said.

"Goodnight, Miss White," he responded, with the trace of a laugh.

Every morning in the week that followed, Sean Laverty presented himself at the door of the Art Room, offering to escort Kathleen to the Staff Room for the coffee break. As they walked he disclosed to her, in a low voice, the foibles of their colleagues, until, in the uproarious wit and laughter with which he commanded the room, she recognised a showmanship that delighted in provoking others for its own amusement. His way of tilting back his chair and pushing up the sleeves of his white coat suggested a studious application to laughter. At intervals his eye would dart sideways and fix hers, encouraging her to attend to the human circus he had conjured. Kathleen limited her response to a quick compression of the lips.

"Have you settled in comfortably, dear?" Mrs Quinn asked her on the Friday.

"Yes, very well, thank you," Kathleen assured her.

"I suppose you'll be going back to Dublin most weekends?" Curiosity hooked the older woman's eyebrows.

"No," Kathleen shook her head. "No. I don't think so."

"Well so, you must come to us for Sunday lunch."

"That would be nice. Thank you." She smiled and, at the same moment, felt the weight of Sean Laverty's fingers tapping her shoulder.

"There's a ballad session in Sullivan's pub tonight, if you want to come along," he said.

Kathleen laughed. "I'll get a swelled head with all these invitations."

"I can call for you on my way down if you like." An eagerness in the brown eyes that started from the man's square, whiskery face defied refusal.

All afternoon, sunlight burnished the heads of her second-year students who, in anticipation of the week-end, maintained an agitation of squeaking chairs and busy whispers, dropped pencils, and clattered unnecessarily back and forth to the sink to replenish their jamjars of water. This little fever communicated itself to Kathleen, driving her to pace the room in a pretence of supervising their work. As she did so, she glimpsed, in a flash of green and white, a parade of boys with hurleys on their shoulders, making towards the pitch behind the school. In passing, one raised his arm to salute her and she recognised her swan-watching companion. She smiled and was about to lift her hand, but faltered when she saw, jogging beside him, the long figure of Tommy Nolan. A moment later, in a hectic spurt, the two boys raced ahead of their team-mates and out of her sight. Her hand dropped back into the pocket of her smock and she pivotted to supervise her class again.

Shadow now striated the dingy white plaster cones and cubes arranged by her on a table at the centre of the room. Glancing swiftly over three or four drawings, she felt defeated by the childrens' failure to respond to this change in the light. She advanced to the table and placed her index finger on the peak of the tallest cone.

"Do you think this looks any different now, to the way it did when you came in this afternoon?" The group, suddenly stilled by her voice, met the enquiry with a blank expression.

"Look at it," she insisted. "And look at your sketches."

Their eyes shifted from the table to their easels and returned a disinterested glance to her. If the silence was protracted for long enough, they knew, she would be forced to answer herself. Impatience set her fingers drumming on the table-top. One girl picked up her satchel, and placed it on her knee.

"Are you going somewhere?" Kathleen asked with asperity.

"It's nearly time, Miss." The girl crooked her head to one side and levelled her eyes at the teacher. An impulse to anger teased Kathleen's nerves.

"Go on, then. Clear up." She swung away from them and returned to the rostrum.

"Did you enjoy the ballad session, dear?" Alice Quinn, girt in a carnation-sprigged apron glanced over her shoulder at Kathleen.

"Yes. Yes. It was quite good."

A rush of steam from the pot of peas being strained by Alice flushed both their faces. Mr Quinn, a haggard, emphysemic man, expectorated and shook his head.

"My husband disapproves of Sean."

Kathleen looked down the table at Mr Quinn who wiped his mouth and brow with a blue check handkerchief.

"Why?"

His wife stooped to open the oven door.

"Well aren't you going to tell her?" he asked and leaned on the table.

"You may tell her since you're the one objects."

"Look," Kathleen intervened. "Don't tell me if it's confidential, or private. Really, I'd rather not know." She twirled the stem of her thimble-sized sherry glass between her fingers.

"Maybe it's better you should." Alice directed an imperative look towards her husband.

"He walked out on his wife and three children not a year ago," he said.

"Well, I'm sure he had a reason for going." Kathleen shrugged.

Mr Quinn tossed his eyes to heaven. "No more reason than itchy feet."

"Ah, Francis, how would you know? Here, eat this and forget about Sean Laverty." Alice set a laden plate in front of Kathleen. "There's mint sauce there, and Francis will pour you a drop of wine."

Mopping his face after a further spasm of coughing, Mr Quinn rose from the table and shuffled into the pantry.

"Don't mind Francis," his wife whispered. "It's only that he's a friend of Sean's father-in-law. So he holds to one side of the story."

Nodding reassurance, Kathleen smiled against the oppression which accompanied this insidious imposition of personal confidences.

An open bottle of white wine clenched in his right hand, her host returned from the pantry, filled her glass and his wife's, but took for himself a tumbler of milk. Their talk ran on generalities, Alice wrinkling at moments into inconsequential giggles while a vapour of convivial heat, adhering to the window, masked the passage of time. They were a childless couple and in Mrs Quinn's immoderate high spirits Kathleen recognised a compulsive maternalism. Mr Quinn vented embarrassment in the deep splutter of his cough and retreated altogether from the room when the meal was over.

"Off to smoke his dirty pipe." Alice expostulated, and began to stack the dishes.

"Let me help with those," Kathleen offered.

"You don't have to, dear."

"Well, I'd like to," she insisted and took up a position at the sink. As hot water swirled into the red plastic basin an annihilating dizziness seized her and the flow was transformed to the inexorable seepage of blood from every crevice of her body. She gripped the cold chrome of the sink edge till her knuckles whitened.

"Here's an apron for you, dear." Alice passed a yellow apron, its creases still sharp from the iron, around Kathleen's waist. "Goodness," she exclaimed. "Are you alright? You look deathly pale."

"I'm fine. Fine." Kathleen shook off the older woman's concern, and, pressing forward against the sink, began to rinse the plates.

"That's nice."

"What?" Kathleen's hand started to her chest. "You gave me a fright," she breathed and flipped shut her sketch pad.

"Sorry," the boy said. "I thought you might have heard us. Here, Max. Max," he broke off his call to whistle long and shrilly through two fingers, until a blonde labrador hove into view. "Good boy, Max. Good boy. Sit." The dog settled back on its haunches and looked up, its pink tongue sliding over its open jaw. The boy plumped down between Kathleen and the dog, and draped his arm over the dog's shoulder.

Kathleen grinned. "You look quite the loving couple."

"Do you hear that, Max?" the boy snorted. "She's jealous. It's great up here, isn't it?" he added, turning to her.

"Yes, lovely." Kathleen stretched her arms forward, then, drawing up her knees, propped her elbows on them and cupped her chin. "It's peaceful." Her eyes dropped over the chequered contour of the hill to the flat, shining pan of the estuary.

"Maybe that's because it's a graveyard."

"What?" She abruptly reined back her gaze and glanced at the boy who nodded.

"It's a Penal graveyard."

She looked round, noting now a series of small mounds such as the one on which she sat.

"That's why there are no tombstones?"

The boy nodded again. "There's a Mass Rock on the other side of the hill. I can show you if you like."

"O.K." Kathleen stood and wiped the grass from the seat of her jeans. "I don't think I like the idea of sitting on someone's grave."

"Come on, Max. Up." The boy called to the dog who had keeled over and spread his legs to absorb the heat of noon. Max lifted and dropped his tail with a languorous thump.

"He doesn't want to move," Kathleen laughed.

"Lazy. That's what he is. Come on boy. Hup." Max raised his head and lowered it again.

"I think he's laughing at you."

The boy cast an exasperated look at the dog. "Alright," he conceded. "We'll go on. He can follow us."

They began the ascent towards the hand-built stone wall that marked the upper limit of the cemetery.

"You know, it's funny," Kathleen remarked as they paused to cross the wall. "I have your dog's name but not yours."

"Philip. Philip O'Shea."

"Well, it's nice to know you, Philip."

"Thanks, Miss White." The boy bowed in a parody of formality.

"Alright," Kathleen grinned. "You don't have to call me Miss White. Except in the school, that is. My name's Kathleen."

"Cathleen ni Houlihan," Philip intoned.

"Not quite, no." Kathleen clambered over the wall. "Come on. Here's Max."

The heavy dog briefly scrabbled his paws in the stone work and cleared the wall.

"He's fit, even if he is fat," she commented.

"I bring him for walks, but then my mother feeds him all our scraps." Philip thrust his hands into his pockets and strode ahead, whistling to the dog. "It's round here," he said, turning the brow of the bald hill, his outline sharpened by the close blue screen of the sky.

"I wish I had my camera with me." Kathleen panted as she joined him. "The light up here is so...so pure."

Together their eyes traversed the straggled line of the village and bent towards the estuary.

"Look," Kathleen suddenly gripped his sleeve. "There they are." Releasing her hold, she pointed to the swans which had scudded into view and sat now on their reflections.

"She'll lay any day soon," Philip said.

"Good. I want to see the cygnets before I leave."

A thin line compressed the boy's mouth and, facing round he gestured over the slope.

"Let's look at the Mass Rock."

"They picked a good spot, didn't they?" Kathleen observed as they drew near to the rock marked by a rudimentary cross.

With his toe, Philip prised up a dandelion that had bolted in the shelter of the rock.

"I'd certainly prefer to listen to mass up here than below in the church."

Kathleen watched him tamp the broken soil. "Do you pray?" Bringing his foot to rest beside its pair, Philip glanced at Kathleen, then perused the air above her head.

"In a way I suppose I do," he admitted. "I like to come up here and, well, just be still. Then I can believe there is something, someone, out there."

His arm described a curve in the air that brought Max trundling towards them. Philip reached down and rubbed the back of the dog's ear.

"What about you?" he asked.

Kathleen shook her head. "Nothing. I used to pray, morning and night prayers, the family Rosary, the lot. Then, I went through the usual rebellion, and now," she shrugged. "I can't pray. Sometimes it comes to me that I would like to. I get a glimpse, or a sense, of how it felt to be sure of God, of life having another dimension, but, if I try to pray, that disappears. I'm stuck with myself."

"Maybe you'll get the knack again suddenly. Like riding a bike." Optimism glimmered in the boy's face.

"On my deathbed probably."
"Well, sure then you'll be saved."
"If I last that long."

Mary's thin hair dropped in hanks across her neck and cheeks as, intent on outlining the model's pose, she leaned into her easel. In this girl's drawings only, did Kathleen find respite from her dread of futility. When the bell rang she beckoned to Mary who swerved away from her companions to approach the teacher's desk.

"Mary, you know I think your drawing is really very good," she began.

"Thank you, Miss White."

"I mean it." Kathleen waved aside the thanks. "But you need to work on your figures. I want you to take this book home and follow some of the exercises in it before the next class."

Mary frowned, but, before she could speak a footfall in the door distracted her and the teacher.

"Only me," Sean Laverty waved. "I'll wait down here." He strolled to the back of the Art Room.

"I'll go so, Miss," Mary whispered and folded the book into her chest.

Kathleen placed a hand on her shoulder. "No, what were you going to say?"

"It's just that I don't have much time. With all the other subjects."

"I know, Mary. I know it's hard. But you have talent. What are you thinking of doing after the Leaving?"

"Well, I'd like to do Law, but that depends on the Points and the Grant."

Kathleen rolled her eyes.

"Everybody thinks it's boring," Mary smiled. "But anyway, I think I should get a job to help my mother, at least until some of the others are through school."

"I see," Kathleen nodded. "Take the book anyway, and if you get a chance try some of the exercises."

"Alright, thanks, Miss." The girl withdrew, pulling the door behind her.

Kathleen walked to the back of the room.

"I see Tommy Nolan is showing his true colours," Sean remarked, swinging the stem of his unlit pipe towards the Bobby Sands poster. "I'm surprised you put it up. Mrs Galvin would have told him off."

"My job is to run with the kids wherever they want to take me."

"Oho," Sean rounded his expression in mock amazement. "So the 'artiste' has no moral responsibility?"

"I'm not sure what 'moral responsibility' means." She threw an enquiring glance at him. "My morality? Your morality? Whose is the right one?"

"An anarchist," Sean half sneered. Then, dropping his tone to an importunate rasp, asked "What did Alice say to you?"

"What do you mean?"

"You know well enough." Sean drew himself up to a dominating pose. "You've been avoiding me for the past couple of weeks. Or was it her cantankerous old fogey of a husband told you? Come on, spit it out."

Kathleen spread her hands as if to maintain her balance.

"Whatever they told me has nothing to do with my attitude to you."

"Ha. I knew it." A malicious triumph fired his expression. "The squinting windows is right."

"I'm going to get a cup of coffee, if you'll excuse me." Kathleen moved away but was halted by Sean's sudden grip on her arm. "Let go, you're hurting," she flared.

"What is the matter with me then?" he insisted.

"Nothing." Kathleen dropped her head. "I just don't want to get too close to anyone at the moment." She cut her eyes back to him. "I just need some air. Now please let me go."

He released her arm which, after a moment of numbness, began to throb.

"What's wrong?" he called as she bent to pick up her bag. "Do you not like men?"

"It seems Tommy Nolan is not the only one showing his true colours," she retorted and left the room.

Instead of going to the Staff Room, Kathleen walked through the courtyard, now a carnival of small blooms, on to the playing fields where the lick of a salt breeze from the estuary abated the anger fevering her cheeks. She was taken with an impulse to lie down and melt into the churned mud of the pitch, but the clatter of studded boots on the tarmac shook her and, briskly pacing the length of the field, she rounded the side of the school building.

When the phone rang she hesitated in a panic of unfamiliarity, then rallied and went to pick it up.

"Hello." A man's voice echoed in her ear. "Hello. Is that you Katy?"

"Michael?"

"Yes, how are things?"

"Fine. You sound as if you're phoning from the moon."

"I suppose from where you are Dublin looks that far away."

"Very funny. What do you want?"

"Myself and a few friends are heading down your way for the long week-end. Can you put us up for a night?"

"I suppose so. How many?"

"Good. Just myself and Paddy and John. You remember them?"

"Not off hand, no."

"Oh. Well you'll know them when you see them. We'll be down on Friday evening O.K.?"

"O.K. Ask at Sullivan's pub. They'll tell you where the house is."

"See you then. Oh. Wait. Before I go. Anything you want from the big smoke?"

"Not that I can think of, no."

"Nothing?" Michael sounded peeved.

"No."

"Alright. See you soon."

"Yes. Goodbye."

For several minutes after she had finished speaking, Kathleen's hand remained planted on the receiver. Surprise at the source of the call oscillated with surprise at her indifference to the caller, and the tightening wire of her anxiety loosened. A drink, she thought, I'd like a drink, but her fridge offered only orange juice and milk, and the sound of voices on the street indicated closing time at Sullivan's. She switched on the kettle and went into the bedroom. Just as she had begun to undress a loud rapping at the door drew her back to the threshold of the room. Voices called indeterminate words. Young voices.

"Who is it? Who's there?" She shouted, without moving.

"A present for you," one answered.

"Special Delivery, Miss White," cried another, a voice she recognised as that of Tommy Nolan.

"Go home lads, go home," she said, stepping back into her bedroom.

After a splutter of giggles footsteps receded down the street.

Tying the belt of her robe, Kathleen returned to the kitchen counter. In the trough of silence that followed the boiling of the kettle, a low moan sounded through the room. She glanced up, dismissed it, and began to stir her coffee. Again, the sound moaned and was succeeded by a feeble scratching on wood. Then, roughly, her name was spoken. She replaced her mug on the counter and approached the door.

"Who's there?" she asked.

"Me, Philip," the words slurred thickly through the panelling. Fear baulked her but, fidgetting the security chain free, she swung the door open.

"Oh God, what have they done?" She knelt quickly beside the boy's naked body. "Are you hurt?" He shook his head. Gripping him under the shoulders she tried to heave him into the room but he lunged from her hold and, tipping himself forward onto his hands and knees, vomited exhaustively into the rose-bed adjoining the doorstep. Kathleen turned away, waiting until he had finished, and begun to crawl indoors, before reaching to help him again.

"Can you stand?" she asked and stretched her hand under his armpit.

He turned his head sideways and rolled his eyes.

"I don't think so," he mumbled. "I'm sorry."

"Alright." Kathleen withdrew her hand. "Alright. Look, sit here." She propped him against the side of an armchair. "I'll make up a bed on the sofa. Just wait a minute."

Philip nodded until his head lolled forward onto his chest.

Kathleen shut the door and, crossing to the counter, measured three spoons of sugar into the coffee which she carried back to the boy.

"Here, try and drink some of this."

He lifted his head and worked his parched lips over the rim of the cup. The milky coffee dripped from the corners of his mouth and splashed onto his chest.

"God. You are a mess," Kathleen grimaced.

Putting the cup down beside him, she went to fetch sheets and a pillow from the bedroom. By the time the bed was made up the boy had begun to snore.

"Come on, Philip," Kathleen shook him gently. "You can't sleep there. Come on. Just a few steps then you can lie down."

He groaned and tried to shrug her away.

"Philip, please, you can crawl. Just three feet." Again he shrugged and articulated a deep snore. Kathleen crouched to manoeuvre him into her lap, and, levering him upright against her frame, tottered to the sofa where she dropped him. Kneeling, she stretched his legs and jammed a pillow under his head. On the point of covering his body, she hesitated, as if perceiving its nakedness for the first time that night. The sheet and blanket still raised in one hand, she allowed the fingers of her free hand track the boy's compact, warm limbs, until, quickened by the graze of the auburn fringe at his groin, she drew back and continued to tuck the covers around him.

The next morning, a wedge of light admitted by a gap in the curtains lay on Philip's brow where sweat had pasted leaves of hair. Padding through the room, Kathleen reached behind the curtain to unlatch the window and release the stink of sour beer and vomit. Disturbed by the slight sound, Philip grunted and cleared his throat.

"Where am I? What happened?"

"Ssshh." Kathleen, a finger pressed to her lips, approached the makeshift bed. "Some of your friends dumped you here last night."

"Oh no." He brushed his arm across his forehead. "It was my birthday."

"Some party."

"My clothes. Where are my clothes? I better get home." His arms fumbled the blanket.

"You appeared as you are."

He blushed and pressed his hands to his face. "Oh no. I'll kill them."

"Who should I see about getting you dressed?"

"Peter McCarthy or Tommy Nolan." The boy replied from behind his hands.

"Here's a towel." Kathleen draped a bath-sheet over the back of the sofa. "You can have a shower in there. I'll leave a pot of coffee on the stove."

"Thanks. Thanks, Kathleen," he said, his face still muffled by his hands. "I'm sorry. I really am."

"Don't think about it." Kathleen flapped her hand. "I'm off now. I'll send one of the boys up," she added and stepped into the clear daylight.

Michael's stubble sanded her cheek as his kiss nudged her ear lobe.

"You're looking well," he said.

Kathleen remained holding the door open. "Where are the others?"

"Who? Oh. They decided to stay in Killarney tonight. I'll catch up with them tomorrow." Michael stood in the centre of the room and sniffed the air. "Something smells good. What is it?"

"There's a chicken in the oven." Kathleen replied, shutting the door.

"Great." He put down his bag and stretched. "I could eat the leg of a table." He sat on the sofa and eased off his sneakers, then, under his usual compulsion to habituate himself to new surroundings, prowled the room, pausing every so often and tilting on the balls of his feet.

"This is nice, this is really nice," he concluded. "You should put a glass door there." He stood before the window giving on to the back garden.

"I'm only renting the place for six months, Michael."

"Still a french window would be nice there."

"I suppose it would," she shrugged, and passed behind the counter to check the oven.

"Look, look. I brought you something." He bounded to his bag and, after a brief rummage, produced a bottle which he set on the counter.

Kathleen smiled. "Very clever."

Feigning bashfulness, he ducked his head. "Well I thought it was appropriate. Now where are your glasses?"

"Up there," she pointed to a cupboard above the fridge.

Michael poured two ample fingers of the Teacher's Whiskey into each tumbler.

"Cheers," he said.

"Cheers," she sipped, welcoming the expansion of alcohol in her chest, and bent to open the oven.

"That's not all I brought." Michael came up behind her.

She straightened up and, turning, met the palm of his upturned hand on which lay a small tin foil packet.

"Columbian Gold," he whispered.

Kathleen caught by a sense of displacement, stared. The hand could have been a stranger's. Yet, once, those fingers used to tighten around hers till their twin joints grafted. Under their chafing she had flushed with passion. Now, she was astonished to realise that she harboured no vestige of what, for the space of six years, had borne the conviction of absolute love.

"What's the matter? Don't tell me you're going to swoon," Michael jibed. "I know: it's Manna. Look, let's forget about the chicken." His fingers crept around her neck. "I've missed you Katy."

Kathleen stepped back and shook her head. "What about Lolita?"

"Christ, you bitch." Michael's hand closed over the hash. "You always did slug below the belt."

A lofty blue sky reproduced it's arch in the transparent dish of the estuary. Beneath the tree Kathleen watched for the swans to emerge from their nesting ground.

"God seems possible on a day like this," she said.

"Mmm." Philip chewed a blade of grass.

Stiff jointed, Max rose and lumbered to her side.

"Yes, Max." She fondled the dogs head until his tail flagged the air and he dropped to roll on his back.

"What's eating you?" She asked. " The exams?"

"Yes, partly," Philip agreed.

"But you're going away anyway?"

"Fast as I can."

"Where?"

"Germany. Or maybe America." He shrugged, then suddenly sprang back onto his hunkers. "There they go."

She followed his sightline to where, carving a channel through the bulrushes, the swans eased onto the open water, while, canted by their parents' wake, six tousled cygnets formed an uneven train.

"They do look odd beside their parents, don't they?" she commented.

"Yes," Philip grinned. "Ugly ducklings. Like babies."

"You're right," she laughed. "I suppose we're all like that at the start. The question is, do we get better or worse?"

"Both, maybe." "How?"

"Well, we get better looking, or some of us do."

"You're no Adonis!" she interrupted in a burst of laughter.

He tilted a quizzical glance at her. "What?"

"Don't worry. Go on."

"But inside we get worse."

"Some of us."

"No." Philip's expression clenched. "I think pretty well everyone, inside, has a dark spot."

"Just when I was beginning to believe in God again." She made a rueful downturn of her lips.

"Sorry about that." Philip brightened. "Maybe we need the bad to enjoy the good."

"You can't have one without the other." Kathleen hummed under her breath.

"Maybe not."

She nodded, but continued after a moment. "I don't want to believe that. Do you?"

"Not really," the boy conceded.

"You've got to focus on the good," she insisted, her eyes fixed on the family of swans. "You've got to try and hone away the bad."

"So, we keep thinking about the ugly ducklings?"

"Yes." She stood and, holding her hand in mid-air, arrested its impulse to brush the back of her skirt. "To hell with our feathers," she laughed.

Philip pushed himself off the ground and stood beside her. "Whatever you say, Miss White."

"Come on, let's go and have a drink," she suggested, linking his arm.

From her bedroom Kathleen heard a loud engine rupture the air and continue to judder after its ignition had been cut.

"Are you ready?" Philip's call punctuated the noise.

"Coming." Kathleen slung the strap of her bag across her shoulder and joined him on the step.

"Wow!" her eyes widened. "I was expecting a Honda 50."

"My brother worked in Germany last summer to buy this." The boy grinned and threw his leg over the broad saddle of the B.M.W. "Here," he held out a black helmet identical to his own.

She jammed it on her head and straddled the bike. Philip turned and raised his eyebrows. Kathleen nodded.

"Ride on Black Knight." Unheard by Philip, her words misted the inside of the perspex mask.

Crossing the bridge over the estuary, Philip slowed the bike and drew in to the parapet where, letting the engine idle, he pointed down the bay. The swans, pursued by two of their ungainly young, moved over the open plain of water. Midway, they stopped, spreading their wings to tumble out the rest of the brood and scoop the two stragglers into the curve of their backs. As the family pushed off again, Philip accelerated and, on a parallel route, overtook the birds, arriving at the town within minutes.

"Is an hour enough time for you?" he asked, rocking the bike onto its stand.

"Plenty," Kathleen nodded. "I've only to fix up with Mrs Brosnan about the bills and the deposit, and to check the trains."

"We'll meet back here at four, so?"

"Fine," she confirmed.

Kathleen returned early to the pier where she sat on a bollard and cast an eye out over the water. There was no sign of the migrating birds. Shortly, a brash hubbub rose on the air behind her. She glanced around but the place was desolate. Again, the clamour rose, frantic as the cheer of a ringside mob. Kathleen stood and wandered down the pier, rounding the end of the high bulwark to reach its shelving foundation of rock. A knot of youths stood here, launching stones onto the water. In the answering spray of foam, she noticed flecks of red. She drew closer to the group but stopped when she saw the swans. Wings outstretched, they reared onto the rocks. Their long necks flailed like a boxer's arms, left and right, and gobbets of dark blood swung from their chests.

"Stop it," Kathleen raged. "Stop it. Stop."

The boys ignored her cries and flung down another volley of stones and broken bottle ends. Through their shouts and her own hoarsening cries, Kathleen began to discern another sound. A succession of eerie plangent whoops culminated in the subsidence of the angry swans. Drooping their jaded necks into their chests, they allowed themselves be towed away by the lilt of the water. The mob, spent too, turned and started towards Kathleen.

Immobilised with panic, she waited, and felt the glaze of their vicarious euphoria pass a sweaty shimmer over her face. When they had gone, she skittered down the sloping rock to the water's edge. Like fragments of broken bread, the dismembered cygnets were cradled in the receding tide. A thin bile of nausea flooded her mouth. Clamping her arms around her waist, she rocked forward on her hunkers.

The touch of Philip's hand on her shoulder drew her upright.

"I couldn't stop them," she lamented.

"I know," he nodded. "I got a chipped tooth and a black eye for trying last year."

"But it's so wrong, so needless."

"It happens every year. Stupid. I always hope that it won't."

"And the swans come back?"

"Yes," his mouth twitched into a wry smile. "They must have hopes, too."

Driving The Minister

Dermot Bolger

At dances he said girls could never tell them apart. I could imagine those rural ballrooms, wind blowing through rocks by the lakeside, bicycles stacked against the concrete wall. They shared a bed till they were eighteen, ate off one plate, played games the other children couldn't follow.

Patrick had the brains, Pascal pushed him. St. Patrick's in the 1950s while Pascal worked the sites in England and sent money back to Patrick. The first teaching post in the village drowning under cement while their new nest-egg grew, waiting for the sixties.

In 1961 Pascal returned. Lights would burn until dawn in Patrick's flat. One slick, one savage, they began their pincer movement - schoolmaster to Councillor, to TD, to Minister - labourer to foreman, to garage owner, to property developer. In the years I grew up the village became a vast suburb with their name above every business in the main street. My father worked in Pascal's garage till a week before he died. I was eighteen, the eldest son. At the funeral, while the minister shook hands with his constituents, his brother placed his possessively on my shoulder.

For eight months since I had been his driver, shuttling between building sites, his supermarket, his ranch like pub on the fringe of town. Sometimes Patrick came to the house.

Dismissing his driver. I'd wait in the kitchen to drive home.

One night the brothers had been drinking heavily when they came downstairs. Pascal had telephoned someone. I was exhausted, relieved to be going home. Instead Pascal told me to drive to the city. It was after one when we got there, the streets almost deserted, the burger huts closed, the night-clubs still churning out music. Near the toilets on Burgh Quay they beckoned me to stop.

Youths leaned on the riverside wall, watching for men, obviously for sale. The eldest was sixteen. The brothers stared at them, then motioned me on. Once it might have been impossible to tell them apart, but politics had lent Patrick a veneer of cosmopolitanism at odds with the raw aggression of his brother. That night as they stared impassively out it was like the polish had slipped and they were one again. I drove with a sickness in my stomach down quays and alleyways where children huddled with cider and bags of glue. Some spat at the slow car others watched with mute indifference. Neither spoke except to say "Slower" or "Drive on".

We moved like a funeral procession through some ghostly apparition of a dead city. Lanes carpeted with glass where street lights were broken, tumble-down buildings and, stranded in the headlights, the huddled figures wrapped in blankets, arms raised against the glaring headlight.

Twice we paused beside a sleeping figure, down a laneway shadowed by the cathedral and the Civic Offices, before I was ordered to stop. Patrick Plunkett was bundled up in an overcoat. In the dark he might be anyone. His brother got out, approached the dazed figure and bent to talk. The youth was perhaps eighteen. He shook his head repeatedly till Plunkett held up money and replaced it carefully in his wallet. Neither spoke and then the youth rose and folded his blanket under his arm and they argued briefly before he hid the filthy covering between two bins.

He sat between them in the back. I knew he was scared. He wanted to ask questions but felt too intimidated. Occasionally

Pascal reassured him or gave me directions. Otherwise we drove in silence. I thought I knew north country Dublin until that night. We passed Rolestown and later a sign for Naul, but generally the tiny lanes we travelled were unfamiliar. Grass grew down the centre and just when they seemed to peter out they joined another. At one crossroads headlights emerged to trail us and this was repeated until we too caught up with a procession of tail lights stretching into the darkness.

We left the tarmacadam and bumped our way across the grass.

In the field before us a semicircle of light was formed by the headlights of cars. We took our place and those behind followed until the rough circle was complete. The minister addressed me for the first time.

"Get out!"

He climbed into my seat and donned a chauffeur's hat from the glove compartment which I had never worn. He fixed his eyes on the floodlit grass. Pascal was standing beside the open boot with the shivering youth stripped to the waist, rubbing liquid into his chest. He handed me the bottle, a sponge and a water container, then placed his hand on the youth's shoulder and steered him into the circle.

From the far side of the circle a second youth was led out, as scared as the first. I knew the man beside him, a factory owner called Wright from Swords who did business with Plunkett.

He jeered.

"Is that your best Plunkett? Must be fierce weak men in the city."

"You sure a grand won't bust your business Wright? It's a lot to lose for a little man like yourself."

The youths eyed each other, desperate to make a deal. But even if they decided to run they would be pushed into the ring by a circle of well-fed men closing in around them. A referee stripped off his jacket.

"Where did you get them?" he asked Plunkett.

"Near Christchurch."

"And yours?" he turned to Wright.

"Tinkers. Camped near the Ward."

"Fifty pounds to the winner boxer. I want twenty-five each off you now."

He turned to the youths.

"Nothing to the loser. Understand? No using your feet, break when I call and the first one to surrender is out. You've five minutes."

We returned to the car. Plunkett put a jacket over the youth's shoulders and showed him how to weave and hit. Two men approached and he went off to cover their bets. The youth glanced at me like I was his gaoler. I wanted to tell him to run but was too terrified, fearing that if he did escape I would be thrust into the ring instead. The winning purse was less than the smallest bet changing hands there. The laughter became a rush of anticipation. Plunkett returned and pushed the youth forward.

"Fifty pounds. Into your hand. Don't let me down."

I followed, noticing Patrick had left the car and was standing unnoticed behind the crowd. The man beside me offered a slug of Southern Comfort and slapped my shoulder.

"Good man," he shouted. "I've a hundred riding on your boy, but watch it, them knackers fight dirty."

There was a roar as both youths entered the ring. They circled cagily while the referee encouraged them forward. For a minute they shadowed each other, fists clenched, tongues nervously exposed. The crowd cursed, calling them cowards. Then the gypsy ducked, got in close and swung his fist. He caught the youth above the eye as he moved forward and flailed at the gypsy.

There were no gloves, no rounds, both fighters punched and clung to each other as the crowd screamed until the gypsy fell to the ground. I expected the referee to count but Wright just pulled him up and wiped the sponge quickly over his face.

Plunkett grabbed the water and raised it to his fighter's lips.

"Don't swallow, spit," he said. "It will be a long night."

Then they were thrust back into action, a graceless headlong collision of blows and head butts. Both bled badly from the face. More frequently now they fell and the fight stopped for a few seconds. Once the gypsy got past his opponent's defence and rained blows against his rib cage. He stepped back and the youth fell, doubled up on the ground. He tried to stay down as Plunkett hauled him up.

"Me ribs, mister, they're broken, broken."

"Get back in there. I've money riding on you! Finish him off or you'll leave here in a box."

The youth stumbled back clutching his side. Bets were flowing onto the gypsy. He approached grinning through the blood, sensing his ordeal was nearly over and as he swung his fist the youth caught him with his boot between the legs and as he fell, again in the face. There was a near riot of indignation in the crowd, their sense of fair play abused. Both youths knelt on the ground while the referee shouted at Plunkett.

"Once more and it's Wright's. You hear?"

The youth rose reluctantly and stared at me. I lowered my eyes and walked away. I could bear to watch no more. To the south the lights of the city made an orange glow. The wind blew against my face. A tree was growing in the ditch. I pressed my face against the cold bark, trying somehow to take strength from it. From the shouts I knew the gypsy was finishing it. They would be watching those final grisly moments before clustering round the bookmakers. I wrapped my whole body against the tree. I had nobody left to pray to so I prayed to the living wood itself, to the memory of someone I had once been.

I walked back. The youth was lying against the side of the car, crying. I found his clothes, helped him into them. I wanted to ask his name but it was too late now. I opened the back door.

"In the front," Pascal shouted.

I eased him gently into the passenger's seat and started the engine.

"Leave us home," Plunkett said, "and put him back where you found him. Bring the car into work at twelve. One word about this and your family will be living on sawdust."

I let them out at his house. Both slammed their doors, and, now they were alone, bowed their heads, discussing the fight. I drove into town. The Mater was on casualty that night. It was almost dawn but the benches were jammed with drunks, with lonely people hoping to fool their way into a bed, girls in party dresses who cried waiting for news of friends. He didn't want to go in, and, if I had not sat there, would have stumbled his way home to that laneway.

Even the nurses were shocked at his appearance. They took

him ahead of those waiting. When he rose, I pushed whatever money I had into his hand. I knew Plunkett had given him nothing. He looked at me but we did not shake hands. The nurses helped him onto the bunk and, staring at me with mistrust, pulled the curtain shut.

It was daylight outside. I thought of my mother, the brothers and sisters I had to provide for. At twelve I would be waiting at the garage to drive him, but now I left the car there and walked the two miles home in some futile gesture of penance even though I knew that nothing would be changed.

Reflex Action

Sebastian Barry

"She was a bit - I don't know how you'd say it -she was rather on the streets the last few years."

My grandfather kept quiet in the front seat. I saw the girl turn to him a moment at the traffic lights. She didn't understand him.

"Did you know that?"

He said nothing.

"Of course she was quite desperate sometimes. She'd come into the Social Security Office looking for all sorts of things. That's why we took the children into care. She was no use to them in that respect."

"You were quite right in doing so," said Papa Haugh.

We drove into a red-bricked terrace, and stopped in the crook of the street.

"This is the house here," said the girl. "I think they've had it fumigated. Well we told them to anyway, and as far as I know they have. Now you're sure you want to go in, Mister Haugh?"

"Don't I have to?" he said, surprised. "I got that impression when you asked me."

"Did you? Well I think it would be better for understanding the court verdict this afternoon, don't you? You might feel easier in your mind. There's a few things of hers you can look through."

On the pavement she said:

"She was found by a young policeman, you see, so the place was in a bad way smell-wise. She'd been up there in her bedroom three weeks."

She nodded at the curtained window on the upper floor.

"Should I talk to him too?" Papa Haugh said.

"Do you think there's any reason?" said the girl. "Oh I think his report will be enough. They'll read it out at the hearing."

She didn't sound very sure that what she said was necessarily true.

"I have a note here - I meant to ask you," she said, fingering through her bag. "Here's the house-key anyway - I better find this before I forget." She removed a torn piece of paper from the leather interior. "Can I read it out? It's just a minor question that the court'll ask you. You might as well be prepared: Did she have a happy childhood?"

I followed them up the short concrete path to a shabby door. I couldn't ignore the fact that the house was dirty looking, like the rest of the town. And there was the same thick grey sky above it.

"Now let's see," said the girl, pushing the door open. "They seem to have been up to something anyway."

She pointed to a dish on the floor of the little hall, with a liquid sitting in it silently. It must have been some product that evaporated in the air, and cleaned it.

A sticky stench came down the stairs in front of me.

"It's a bit rough all the same," she said. "Do you have a handkerchief, Mister Haugh?"

Papa Haugh hitched his overcoat, and swept out a fold of white linen, and offered it to her.

"Oh no, I'm used to it. I thought your grandson."

"No, thank you," I said.

I went into a bare room on the right. They stayed talking behind me. There was a plastic-topped table against the wall, and two uncomfortable chairs pushed under it. In a corner was a slouching couch, with its cover dragged from being sat on. Papa Haugh and the social worker came in after me.

"There's not much here," she said. "But I think you could take anything you wanted."

There was a calendar on the wall beside the grate: Church of the Divine Encounter.

"Look," I said.

"She changed her religion every second month," Papa Haugh said.

"Why don't you take that radio, Annesley?" he said, when the girl was looking behind the couch.

The transistor was on a low table, under the window. I bent down and examined it. It was grey, with a band of tarnished silver. Around the dials, and in the protected part of the surface, there was a lot of grime. The body was bound round with sellotape. I could imagine her using it.

"Go on," said Papa Haugh. "It's quite in order."

I wasn't sure if he meant the radio or the taking of it.

"I don't think so," I said.

"Will we go upstairs now, Mister Haugh?" the girl said. "I believe there's a wardrobe in her bedroom that needs checking through. There'll be men in here in the next week or so, clearing her effects. The house can't be left empty for any time longer."

"After you," said Papa Haugh politely at the base of the stairs.

I went up behind them. All the doors on the landing above were open, leading into small shadowed rooms. Half way up the stairs the stench grew more powerful. I was breathing through the sleeve of my coat. I felt the smell settling on my eyes.

"That was the children's room I think while she had them," the girl said, indicating a room with a softly glowing chest of drawers inside.

"This was her bedroom."

They entered in where the smell seemed most repugnant. I lingered on the landing, to see if I could feel less ill before I followed them. They didn't need me of course, but it was lonely on the landing without them.

There was a handbag on the table outside her bedroom. I looked inside it with my free hand, influenced by their spirit of searching. All it held was three pill-bottles, with a few capsules rolling about at the bottom of one of them. I thought I'd show them to Papa Haugh, in case they meant anything, and stepped into the room. The stench seemed to be alive there. It felt as if the air was thicker inside the door. I saw that my three small bottles meant little. The bedside table was littered with similar containers.

Papa Haugh was gazing down at them.

"It looks a lot," said the girl. "But you see she always liked the doctor to give her a three months' supply. It's a common practice. It means she doesn't have to see him every week."

"Whiskey, too," said Papa Haugh.

He didn't bend down to touch the clouded bottles on the floor.

"The usual mixture," said the girl. "She used to complain of seeing her grandmother at the side of her bed sometimes. Just illusions. We put them in her notebook. Do you think there's any reason for that?"

"She lived with her grandmother as a child," said Papa Haugh. "She was very fond of her of course," he said, turning to the girl and nodding.

"What the pathologist thinks," went on the girl, "is that she took some barbiturates before sleeping, and woke up later in the night in a rather desperate state, and swallowed down more pills than she should have, to return to sleep. He says it often happens. It's not necessarily her intention to take too many. It might have been a sort of reflex action, if you like."

They moved away from the bed. I saw it hadn't been stripped completely of its covers. The mattress and the bottom sheet remained. I noticed the rest of the bed-clothes in a corner.

They were covered in a white powder. And the sheet on the bed was covered in it too.

Down the middle of the sheet was a weal of dark damp brown. It was a stain. I thought the smell came principally from there. It stretched from pillow height to the foot of the mattress. I wanted to leave.

The girl saw Papa Haugh looking at it.

"You must remember she wasn't found for three weeks," she said. "Things get a bit soft in that time. She really wasn't very easy to identify once she was moved. The policeman knew her face when he saw it. It's a hard thing to move intact. But it saves you having to identify her, Mister Haugh. They're satisfied with the policeman's report that it was her."

"I'm sure it was," said Papa Haugh. "I'm sure it was."

I regarded the stain. They opened the wardrobe, and sorted through the clothes I could make the clothes out dimly in the gloom of the room, coats and dresses. But the white of the sheet made the mark on the bed hold my eye. I wanted Papa Haugh to come away. I felt the stench was inside me somewhere. I couldn't go downstairs alone, because of the radio, and the couch, and the calendar on the wall.

The girl drove the car away competently.

"There you have it," she said. "That's the worst part. There's just the court now and you can go home to Ireland."

"Yes," Papa Haugh said.

"I don't think, everything considered, they'll return a verdict of suicide," she said.

"No, she wouldn't want that," he said.

"As her father of course, you'll be able to say something in her favour. It'll hinge on the evidence of the policeman and the doctor though. There's the question of the reflex action."

"I'd like to be able to do that one last thing for her," Papa Haugh said.

"And there was no sign that she wanted to kill herself," said the girl.

The Quiet Man

Gabriel Byrne

When I return to my hotel in Vienna, there is a phone call.

A friend of mine is leaving for the States on holiday and wonders if I'd come to spend a month at his cottage in Ireland.

"Come and play the Quiet Man," he says. For real. Because there is an ongoing strike in Hollywood I accept at once and book a flight for the following day.

"Well you can tell the party of the first part that I go for it."

The rattling train from Dublin defeats sleep and three hours later I step onto the platform at a tiny station in a shower of early evening rain.

"A fine soft day in the spring it was when the train pulled into Castletown and himself got off."

The tarpaulin on the roof of the bus flaps wildly in the wind and sunlight hits the window giving it a mad flashing eye, as it charges over the hill towards us.

We climb aboard, an old man in a cap with twine shopping bag and myself. We swing out of the town into the blue black hills. The old man sways towards me holding the seats to steady himself.

"Are you who I think you are?"

"I hope I am who you think I am."

He thrusts a pencil and a torn cigarette packet in my hand.

"What name will I write?"

"Your own of course." A reprimand.

"Are you down making a film or what?"

"No, just holiday."

"And other things, Mickeleen. Other things."

Now and then, the doors of the bus open in a hissing sound and, without losing speed, bundles of newspapers are thrown to land on pavement or gravel or in shop doorways. Down the hill, and the last of the day dying, to finally halt under a sign that says CIE swinging rusty in the wind.

The clock on the town hall tower is stopped forever at twelve-twenty exactly, and under it a group of men are smoking and playing pitch-and-toss. They stop to watch me, the stranger among them. The bus turns and heaves itself back up the hill, canvas still flapping madly over the hedgerows. I approach the men, purposefully. I enquire of them the whereabouts of my friend's cottage.

"Christ you've a step to go yet. You've a right to go over to Kellys and root out The Vampire. He has a sort of Taxi." They laugh.

"Can you tell me the way to Innisfree?"

"Innisfree is it?"

"Happen you know the road to Aughanure?"

At the bar a man who looks as if all the blood has been drained from his body is watching the Nuacht. On the TV, Yasser Arafat smiles into a microphone.

"You see that hoor with the dish-cloth on his head? That's a crafty hoor if ever I seen one."

We shake hands. I offer him a drink.

"Well that being the case, it is a pleasant evening and I will have a drink, Sean Thornton."

"So you'll be staying out at the Lake-House, far from the maddening crowds is it? A blowy spot but if it's peace and quiet you're after, no better place."

"Innisfree?"

"This way!"

It begins to rain again. Long nails of rain in the carlight. The rubber from the windscreen wiper is missing and it scrapes across the glass. Dave Fanning talks low on the radio. Suddenly, without warning, two white ponies stand in the roadway before us staring us to a swerving standstill. Dave Fanning's voice fills the night, and my heart is exploding in my chest.

Further on, cars are parked outside a football field. Men lean against them with shoulder bags and hurleys, staring and saluting as we pass. A man in a vest is frozen momentarily by the headlights, one leg in his underpants, his backside bare to the night. The Vampire rolls the window down as the man dances for cover.

"By jazes Finnegan, you've a lovely arse, God bless it!" The journey seems endless.

"The young May moon is beaming love, the glow-worm's lamp is gleaming love."

"It's a good job you can't see where we are now," says the Vampire.

"Why is that?"

"Oh, that's why," he laughs.

At last we arrive. A light shines from the cottage set among trees. We part on a handshake.

"Tis a nice soft night. I'm thinking I'll go and talk a little treason with my friends. Goodnight Mickeleen Og. Goodnight Sean Thornton."

I find thc kcy under the stone by the door. A fire flames in the grate in a crooked blue room. Sleep comes fast in a settle bed.

I awake to the morning and call of birdsong, and a wind that moves the trees outside the window. These only disturb the stillness and I realise that these sounds have become alien to me, and I must learn to listen again.

I open the door of 'White O'Morn' to the garden and a wooden gate that gives on to a sloping field of dandelion and daisy. And beyond this the lake. The water is a sheet of grey glass furrowed by tiny waves that break regular as breathing among the tall reeds. A scatter of swans moves slow in the still day, and a heron flies heavy-winged above.

The hills beyond the lake lie like dark cats waiting to pounce. There is something dangerous, threatening about them even in sunlight as they cast shadows and take on the moods of sky and water.

Of course I am aware that my stranger's eye sees it so, but still it is not the chemically coloured Innisfree of a film director's romantic imagination. And I am victim to the fallacy that this landscape has always been thus. It is pagan and timeless, yes, but the only constant in any landscape is change, however imperceptible. And so for a time I feel I belong here, for there are times when the feeling of being part of a landscape is greater than the sense of being outside it.

On my walks I notice everywhere small battles between growth and decay, between man and nature. The nettle that grows solitary from a concrete wall. The Massey Ferguson abandoned in the corner of a field, grass growing in the gearbox. The hare that starts from under a broken boat, a waddle of ducks bending under a rusting gate.

By the railway track, unused now, for many miles I walk till I come to the station house. A ruin, where rooks have built their nests and groundsel grows in the waiting room. And if I look to the distance, it's Sean Thornton I see, his face as dark as the black hunter he rides along the tracks to the waiting train. And she, Mary Kate Dannaher with her freckles and her temper and her flame red hair, leaning out the carriage window as she waits for him.

"Don't go Mary Kate. You've married a better man than you know. Tis Sean Thornton loves you surely."

And he kisses her upturned mouth as the smoke of the engine swirls about them.

"Oh there'll be no bolts or locks between us Mary Kate, only the bolts and bars of your mercenary little heart."

A shutter on a broken hinge bangs closed.

Across the boreen from the cottage there is a wood, dark and mysterious. Easy to imagine Grainne against a tree there asking Diarmuid if a droplet of water on her white thigh is more brave than he. And among damp grass, splashed with wildflower there are paths that meander drunkenly, yet logical and ancient as the trees themselves. In this, the most secret and pagan of places, the peace of a chapel pervades. Once surrendering to a delinquent urge to shout out, I am immediately shamed with a feeling of desecration. This wood is for silence, or at the most for whispers only.

Hours I spend in the garden, watching the beginning of lilac and apple-blossom, pink and white ignite in the branches of a fallen tree. Through an ivy-covered break in the wall, a view of the lake beyond. Behind an outhouse, plum trees have been planted and everywhere bees hang in the bells of flowers. Now is the season for nettle soup, but a poem by Peter Fallon haunts me still and I cannot think to pluck them.

My nearest neighbour lives across a field in a mobile home, sheltered by the ruins of his former home. An old Bosch fridge door serves as his gate and in the pathway, in rain or shine, his old rag of a dog lies sullen and sad dreaming of long ago sheep. He talks across the hedge to me with the shyness of a child.

"You that's been abroad, what would you think of this place now?" He offers me a Silvermint and watches me under his eyebrows. Between the peak of his cap and his forehead is a birthmark of red skin. Once, he tells me, he caught a great black bird, a stranger to the lake, dragged it home and tied it to a post with ropes, till it died screeching a week later. At night he comes with poteen and he talks of a brother beyond in America.

"Cincinatti?"

"No. Pittsburgh."

"Oh aye, Pittsburgh, Massachusetts, where the steel and pig iron furnaces are so hot a man forgets his fear of hell."

We talk of the Quiet Man and the little fella with the horse called Napoleon and Maureen O'Hara giving lip to John Wayne and the way he put his shoulder to the door in the storm and thrun her down on the bed and it broke under the weight of them. "That was a great pitcher. Very true to life," he laughs.

More poteen in his blue mug.

"I never married, no, I suppose I was kinda choosey, and the Mother, God be good to her, wouldn't hear of another woman in the house. Sure everyone has some fad or mi-adh on them. That was mine I suppose. When we were childer we came visiting in this house and we'd sit in the corner there by the fire and look up the chimney and count the stars."

Maire is his sister, a tiny timid woman who never speaks and moves like a ghost between the caravan and the fields. She hides her hands under a spotted apron and they move in there like little trapped birds.

"There are some things a man can't forget Mary Kate."
"Like what, supposin?"
"Oh the sight of a girl in a field with the sun on her hair."

On Sunday I go to Mass. The men stand outside the railing till the last bell calls them in, stamping out their cigarettes which they hold under their palms away from the wind. The chapel smells of damp. I stand at the back among the latecomers, the women in scarves, the men kneeling on handkerchiefs to protect Sunday suits. After the silence of the Consecration, an explosion of coughing and then the slow eye-roving procession to Communion. I walk the three miles home, passed by men on bicycles who say morra, and cars stuffed with gawking children beep their horns in salutation to the stranger among them.

I stop at the shop named Open and buy the papers from another world and cigarettes for the long Sunday afternoon in the room where the clock made in Romania ticks crazily backwards.

Sadly it is time for me to leave. There will always be the coming and the going, the breaking of camp, the journey towards something else. The goal is always another place.

I have lit the room with candles that shiver in the draught from underneath the door and throw my shadow huge across the room. I will miss hearing the chimney winds and the spitting of rain against the crooked window and the drip of it from the thatch. And outside in the darkness, the bleat of sheep and the call of wildbirds and the twisty fingers of trees against the sky. Tonight clouds cover the stars, but as always you watch for one that falls and tells a soul to heaven goes. No houselight shines in the distance near or far, but only some pulse of yellow light unknown to me, flickers in the trees beyond the lake.

Are the swans sleeping now? And the cows, immobile as ornaments all day, gone happily home? Have the ponies galloped away beyond the hills?

"Living in a shack near the slag heaps White O'Morn and Innisfree come to mean a little bit of heaven, Mickeleen Og."

I keep it all like a movie hidden in the vault of memory, to be screened at will, at any time of day or night, wherever my road may take me.

Now and then a dog is barking but if I listen now, the silence answers back across the water and along the fields of night.

The Strangest Feeling In Bernard's Bathroom

Aidan Matthews

Bernard was almost sixty, and still happy. He liked to bring this up in conversation. It was his only vanity.

"I don't expect much," he said. "That way, I'm never disappointed. Other people want the sun, moon and stars. When they don't get them, they become bitter. Honestly, there is so much bitterness in the world. If only people were happy with what they have. That's what I always say."

All his friends in the staff canteen would nod when he said this.

"You're a philosopher, Bernard," they used to say. "You're a wise old bird."

Jack Barrett, his oldest friend, who managed the Curtain Material Section, would chip in here.

"If there's one thing better than an old head on young shoulders, it's a young head on old shoulders," he said, wiping bits of pastry from the corners of his mouth.

And Bernard would come in on that cue.

"The young people want their houses curtained and carpeted before they move in. They want everything at once, just like that. It was different in our day."

"A damn sight different."

Then Carmel Timoney, who worked in the Stationery Department, would bring the whole thing to a close. She would punch out her cigarette at the edge of her saucer, and speak for them all.

"No wonder you look so young, Bernard," she always said. "The right attitude is worth a hundred trips to the doctor."

"Or to the psychiatrist," Bernard would say, but only if the girl from the Information Desk was sitting at another table, because one had to remember, all said and done, that her brother had been in and out of homes ever since the accident on the motor-bike. If she was sitting with them, he would say something else.

"Or to the priest," he would say.

"God forgive you, Bernard Brennan," Carmel would say in mock horror. "Wait until I tell your wife."

That was the pattern of Bernard's life. When you thought about it, there was a lot to be said in its favour. It was all very well to talk about action and adventure, but the truth was you had enough to contend with from day to day. Bernard's life was full of days. It took him all his time just to get through them. Sometimes he thought they would never end. Still, he was good humoured about that too.

"Time probably does fly," he used to say, "but you have to wait a long time to get clearance for take off."

They loved that.

"You're a laugh a minute," Jack would say to him.

But his wife had heard it too many times.

"Would you ever think of another one?" she said.

So the next time the topic came up for discussion, he changed it slightly.

"Time probably does fly," he said to Janet while she was folding shirts in the kitchen. "But it flies on one engine."

Secretly he preferred it the other way.

Bernard's day began with an erection, and ended with anti-flatulent lozenges. He hated taking them, even the lemon-flavoured ones, because he had to get out of bed to wash his teeth again. If he didn't take them, the inevitable happened. Then Janet would turn over angrily, taking most of the eiderdown with her.

"It's not fair," she would say. "It's just not fair."

His erection she never noticed. Once he had pretended to be asleep, and rolled over to her side. But she never said a word, then or later. Anyhow, that was years ago. There was no point in wondering about it now. Instead, Bernard wondered about other things. Rainbows, for example. They had to do with reflections and the spectrum, but most people never bothered to find out. They just darted home between showers, or gave out about the weather forecast. But they never once stopped to think: how extraordinary rainbows are. In fact, there was no end to what you could wonder about. Teachers nowadays understood that. When he was at school, you never heard about nature trips. And what about the way in which Religion was taught? You didn't just parrot off any old rubbish anymore. You talked about things, you were open to discussion. Of course, certain questions could never be answered. Take a sixty year old dead person. Would that person be raised up as a baby, a boy, a man, or an old man? Not even the priests with beards could tell you that. Or take the way people were different. Why was one person a millionaire, and another man with a spastic child? As to sex, you could wonder about that until the cows come home.

Bernard spat out the hydrogen peroxide he had been gargling. Then he rinsed his mouth with warm water.

"You're a great man for questions," he said to his image in the mirror.

A face that was almost sixty, and still happy, looked back at him. Its lips were white with toothpaste.

That was where things stood, the day Bernard walked into the bathroom without realising Janet was in the bath. He was the kind of man who likes to shave twice a day. Besides, doing it the old fashioned way with cream and a naked razor gave one a few minutes by oneself after a day spent behind the counter without any real opportunity for privacy. It made you fresh and alert as well. Most of all, it was a good discipline. Bernard had always known when the rot sets into a man: if a chap stopped shaving, he stopped making the effort. He might as well pack it in. His cards were numbered.

It was a good thing Janet had turned on the warm-air heater over the towel rail. Otherwise she might have heard Bernard opening the door. As it happened, she was sitting with her back to him, fiddling with the taps. All her hair was up under the shower cap that had the design of the little Black and White Minstrel men running round musical chords on it. She was bent forward so that her spine stood out. Bernard could see the red mark of her brassiere strap and, just above the water, the thin print that her panty hose had left across the small of her back. It was ten years since he had last seen her like this. Perhaps it was more.

"Janet," he said, and was amazed that he had.

But she never heard him. The taps were going full blast, and the steam was rising in clouds. She started punching the water between her legs, and then whisking it, to make more foam. Bernard could see the slippery corner of her breast, and the white puncture-marks of the vaccination weal on her shoulder. Her body seemed very tired somehow. He felt terribly sorry for it, and for her too. In fact, he had never quite experienced such an odd feeling before; he was at a loss what to call it. He had always been very fond of her, of course, but one assumed that.

When they had been married at first, there was the other too as well, for a while at least; and then there was the Christmas feeling, good-will and so forth, from time to time. But that was par for the course. That was run-of-the-mill stuff.

Janet screwed the taps shut with both hands. Now he could hear again the high humming of the warm-air heater, its dry gusts reaching him across the length of the bathroom. He was afraid she might sense him then, or feel a draught, or lose the soap and turn around, groping for it in the bath. She wouldn't understand, she would think he was some kind of peeping tom, she would have no idea of the sadness he felt as he saw her sitting there, looking ridiculous and forgotten-about and delicate. He felt if he touched her she would come out in a rash around the mark of his finger. If she fell getting out of the bath, her skin would be bruised. If her ankle knocked against the spigot of the tap, the tissue would blacken. Anything might happen. Without her clothes, she was so terribly naked.

Bernard shut the door quietly behind him, and stood for a while in the passageway. Suddenly everything had gone quiet. He couldn't hear the warm-air heater now. His own body-sounds made the only noises: his heart and stomach juices, his lungs taking in air.

"Janet," he called.

The heater was probably too loud. Or perhaps she had water in her ears. Or maybe she was washing her hair. Would she wash it sitting in the bath or standing beside it, bending over? You could be married twenty-eight years, and not know these things.

"Janet!" he shouted.

"I'm in the bath," she called out. "I can't hear you."

Bernard was determined to make more of an effort that evening. It was never too late. If there was one thing people agreed about, it was that. Of course, it would be silly to talk in terms of a resolution. That kind of talk got you nowhere. It would be better to think in terms of giving up cigarettes. When you stopped smoking, you did so quietly. You told no-one. You just hoped for the best. If you made it through Monday, the chances were you would last through Tuesday too. But there was no use worrying, or looking back. The main thing was to stick at it. That would be his approach. Anyway, if he was suddenly to become attentive, she would probably suspect him. It might even alarm her.

After supper, he began to stack the dishes.

"What's got into you?" said Janet.

"I thought you might be tired," he said.

"Thanks very much." But her tone of voice took the good out of it. "I've been tired for twenty-five years. Watch where you let that gravy drip."

Still, she seemed pleased. From the way she swung her sandal by the toe-strap he could tell she was chuffed. That was one thing he knew about her.

"You're in good time for your programme," he said.

"It's on late," said Janet. "That's why I had my bath early. There's some football match on, with a satellite link-up. My programme isn't on until ten."

She cocked her head to one side, and shook it a few times. For a moment, she became strange to him again. He was slopping the dinner plates into the pedal bin, but he stopped to look at her.

"Water," she said, wagging her finger in her ear.

What was the point? After twenty-eight years, you could hardly walk up to your wife, and say to her "I saw you in the bath this evening, and I was shy, but not for the reason you might think. It was because you seemed so small really, so helpless almost. I wanted to put my arm around you, although it was not a sexual feeling. It was more a feeling of sadness."

"You're only making work," she said to him. "You're making a mess."

She was picking peas and a potato-skin off the floor. He let her take the plate from his hand. Then he peeled off the kitchen-gloves. Perhaps it was already too late. Perhaps it would do more harm than good.

Janet examined him closely.

"You're in strange form tonight," she said. "You didn't even shave when you came in."

When she was fast asleep, Bernard put his bedside lamp down on the floor, and turned it on. Then he could look at her without fear of waking her. Something of what he had felt in the bathroom revived in him, but it was not as strong or sudden or strange. In fact, he had to work at it a bit. Face-cream glistened on her cheeks and forehead; her lips were tightly shut. After a while, he experienced a kind of affection, a sort of peace; yet it all seemed willed. What had happened in the bathroom was unselfconscious, and he was wistful about it now. But perhaps it would happen again. Perhaps it would happen more and more often, at the most unlikely times, in the most unexpected places.

Bernard pressed another anti-flatulent out of its foil sheet. He let it dissolve slowly on his tongue. Then he made his way to the bathroom. He could still see the prints of Janet's feet where she had stood under the heater to dry her shoulders and hair, tapping clouds of talcum powder onto her legs so that the white and lemon dust settled around her on the dark carpet. After he had washed his teeth, he sat down on the toilet, and looked at the prints. They were like the marks you see in the snow: bird-marks or hoof-marks. There were animals in Asia that had never been seen, Bernard thought. They were known only by the prints of their paws. He had forgotten how small Janet's feet were. They were almost petite. Yet she was not a small woman. She came up to his shoulder.

When Bernard got back into bed, his hands were so cold that he couldn't touch himself with them. He held them away from him until the heat of the bed made them warm again. He knew it would be an hour, perhaps an hour and a half, before he slept. But he was used to that too.

Bernard's third-best suit had a blurred look at the collars and cuffs, and a glazed look at the seat and elbows. In the morning, he put it on, and went to work.

"Have a good day," he said to Janet.

"I don't know how you get away with that suit," Janet said. "Jack Barrett is always dressed like a lord."

He could see that she knew he was behaving differently. It made her uncertain.

"Don't just stand there," Janet said.

He could say it now. He had twenty minutes to spare. Janet was still in her dressing-gown too. It was strange how defenceless people seemed in their night clothes. Their work-clothes made them hard again: when they were dressed, they would fight you tooth and nail. But they were clumsy and bashful in their pyjamas, smelling of toast and sleep. He could see why the secret police made dawn-raids. It would be a good thing if the United Nations were to meet in dressing-gowns. Then there would be fewer wars.

"Will you not just stand there?" Janet said. She gathered up the collar of her dressing-gown, and covered her throat with it.

He would say it that evening. Friday night was a good time for speaking out.

"Goodbye so," he said.

A young black in a brightly coloured shirt sat opposite Bernard on the bus. If you look at them, Bernard thought, they imagine you're being critical; if you look away, they suppose you're being contemptuous. He wished he had bought a newspaper on the way to the bus-stop. It might be a time before he could offer his seat to an old lady. The bus was only half-full, and old ladies made a habit of getting up later in the morning. It would be foolish to stand for a young woman. After all, he was almost sixty. Besides, if they wanted to wear trousers, they could go the whole hog, and stand in buses as well.

Bernard stared out the window, lifting his hat from time to time as the bus passed a church. He had never been very consistent in this practice. At times, he liked to raise it at any and every church, whatever the colour of its money; at other times, he would tip it intermittently, once in five perhaps, or once in six. Today, he touched his hat-brim whenever he saw a church; and he was a little surprised, as he had been before, at how many of them there were, on the way into work.

What had happened in the bathroom was not sexual; and if it was, it was also more than that. Seeing a pretty girl sauntering along the street, and wanting, let's call a spade a spade, to reach out and pat her behind, was one thing; but to walk into your own bathroom, to see your wife sitting in the bath, and to feel sad and shy about it, was another. Not that Bernard was a stranger to emotion. He had his feelings, even if he didn't parade them. Only a week before, he had gone out of his way to minimise the fuss when a young woman was caught with a pair of lisle stockings in the Religious Objects Department. Jack Barrett, for all his palaver, would have prosecuted; but Bernard had talked to her nicely, and said it was obviously an oversight, and would she go back to the hosiery section, and pay for the article there. In the end, she made a bee-line for the side-exit.

Bernard looked down at the black hands in the lap opposite him. Why were the hands of black people, and brown people for that matter, so beautiful? Their fingers were long and tapering; they were like pianist's fingers. It was no wonder the blacks had invented jazz. Now if it was Jack Barrett on the bus, he would not have noticed the delicate black hands. He would have saved up some comment about squashed lips and noses. He would not have been open to the beauty that you can see in blacks, if you take the trouble to look. But that was the whole trouble with Jack. He was a very nice oaf, it was true; first and foremost, though he was an oaf.

Bernard stood up. He had reached his stop.

"I beg your pardon, sir," he said to the black.

The man was confused. His legs were not in the way. Still, he drew them in, and watched the nice old chap with a kind of happy face stepping down off the bus.

When the lunch-hour was almost over, Bernard decided that he would, after all, tell Jack what had happened. Carmel had turned away, and was chatting ten to the dozen to the girl whose brother had had the nervous breakdown.

"I walked into the bathroom last night," he said to Jack, "and I saw Janet just sitting in the bath. I..."

"Carmel," Jack called. "Come and hear about Bernard and Janet in the loo."

"Bernard Brennan," said Carmel. "Now at last we know how you manage to stay looking the way you do. I'll have to keep an eye on you, I will."

"But it wasn't that at all," Bernard explained to Jack. "It was the strangest feeling."

"I think I know the feeling," said Jack, winking elaborately at Carmel. "I had a touch of it myself this morning when I went the short way through Trousers, and what did I see?"

"Tell us then," Carmel said.

"A young lady who was nameless and shall remain so, stretched out on the floor of one of the cubicles, with her feet out like so, as if she was having a baby."

Jack pushed back in his chair and swung his legs high. There were whoops of laughter. Bernard gave up, and joined in.

"What was she doing then?" he said.

Jack puffed and panted his answer.

"She was holding her breath, and sucking in her tummy, to get the bloody designer jeans on. But her arse wouldn't go in."

Carmel covered her face, and howled with glee.

"Yes," said Jack in his normal voice, "I know about strange feelings. You're a clever old bird, Bernard. A wise old owl."

Bernard looked at the clock on the canteen wall.

"Time flies," he said.

"Are we ready for take-off?" Jack said, twisting round to squint at the hands.

"No," said Bernard. "we're just coming in to land."

On the way home he had an inspiration.

A priest would listen. In a sense, and without any disrespect intended, that was what they were paid for. It was downright stupid to have even tried talking to someone like Jack Barrett. What could you expect of a man who put brown in his hair, and wore a gold chain around his wrist? Jack had an answer for everything: it was the easy way out. But a priest would understand. At the same time, of course, it would be unreasonable to suppose that a priest would have had any very similar experiences. That was what the whole argument about celibacy was concerned with. On the other hand, they were men who read, and travelled. They know a lot, and they meant well, even if they did go on a bit about the joy of service, and the joy of faith, and whatever. It was easy known they had never sold a pair of shoes across a counter.

Finally, Bernard got off the bus one stop short. The Church of the Incarnation was only a stone's throw. Anyhow, he would just nip in, and see what happened; if he changed his mind, he could walk home through the park. But he hesitated at the church railing, and was even more unsure in the church porch where two small boys were playing conkers with a young curate. His fingers stung when he dipped them in the font: holy water had a way of being cold.

Am I behaving oddly? Bernard wondered.

Inside, there was an old woman leafing through a parish newsletter, and a file of six or seven persons waiting for Confession. Bernard sat down at the end of the bench, and shifted farther up it whenever the queue shortened. He used the muscles of his bottom to do this. It was strange how it brought back his childhood, when his legs didn't reach to the kneelers, and he had to shuffle along the seat on his bare thighs, with the waxed wood cold against his skin. That was what Bernard hated most about churches: they always brought you back to your childhood, as if things were not already difficult enough.

And what was he going to say to the priest? That he was a

man of feeling? That would be some kind of start, but it might well seem unusual, the more so if the man hearing Confessions was one of the old school, all gate and no garden. In a way, it was odd to be coming to confess at all. It wasn't even a matter of slip-ups and stabs of conscience: it was more the desire to confess the strangest feeling, and one that, in spite of its own bizarreness, Bernard rather hoped to have again, and even again, if that were possible. Because he had no other feeling to measure it against. True, he remembered seeing the blind children coming out of the home the nuns ran, and being emotional about that, especially when they filed across the road at the zebra crossing, each holding onto the one in front, with an albino at the top of the line. Still, he hardly ever thought about that now. Besides, you would want to be a monster not to be upset about blind children. A middle-aged woman sitting in a bath with a shower cap on her head, and no Brigitte Bardot, be it said, was a different thing entirely.

He was almost the first in the queue. This priest was a quick one. Other persons had filled the bench behind Bernard: a policeman in uniform, which was quite extraordinary when you thought about it, a quite young girl with cold sores on her mouth, and a father and son, the son looking rather fed-up, if the truth be told.

Bernard was next. This was ridiculous. He couldn't walk into a Confession box, and rattle off a story about surprising his wife in the bath. The priest would think he was mad. He might even ask the policeman to throw Bernard out. Worse, he might decide to keep Bernard for ages. He might be one of those very young priests who should have been psychiatrists, and would like nothing better than to open the prisons or sell off St. Peter's and all its treasures. If he was, and he found out about Bernard not seeing Janet in the buff for however many years, he would probably go on and on, and end up by wanting to see them together. In the meantime, you would have all those people outside, just wondering why on earth this particular confession was taking so long.

The other people in the queue were a bit surprised when the old man who was next, and had a nice, happy kind of face, stood up and walked off. He must have something pretty weighty on his mind; or perhaps he was a crank; or maybe he had left his gloves somewhere, and just remembered where.

Everybody moved down one along the bench.

When Bernard arrived home, and walked upstairs, he found that Janet was in the bath. At least, she was in the bathroom. He listened at the door, but he could hear nothing. The warm-air heater was on.

"Can I come in?" he shouted.

"What?" Her voice was not terribly pleasant. Of course, she hated shouting.

"May I come in?" Bernard said.

"I can't hear you," she cried. She was certainly exasperated.

"Please may I come in?:" Bernard shouted for all he was worth.

"I'm in the bath," she screamed.

So he went downstairs again, and hung up his coat, and straightened his tie, and ran a hand through his hair. There were plums in the bowl on the sideboard in the living room, but perhaps they were meant for later. Instead he took a Turkish Delight out of the second layer in the box of chocolates. There were some left in the top layer, mostly nougat, but he didn't care. He would go down to the second, even if she criticised him for doing so. After all, who had bought them?

Bernard sat down, and thought about his day. Perhaps it had been impetuous of him to leave the church. Perhaps he would mention the whole thing from start to finish to Carmel Timoney. He had talked to her about other things, personal matters, in the past, and she had always been helpful. When you thought about it, she was a most obliging woman. Why had he not spoken to her instead of to Jack? But perhaps Jack meant well beneath it all. You never could tell.

Bernard went down to the second layer again, and took out a hazelnut this time. He could hear Janet letting out the bathwater.

Perhaps he had misunderstood himself the night before. Perhaps he had been startled by Janet's plainness and fat. Perhaps he had been a bit appalled that she couldn't make more of herself. No-one was asking her to be Greta Garbo, but she might make the effort. Or perhaps he had been tired, or depressed. He had a perfect right to be, sometimes. Maybe it was just as well she hadn't let him into the bathroom with her.

Where was the orange one?

Bernard leaned back, and chewed the chocolate on his good side.

Perhaps it was just as well.

Goodbye To The Hurt Mind

Hugo Hamilton

You're full a shite.... he said, looking straight over at me.

I don't go looking for trouble. Not when I hear a Belfast accent, anyhow. But there was no mistake here. His small, black eyes were on me; either with intense rage or intense stupor. I hadn't opened my mouth.

I half knew the woman he was with, Helen Connors. All cleavage. Dress designer, I think. She frowned at him or at the floor underneath him and said nothing. He was well gone; slumped down on his elbows. The candle at the centre of the table made everything look darker. Made the line of her cleavage that bit more unstable. Even the wine looked black in the glasses; black as H Block flags or black plastic bags used to make H Block flags. The music was just about loud enough to pretend nothing was happening.

Full a shite.... he repeated once more.

How long can you ignore that? I looked away; pretended to be intensely interested in the band just then. I could see the waitress at another table with her back to us. But his solid, black stare had attached itself to me. And the candle seemed to give everyone pale flesh tones. I thought of pale, degraded election posters.

I had nothing to say. What does he want? And then you begin to think he might be half right. Maybe he knows something.

The Belfast accent beats me too. I could never be sure whether he said "shite" or "shout". So many words seem interchangeable. There's a lot of shouting. Paisley used to shout all the time. And Gerry Adams shouts through his teeth, without taking the pipe out of his mouth. And Margaret Thatcher doesn't need to shout any more, ever since the Brighton bomb. The Northern accent bewilders. Twice I've been up there for some fishing and they keep talking about fashion... fashion, fashion.

I can't help taking another look at Helen Connors while she's looking away towards the band, but Belfast there keeps staring across at me. I can't make him out. Beside the candle, there was a pale blue menu card jammed between salt and pepper and a small vase containing a single daffodil. This was repeated on every table.

Janet wanted me to collect her mother from the hairdresser. Her mother always pretends at the hairdressers that I'm her lover. Here's my Romeo, she says. I wait in the cane waiting-chairs without picking up one of the magazines on the glass table. They offer me coffee. No thanks! There are cane frames around the mirrors. The image must have been decided on from the beginning; cane along with red towels. I can see half of Janet's mother's face in the mirror. Somebody sweeps up the cut hair around her on the floor. I hear an ad on the radio for late night shopping. An oval mirror is held up at the back of Janet's mother's head. I concentrate on telling her that her hair looks great. Janet's mother links arms as we leave the hairdressers and the girls smile. The scent of hairspray fills the car.

I saw Helen Connors make a move. She stood up and put on her coat, gave Belfast a slap on the shoulder with the back of her hand and said: Come on you. She treats him like a schoolboy. Up you get. He's got difficulty on his feet; makes the bar look like a ferry. She plunges again down towards us to pick up her bag, looking at me with a half smile as if to apologise for him before she steers him through a gap between the tables, past the stage and out the door.

I'd never hit anybody. I'm sure they can see it a mile away. To be honest, I'd be afraid to. In fact I've only ever hit one person in my life and I still recall the sight of my fist leaping back from from that bleeding lip. Janet hit me once. That's when she was pregnant. I was asking for it.

As soon as he was gone, somebody told me he was an artist. So bloody what, I thought. But he was going to be a big noise one of these days, they said. I left, not long after that myself. My ears were ringing with the music. And the house seemed unusually quiet when I got home. The sandwiches and flasks stood ready for school in the morning. I sat down in the kitchen, switched on the radio and refused to think about next day. I knew Janet was already half way through it.

The next time I saw Helen Connors, she was standing completely naked in a field with a helicopter overhead. Voyeurs? The army as voyeur? Or the artist as helicopter?

Graham Hoban. I had forgotten the man's name completely and walked into the gallery just to pass the time. But I recognised her instantly. There was no mistake. It was Helen Connors without clothes. She seemd fully aware of the helicopter above. I had never imagined a dark shading around her nipples. Or that her hair would be black. Never imagined her at all. Breasts are like eyes; or bogus eyes. I felt Helen Connors looking at me the way Dalmatians look at you when you don't know where their eyes are. So I did a tour of the gallery. I crossed the path of a nun and found it odd not to say hello; to seem so intensely interested in the exhibits. When I got back to Helen Connors, there were two women examining her.

I never look into Janet's eyes. Then sometimes I feel a desperate urge to look her straight in the eyes. Janet, look into my eyes, I shout at her. Janet, look at me. Once, I grabbed her by the hair on top of her head and turned her round to face me. She spat into my eyes. I asked her to.

I can't bear repetition. I like things to happen once.

When Janet's mother comes around for dinner on Tuesday's she wears her fur coat. She likes to pretend this is a special occasion, her first ever visit to the house. I hand her a glass of sherry. She takes my arm and says to Janet: you don't mind if I borrow your husband for a moment. Janet's mother tells me about a famous dentist whom she could have married. He was mad about her. Extremely intelligent man. Had asked her many times to marry him but she turned him down. Gave him back a ring he once gave her; they were on a train at the time from Limerick to Dublin when he took the ring back and threw it out the window of the carriage.

Why didn't she marry him, I ask? Janet's mother can't answer that. Everybody usually wanted to know if she remembered the spot where he threw out the ring. She laughs. That was an expensive ring.

Over dinner, Janet's mother remembers to suggest a new carpet. She had mentioned it the week before. How long can you ignore that?

After dinner, Janet asks me to put on a waltz for her mother. She likes the Blue Danube. Janet's mother once stayed in Vienna. Janet's mother is a woman over whom an expensive ring was flung from a train into a ditch. It was in Vienna that she learned to dance. Mere contact with the city was enough. - Zwei mal hin, zwei mal her, rund herum, das ist nich schwer.- Janet's mother askes me to dance with her. I'm much taller than she is. But not firm enough. Too stiff. Too stiff. Ah, you're no use at all, she says. A man should lead. Are you a man?

Janet danced with one of the children. Their movements are exaggerated.

I was bound to run into him again at some stage. Belfast. When I did, a few months later, on one of those fishing trips up north, it was a bit of a shock and perhaps a small victory too. He must have felt it. We had both been invited by the same people; I was merely told a few northern lads would be on the trip. I don't even know why I go on these fishing trips since I've got no patience and no interest in fishing. I never touch a rod.

We pretended never to have met before; Graham Hoban. We had to. And of course I pretended not to know that he was an artist. Nothing was said about the first meeting either. There was an unspoken agreement between us. Do you remember calling me a shite, I felt like asking him a few times. But I left it alone. We got on well; surprisingly well. We talked and drank in the pubs after the day's outing until I began to think that he had forgotten or never even remembered. There was too much of a conspiracy. He never mentioned Helen Connors either and we never met alone so nothing was ever brought out in the open.

We can talk about anything. Fishing, music, women. No politics. Mostly we talk about women and as time goes on I just can't ignore it any longer and suddenly burst out for all to hear: they're all full a shite. But then everybody was waiting for me to expand when I really had nothing to say since all I wanted was to say the words so that Hoban would hear them. I'm always afraid of saying things I don't mean. Or things I can't back up. Everybody thought I was drunk.

But Hoban knew what I meant and soon took up the challenge.

You know, he said, a while later so that everybody would hear him, I think people generally get on much better when they dislike each other. Men, women, everybody.

Everybody was listening. Again we faced each other across a table, this time covered with a plantation of drinks in a bar which was thick with smoke.

Take Belfast there, he argued. In Belfast you can say anything you like to your best friend and he'll still be your friend. Call somebody a scabby bastard, he'll like you all the more for it. Inverse flattery, I suppose. Just being the object of attention is a compliment in itself. The girls love it too. In fact they'd be insulted if you didn't call them names; the same way a fish would be insulted if you didn't eat it after you went and caught it.

On the way back to the hotel along the pitch-black road, the two of us walked together. The rest of them got separated. I could hear them laughing ahead. He stumbled against me and put his arm around me for support when I was hardly in a position to provide it. Anyhow, I still hadn't forgotten.

I thought of Helen Connors. Then he began to tell me what he liked about women when I least wanted to hear it.

I like the way they ask me to draw on their white flesh with lipstick. I'm an artist you know. And I like the way she puts her arse up to your eye and turns around to say: Come on---you bastard.

Janet is able to repeat things. She can relate the same thing twice or even three times in successive phone calls.

When I read a book I hold it so that it looks almost unread when I'm finished. Janet cracks the spine and leaves books face down on the sofa while she's on the phone.

Janet remembers some strange things. Forgettable things such as names and street names. She still knows the name of the shopkeeper at the end of the road in Wood Green: Mr Crawley. She still knows the name of every street and how many bells were on the front door and all the names with the bells.

I can remember an upturned ice cream cone under the seat of the bus the day we went to visit her uncle and I can still think of nothing more inedible. Janet remembers what pub we drank in that night: The Tankard. It's so easy, I always forget.

Janet hates bringing the car to the garage. She says it reminds her of a gynaecological examination every time a mechanic starts poking underneath the bonnet. She never remembers to check the oil in the car because that's something I always remember. I often think of motor oil.

It is Janet who asks me if I'm finished with the papers so she can throw them out.

It is me who collects the car from the garage. It is me who first grips the oily steering wheel when I get into the car. It is the mechanic who sees me searching for tissue papers and points to a large drum of blotting paper on the wall. Both Janet and her mother are at the hairdressers today. I couldn't collect them with oily fingers. It is me who remembers to say that they both have very nice hair.

Long after Janet's mother is gone home again, Janet asks me if I remember the name of a pub in Kensington. I ask her if she knows the colours of Lufthansa. She asks me what the name of the bakery was; Russell's, no Hoffer's.

While I lie on my back in bed that night, I cannot avoid remembering the name of the garage: Huet Motors. I continually see the petrol pumps and the interior of the workshop. I keep thinking that we've gone to bed on the floor of the workshop. It is me who keeps thinking about engines. It is Janet who first embraces me.

Mind you don't get any oil on my hair.

There is nothing in the world but the thought in my head.

I was on a train once in Germany. A woman came into the carriage and sat opposite me. We began to talk. She could speak little English and I could speak no German. I asked her why she was dressed all in white like a nurse. She said she was a nurse.

I asked if she would get off with me at the next station. She said she was getting off at the next station anyhow. GelsenKirchen. There's a big hospital there. When I saw a white bathtowel, I began to ask if she wasn't overdoing it with the colour white. Did I not like white? I do except on cars and pianos. Before I left, she suggested we meet again.

Janet's mother says I've got a weak handshake.

The last time I met him was outside Trinity; along the railing. It must have been around five o'clock in the evening. People were going home. The windows of a passing bus were steamed up. Some passengers upstairs had already cleared a circle with the sleeve of their coats; enough to look at the street and the railings of Trinity and the people walking by. He stopped and asked me if I was doing anything. I can never describe what I'm doing.

Come on you bastard. Let's, murder a pint.

On our way to the pub, we saw lots of people waiting for buses. As usual, there was a man selling evening papers at the corner of Westmoreland Street. As usual, I remembered the names of streets as I passed through them and forgot them again as soon as they were behind me.

He told me he was getting out. Australia. He had organized a place to work there.

You bastard!

He said he had engineered an exhibition for his paintings and a studio on a beach near Sydney.

You dirty bastard!

In the pub, I remember to look at the time. After a while I forgot the time. Let's make a disgrace of ourselves, he said. But I was taking it easy.

Goodbye to Ireland, he kept saying as we left the pub. Goodbye to the hurt mind. The barman said nothing and just laughed; he seemed glad to get us outside.

As we arrived around at Helen Connors house, he fell asleep on her doorstep. He couldn't even make it into the hallway. I had to pretend I had never seen her body naked before. We carried him in and laid him on the bed. I took off his boots. She took off his jacket.

Skin

Neil Jordan

The odd fantasies we people our days with; she had just pierced her finger with the knife, and from between the petals of split skin blood was oozing. It was coming in one large drop, growing as it came. Till her detached face reflects in the crimson.

But in fact the knife had missed her forefinger. It had cut round the gritty root of the lopped-off stem and was now splicing the orb into tiny segments. Her eyes were running. Cracked pieces of onion spitting moisture at her, bringing tears, misting her view of the enamel sink. The sink that was, despite the distortion of tears, as solidly present as it had been yesterday.

She was absorbed in the onion's deceit; its double-take. She had peeled layer upon layer from it and was anticipating a centre. Something like a fulcrum, of which she could say: here the skin ends; here the onion begins. And instead there was this endless succession of them, each like a smaller clenched fist, fading eventually into insignificance. Embryonic cell-like tissue which gave the appearance of a core. But in fact the same layers in miniature. Ah, she sighed, almost disappointed, looking at the handful of diced onion on the draining-board. She gathered these in her hands and shook them into the bowl. She washed her hands, to dispel the damp oily feeling, the acid smell. Then she turned her back on the sink, gazed absently on the kitchen table.

She had an apron on her, something like a smock. Flowers bloomed on it, toy elephants cavorted on their hind legs. There was lace round the neck and a bow-tied string at the back and a slit-pocket across the front into which she could place her hands or dry her fingers. Above it her face, which was uneventfully trim, and just a little plain. She was wearing high-heeled house slippers and an over-tight bra. Her shoulder was shifting uncomfortably because of it. When one rests one notices such things. She was resting. From the diced onions, carrots, chunks of meat, whole potatoes on the draining-board. From the black-and-white pepper tins on the shelf above it.

There were two large windows on the sink side of the room. On the wall opposite was a row of small single-paned windows, high up, near the roof. The midday sun came streaming in the large window from behind her. She saw it as a confluence of rays emanating from her. When she shifted, even her shoulder, there would be a rapid rippling of light and shadow on the table cloth. Blue light it was, reflecting the blueness of the kitchen decor. For everything was blue here, the pantry door, the dresser, the walls were painted in rich emulsion, varying from duck-egg to cobalt. And the day was a mild early September, with a sky that retained some of August's scorched vermilion. The image of the Virgin crossed her silent vacant eyes. She had raised her hand to her hair and saw the light break through her fingers. She thought of the statue in the hall; plastic hands with five plastic sunrays affixed to each; streaming towards the feet, the snake, the waterbowl. Mother of Christ.

She had been humming the first phrases of a tune. She stopped it when she returned abruptly to the sink, to the window, to the strip of lard - sparrow meat - hanging outside. She chopped the meat into neat quarters and dumped them with the vegetables into a saucepan. She placed the saucepan on a slow-burning ring. Then she began washing her hands again. The scent of onion still clung to them. Pale hands, made plump by activity, swelling a little round the wrist and round the spot where the tarnished engagement ring pulled the flesh inwards.

She massaged separately the fingers of each hand, rapidly and a little too harshly; as if she were vexed with them, trying to coax something from them. Their lost freshness.

Several inches of water in the sink; a reflection there - two hands caressing, a peering face swimming in the mud-coloured liquid, strewn over with peel. She grabbed hold of the knife and plunged it, wiping it clean with her bare thumb and forefinger. And again came the image - blood oozing, in large crimson drops. But her finger didn't gape. The knife emerged clean.

She pulled the sink plug then, hearing the suck, scouring the residue of grit and onion skin with her fingers. She dried her hands, walked with the towel into the living-room.

There there was a low-backed modern sofa, two older tattered armchairs and a radiogram piled with magazines. She sat in the sofa, easing herself into its cushioned supports. She fiddled with the radio dial, turned it on, heard one blare of sound and switched it off again. The silence struck her; the chirp of a sparrow outside, clinging to the strip of lard. In another minute she was restless again, leafing through the magazines, flicking impatiently over their pages.

A housewife approaching middle-age. The expected listlessness about the features. The vacuity that suburban dwelling imposes, the same vacuity that most likely inhabited the house next door. But she was an Irish housewife, and as with the whole of Irish suburbia, she held the memory of a half-peasant background fresh and intact. Noticeable in her dealings with the local butcher. She would bargain, oblivious of the demands of propriety. She would talk about childhood with an almost religious awe, remembering the impassioned innocence of her own. And, although house-proud, rigorous tidiness made her impatient; she had a weakness for loose-ends.

And in her the need for the inner secret life still bloomed. It would come to the fore in odd moments. A fragment of a song, hummed for a bar or two, then broken off. A day-dream. She would slide into it like a suicide easing himself into an unruffled canal. She would be borne off, swaying, for a few timeless moments. She would hardly notice the return. And for occasional stark flashes, she would be seized by a frightening admixture of religious passion and guilt, bordering on a kind of painful ecstasy; the need, the capacity for religiously intense experience of living; and in consequence of the lack of this, a deep residue of guilt. At times like this she would become conscious of anything red and bloodlike, anything blue or bright, any play of light upon shade.

But if she were asked how she lived, she would have replied: happily. And if she were asked what happiness meant she wouldn't even have attempted an answer.

She found herself rummaging among the magazines searching out one she had been reading yesterday. She recalled a story in it about the habits of Swedish housewives. Certain of them who would drive from their homes between the hours of two and four in the afternoon, out to the country, and there offer themselves to men. The event would take place in a field, under a tree, in a car. And afterwards, they would straighten their clothes, return home to find the timing-clock on the oven at nought, the evening meal prepared. It had disgusted her thoroughly at first glance. But something in it had made her read to the finish. The image, perhaps, of a hidden garden, sculpted secretly out of the afternoon hours, where flowers grew with unimaginable freedom.

Now she was feeling the same compulsion. 'Weekend' was the name, she remembered, selecting one from the pile. She opened it at the centre page. A glaring headline there, in vulgar black print: 'SWEDISH HOUSEWIVES' AFTERNOON OF SIN'. And a picture: a woman standing by a clump of trees, in a shaded country lane. A man in the distance watching her. A parked car.

She closed it instantly. It had disgusted her again. But as she sat there, the sound of distant cars coming to her from the road, her fingers began drumming impatiently on the wooden top of the radio. Something about it drew her. The sun, the glossy green of the foliage. The man's dark predatory back. Not the cheapness, the titillating obscenity. Not that.

Then she was moving towards the front door. Her tweed walking coat was hanging in the alcove. Outside, rows of starlings laced the telegraph wires. Motionless black spearheads, occasionally breaking into restless wheeling flights, to return again to their rigid formations. The same expectant stasis in her, her drumming fingers, like fluttering wings. She was a starling.

The sudden, unconscious burst of disquiet. The animal memory of a home more vibrant, more total than this. The origin track; the ache for aliveness.

All the way through the hall, out the front door, her fingers drummed. As she turned the ignition key in the dashboard the engine's purr seemed to echo this drumming.

Howth was facing her as she drove, answering her desperate need for open spaces. Slim spearlike poplars passed her on her left. Oaks gnarled and knotted to bursting-point. Ash and elder, their autumn leaves discoloured by traffic dust. She drove mechanically. She hardly noticed the line of cars coming towards her. Only the earth to her right, a dull metal plate today. Beyond it, as if thrusting through its horizon with a giant hand, the Hill of Howth.

Her forefinger still tapping on the steering-wheel. Scrubbing vegetables had banished most of the varnish from the nail. Today she didn't notice. A car swerved into her lane and away. She had a moment's vision of herself as a bloodied doll, hanging through a sharded windscreen. She drew a full breath and held it, her lungs like a balloon pressing at her breasts.

She pulled in at a causeway that led across marshlands to the open sea. She quenched the engine and gave herself time to absorb the shock of silence. Then she opened the door, got out, her fingers drumming on the metal roof.

Sounds that could have been the unbending of grass or the scurrying of insects. The lapping hiss of tide from the marshlands, its necklace of canals. But now she was here she wasn't sure why she had come. What to do with 'this' - as if the scene before her were some kind of commodity. It was the silence. The sheer pervasiveness of it.

She ran from the car door to the edge of the causeway in an attempt at the abandonment she imagined one should feel. There was a drop there, then mud-flats awaiting tide. Nothing came of it, however. Only the sense of her being a standing, awkward thing among grasses that crept, tides that flowed. It didn't occur to her to fall, flatten herself with them, roughen her cheek with the ragwort and sea-grass. She began to walk.

There were ships, tankers most likely, on the rim of the sea. As she walked through the burrows she saw hares bounding. She saw the sun, weak, but still potent. She saw a single lark spiralling towards it. She saw, when she reached it, a restful strand dissolve on either side into an autumn haze. It was empty of people.

The sand rose in flurries with her steps. She had worn the wrong shoes - those high-heeled slippers. Useless, she thought, slipping them off.

The sea amazed her when she reached it. Surging, like boiling green marble. Very high too, from yesterday's spring tide. There was a swell, beginning several yards out, that reached her in ripples. Each wave seemed to rise like a solid thing, laced with white foam, subsiding into paltriness just when she felt it would engulf her. Swelling, foaming, then retreating. The sun glistening coldly off it. She felt spray on her cheek. Wet, ice-cold, the feel of church floors, green altar-rails.

She decided to risk a paddle. She glanced round her and saw nothing but a black dot, like a rummaging dog, in the distance. So she opened her coat, hitched up her skirt, unpeeled her stockings. She'd stay near the edge.

She threw them, with her slippers, to a spot she judged safe from the incoming tide. She walked in, delighted with the tiny surging ripples round her ankles. Her feet were soon blue with the cold. She remembered her circulation and vowed not to stay long. But the freshness of it! The clean salt wetness, up around her calves now! It deserved more than just an ankle-paddle. And soon she was in it up to her knees, with the rim of her skirt all sodden. The green living currents running about her legs, the rivers of puffy white foam surrounding her like a bridal wreath. She hitched up her dress then, the way young girls do, tucking it under their knickers to look like renaissance princes, and felt the cold mad abandon of wind and spray on her legs. A wave bigger than the others surged up wetting her belly and thighs, taking her breath away. The feel of it, fresh and painful, icy and burning! But it was too much, she decided. At her age, skirt tucked up in an empty sea.

She turned to the strand and saw a man there, a wet-tailed cocker-spaniel at his heels, bounding in a flurry of drops. She froze. He had seen her, she was sure of that, though his eyes were now on the dog beside him. The sight of his tan overcoat and his dark oiled hair brought a desolate panic to her. The shame, she thought, glancing wildly about for her stockings and shoes.

But the sea must have touched her core with its irrational ceaseless surging. For what she did then was to turn back, back to the sea, picking high delicate steps through its depths, thinking: He sees me. He sees my legs, my tucked-up skirt, the outlines of my waist clearly through the salt-wet fabric. He is more excited than I am, being a man. And there was this pounding, pounding through her body, saying: this is it. This is what the sea means, what it all must mean. And she stood still, the sea tickling her groin, her eyes fixed on the distant tanker, so far-off that its smoke-stack seemed a brush stroke on the sky, its shape that of a flat cardboard cut-out. Around it the sea's million dulled glimmering mirrors.

But she was wrong. And when she eventually turned she saw how wrong, for the man was now a retreating outline, like the boat, the dog beside him a flurrying black ball. And she thought, Ah, I was wrong about that too. And she walked towards the shore, heavy with the knowledge of days unpeeling in layers, her skirt and pants sagging with their burden of water.

Brothers

Desmond Hogan

The whole scene converged on him under the bridge, the illumination of sky, of trees, of water, the whole outworld of the small Irish town assembling in Paul's mind, trees rallying towards the blue of the sky, church steeple issuing from behind them reflected in the intermittent pools, water extending itself in different directions, conveying the blue of the sky, pink skins collecting on it, hailing from the surrounding trees, the residue of a protracted spring.

He had wanted to come to this place, to secrete himself in it, ever since he heard his brother had been killed in action in Vietnam. It was the one place he associated with his brother, having wandered here with him on afternoons of childhood, picking their steps amid the stones.

Their home lying nearby - guarding the scene - upholding itself in its five storeys. The local bank house - walls rising to the afternoon sun - lane fading into a powdered perspective behind them.

'Gig' his brother had been called, the name hovering in the little boy's mind, about to topple over into some area of jocundity, of knowingness.

From here Paul could see the red seat under a distant clump of foliage where his brother used to meet a nurse, their figures embraced in shadow, leaves assembling about them, procuring an intimacy of pose, invoking the red and white of the girl's uniform.

The youth standing over her, manifesting his stature, the girl huddled to one side, secure in her demand, in her seniority of five years, the two of them engrossed in one another.

The affair weighted in a period of years, integrating itself in the afternoon shadows of school-days, a world of Latin books, of mathematical problems of blue and white lined copy-books, Gig's parents violently refraining from the relationship, withdrawing from this early show of sexuality, of physical need, maintaining themselves in their bank house, accommodating themselves in their fur coats, in their suits, incarnating themselves at bridge parties, at golf-club socials, secreting their lives in the patterns at the backs of cards.

Paul rarely encountered his older brother in those years, the youth occasionally escaping into his imagination, stalking naked about the upstairs room, his sexuality conserved in reds, in purples, hair bunching about it.

Sometimes the little boy overheard him making love to the nurse in the old van in their back yard as the affair became more serious in portent, the vehicle creaking with their efforts, the noises replenishing the night air, gripping the boy's mind, encompassing some childhood fear in it, enlarging it.

But Gig was basically a waster, floundering at examination, rows fermenting.

These rows were closed from Paul, the little boy fleeting to music lessons each week, fragile in intent, a violin under his arm, the ivy-covered house, which was liver coloured in autumn, waiting for him on the waterside of town the blue-haired lady who taught him music, assembling the pieces he'd learnt over the week.

A final row occurred between Gig and his parents the night he failed his examination for the third time - voices sounding from his room into the small hours - Gig deciding to go away.

He left in the following days - taking his suitcases - reassembling his life in New York.

Two years elapsed - procuring a peace for the inmates of the bank house - a sense of exorcism.

Then they heard that Gig had been sent to Vietnam, news of the war first reaching them from the freshly-formed Johnson regime, encompassing them.

A little world ranged on an old desk in Paul's schoolroom, extending itself in blue, demonstrating the country in which his brother was fighting on one of its furthest edges.

Letters arrived from his brother as he grew up, forming in the little boy's mind, tangerine stamps on them.

He inherited his first summers of loneliness, other young people distilling colours, walking the streets in dark glasses, in floral shirts, in flared trousers.

He often stood at the window in those summers, his figure convened amid the intransigent lace curtains, his violin discarded amid the drawing-room shadows within - the world withholding itself outside.

But he grew to an appreciation of himself, a formulation of himself in the pictures which ranged in his room, Simon and Garfunkel conversing over his bed - heads inclined towards one another - the photograph of a girl hovering alongside them, that of Katherine Mansfield, ghostly hair parted on her forehead, the artist who'd consummated the experience of love, of loss, in the books by his bed.

The presence of Vietnam to his life assailed for the first time, the images of the war performing a nightly persuasion upon his brain, veering towards him from the television, helicopters swooping like birds of prey, men shrieking, guns exploding, assembling a response in him, a mediation with his brother's philosophy.

He realised the intrinsic evil of the cause for which his brother was fighting, the intrinsic evil which he was helping to perpetuate. He grapsed a politcal philosophy in repudiation of his brother's beliefs, the heads of political leaders, joining those of transitory pop stars, that of an American negro, a noted assailant of the system his eyes large with agony, with remembrance.

A hope stepped out of those pictures, declaring itself in the promise of a shape, an integrity to his life, assailing the cartoon poster, the unpremeditated expressions of the faces of Toulouse-Lautrec characters, prostrating them in a new pose, in an indefatigability of colour.

This integrity was threatened by his brother's position, by his betrothal to violence, the blue holocaust of gunsmoke on television each night discharging in Paul's mind, ramifying his brother on his beliefs, in their innegotiability of tenure.

A gap exposed itself between the two boys - transfixing itself in the crucifix in Paul's room - in an utter irrevocability of stance.

A landscape of devastation replenished the youth's mind at night, distilling itself in plasticine colours, embracing in little fires. Eyes appealed to him from this background, the heads of children clamouring at him, demented planes in the sky behind them. The images of the suffering convoked, demanding an account in him, exercising his capacity for sympathy.

His brother was subsequently banished into some out-area of the mind, relinquished amid the despots of the world, abandoned to the surfeit of their crimes.

But a statue of a Greek Athlete stood on the hall-stand, negotiating with the flowers alongside it, the outreaches of seasonal colour, defining itself in a muscularity, delineating itself in light, attesting to all his brother had possessed, all that was wanting in himself.

It wasn't until today when he heard his brother had been killed, a Vietcong bullet tearing through his chest, that he realised the fact of his brother, of their separate existences, of the separate allegiances.

It wasn't until then that he reconciled himself to that part of himself which his brother had subsumed, leaving him vulnerable to a nature which protracted itself over the afternoons of adolescence, afternoons of wavering curtains, of unremitting self-abuse.

It wasn't until that moment that he conciliated with the forces of life, bringing the proceeds of his existence to this place, discharging it amid the ferment of blues, of greens.

A whole new intuition of himself collected about the figure of the youth in the red and white striped tee-shirt, delivering him to the afternoon, remitting him in the blonds, the duns of his hair, the vagaries of his appearance.

A butterfly, a woman on a bike, a child with a blue fishing-net, careered into a single instant, diffusing in him, protracting themselves in an intensity.

The images convened, collaborated, administering a final image of his brother, that of a rather bulky youth in a green American uniform, dark hair crouching over the handsomeness of his features, a helmet in one hand, a guarded solicitude about the pose.

They assembled in an elegy to his brother, an elegy to a rather bereft relationship, seeking a final assimilation, finding it in the newly-realised intensity in Paul's mind.

The entire perspective of their lives assailed him, rising from the surrounding images, concurring with them.

There had been an apartness between himself and his brother, they'd opted for different sides, they'd been decided by their presences to one another. But they'd been together in one thing, in an orientation towards life, a fundamental inclination towards living.

It was this inclination which was shattered in Gig now, arrested by the powers which operated under flags, under the guise of nationhood, of self-preservation.

A jet transversed the sky, unfurling itself in white, concelebrated in blue, inducing the entire afternoon into one embrace, into one gesture.

The American flag flared in Paul's mind, the entire afternoon consummated in a repudiation of it, in a disavowal of it.

Two little boys ran alongside the river-edge, fleeting into a statement about life, about death.

The House

Anne Devlin

It's my own fault that I ended up here. I have no one to blame but myself. I trusted her, you see. I don't mind any more, sometimes I even enjoy it; sitting by the window most of the day and they leave me alone now. I still get visitors: she always comes. She needs my approval even after all this time. In the beginning when she started to go I used to cry a little. Now I don't shed any tears at all. The pain is like a knot in my chest, it tightens the worse the noise becomes. And it usually happens after her visits. Sometimes the knot is so tight I think I am going to cry out. But I usually manage to control this urge. I don't talk at all now, I learned my lesson. It was opening up to her in the first place which did it. I should never have started to talk, let alone listen; and yet I so longed to have an intimacy with someone. I kept remembering '78 and wishing I could go back to a time before I met her, when she was just a nodding stranger on the road.

It began with a dream: the image was that of the interior of a house. It was the house I lived in as a child, fused with the house Paul and I shared when we married. In the dream I started at the top of the house – in the attic, where I had my darkroom – and began to run down all the flights of stairs to the bottom. As I approached them, the stairs became greatly exaggerated and seemed endless. I ran down each flight never expecting to do more than descend to a landing at a time; but to my surprise, I ran down flight after flight without stopping and right out through the front door and into the street. I left my job a year after that dream began to haunt me; that was how she entered our lives.

I worked as a teacher in the Art Department of a school in which Paul was Head of Mathematics. We had worked there together for several years. I am not sure whether the dream propelled me into this action or whether it was a symptom, but I had never been very happy at the school. Until I finally found the courage to tell Paul that I wished to give up teaching Art to apprentice boys and concentrate on making it as a photographer instead. It meant that for the first time in our marriage I would be dependent on Paul in the only way a man hates a woman to be dependent – financially. I say this in retrospect, at the time he assured me he would be glad to support me: so I gave up teaching.

She was my replacement. And this more than anything frightens me: I made way for her. It's very strange how every detail of her arrival, her appointment, her comings and goings, attached themselves like side glances to my consciousness. Everywhere I looked she was there, not in the centre of my pictures but somewhere in the far corner, tucked away and watching, like an incidental presence quietly moving across the lawn towards the house. On the day she was appointed to my old job at the school, Paul came home and said: 'The new Art teacher is smashing; they picked her because she was so like you. You'd love her. She's very sensitive.' I hate being driven into friendships, so I did not respond. The rest was inevitable: I was not going to be allowed to ignore my replacement. The next thing I heard about her from Paul was that she badly needed somewhere to live before the start of the new term. 'Could she possibly stay with us until she finds somewhere?' he asked. To which I responded with alarm because I fear such intrusions: 'She's a stranger. How can we share our house with an absolute stranger? We know nothing about her.' I have such fears about new people entering my life – and always have had; it has something to do with the fact that strangers bring with them wounds about which we cannot know because we have not witnessed the progress of the stranger through a community known to us. But most of all I have a heightened paranoia about outsiders, fostered by a Catholic childhood. 'Never talk to strangers!' were my mother's parting words as I set off to school as a child. I think she may have impressed this on me too effectively, because at the same time I am not a confident enough person to live in a house with anyone I haven't known for a very long time. And I regarded Paul, who took up with people effortlessly and would tell his life history to the man at the bus stop or the woman at the launderette, as a fool to live so dangerously. He in turn dismissed me as aloof, ungenerous and neurotic. 'If you met her, you'd change your mind,' he said.

I stayed clear until Christmas, when I met her at the staff Christmas Party at the school. The trouble with giving up teaching was that I hadn't really left the school: my friends were still there. I was too isolated and too wrapped up in my work to make other friendships. It was the first time that I was able to observe what my withdrawal from the group had done: I was in the rather peculiar position of not being a member of staff any more; my place had been taken, my substitute was there, but so too was I. Alice, for that was her name, had naturally allied herself at school with Paul; and indeed, because he was missing the comradeship at work which we both shared once, he had naturally teamed up with her. It was clearly an easy, effortless friendship. (He never did make friends with men). And she filled the gap at work which my departure left. Paul had always been a very adaptable person – on the surface. In fact he never adapts but makes the circumstances adapt to him. He hates disruption and never wastes time worrying about the effects of change. He would look around for something ideally similar and either make it the same as the past by the sheer force of his personality or blur the differences so that he didn't see them. I am, on the other hand, one of those people who believes that we pay for such naivety – for taking such easy exits. Instead of coming with me, of seeing how our relationship could adjust and would be changed by what I had chosen to do, he had not moved at all in my direction. He had stayed with Alice. This was how I perceived the situation that night before Christmas when I stepped into the festooned staffroom.

I had come on later because some photographs were still in the developer and I couldn't leave them. Paul, irritated at having to go on alone, had nevertheless gone ahead because he said that he had promised to be there earlier to set up the drink. When I arrived, the room was already full of the familiar faces of my teaching days; but something in the way they stood together, side by side, not talking, something in the arrangement of the group told me clearly: Paul had stayed with Alice.

She was small and colourless, in fact if I recall anything clearly about her in those early days, it was that she wore black and sometimes toneless things like white and beige. I was, on the other hand, fond of bright yellows and oranges. That evening the contrast between us was one of colour; in every other way we were the same. We both had dark hair and dark eyes and the slim figures of girls. In the way some men sense a woman's sexual waywardness almost as soon as she's begun, Alice sensed my insecurity the moment I arrived. 'Gosh!' she said. 'As well as everything else I've heard about you – you would have to be beautiful!' She laughed, biting her lip. I was foolish enough to believe that when a man or a woman tells you that you are beautiful it means they like you. If I have learned anything from that time, I have learned what a fallacy that is. Beauty does not excite pleasure; more often it inspires envy, resentment, anger, hate, but rarely pleasure. In my experience most human beings are too maimed to let beauty pass them by; few have the humanity to leave the wild flower on the hillside, to take their moment of pleasure and be gone with just looking. Lately, I have become fat and dull, I don't attract their anger or hate or resentment anymore. And if I'm quiet even the nurses won't bother me. I like it better this way. 'Paul never stops talking about you,' Alice breathlessly assured me. 'And as for the kids, they say that no one understood them like you. You're a hard person to follow. I feel like Miss Mouse beside you.'

Plainness makes some women manipulative: Alice was one of these. She spun a web of flattery into which I tumbled without regard. She really is a sensitive woman, I thought, when she told me how insecure I made her feel. Before long we were competing for who was the most insecure. 'Never mind how I look,' I said. 'This is just bluff. Inside I'm scared stiff.' From that moment in the evening until I left with Paul, Alice and I could not be parted or interrupted by anyone. Paul was not sure whether to feel pleased or annoyed; he had been ignored all evening by both of us. 'Have you found anywhere to live yet?' I asked, as we were preparing to leave. 'Well, no, actually I haven't found anywhere suitable and I'm feeling pretty miserable about the whole business.' 'Why don't you come and stay with us until you find somewhere?' I said, as though I had just thought of it. 'Thank you' Paul said, squeezing my hand as we left. 'You really are a generous person.'

I invited Alice to stay in order to prove to Paul that I was capable of forming friendships with women. He had often accused me of a defensiveness in relation to other women. I explained it had nothing to do with our relationship, I simply found men easier – they were less preying. My mother had warned me as a child that there were three things I ought to be afraid of and on my guard against in life: they were fire, water and other women. Perhaps I had decided that the time had come to challenge my mother's wisdom; because I set out to make Alice my friend.

She moved in with us on the first of January, and I remember I never greeted a new year with more hope than that one. However, my dreams were to leave me no peace. If anything, they intensified, and sometimes were so noisy and the voices in my ears so strong that I woke up in a sweat and spent five minutes grappling for the light switch. After three nights of bad dreams, I woke up finally and said to Paul, 'There is evil all around me. I am being warned about something but I don't know what!' Being a hard-headed mathematician, Paul was, to say the least, unsympathetic to my fears. He had no time for what he described as my primitive instincts. He hated all forms of religion and mysticism. As a Methodist from a working-class background, Paul's idea of wickedness amounted to no more than overspending, living lavishly, and getting sick – all of these things got in the way of work. If he had any God which was personal to him, I would say it was work. He was an only son whose delicate mother killed herself through long hours of strenuous labour in a spinning mill in Belfast. And I have often felt that he grew up with the impression from then on that no other sacrifice short of that from a woman would be good enough for him. His mother set too high a standard for anyone else to follow. I wish I had had the courage to give him up when I realized that was all that would satisfy him. It was Paul's idea of what proper work consisted of that eventually drove us apart. I think that, every morning he left me at home, and dashed off to make his nine o'clock classes with Alice, he resented me for what he could not see as work.

When we first met I was an art student with a massive loom in the hall of my flat – the loom was imported from Donegal. It came in the back of my father's car like a box of firewood, and together we had assembled it. The loom romanticized me for Paul; he saw in me the weaver his mother had been. But I moved away from producing wall hangings and rugs and became more interested in photography, and this he could not grant the same seriousness, it was not physical work like weaving. And in a year when he could see less and less output, he resented me even more. In such an environment I could not work and the isolation I felt was incalculable. Most mornings when I did get up, I cried in the bath. And I believe I had a phase of lying in my room and staring at the ceiling. Eventually I stopped taking pictures. It was then I turned to Alice. It seems we both did.

In the beginning she and I had long soul-mate conversations: Paul never talked much about his feelings and I was glad to have someone round to console me in my down periods. Alice always supported me. But I noticed that, when she encouraged me in a course of action away from Paul, she was always on hand to step into my place. When I didn't want to go out to dinner with him, or I didn't want to go to any more school parties because I wanted a more independent existence, Paul, feeling rejected, simply shrugged his shoulders and went ahead, not alone but with Alice. I am not blaming her, the ideas were my own, but she seemed to undermine my position by stepping in so readily when I stood up to Paul. As long as there were women like Alice, men like Paul would never accept the validity of my position.

Instead of finding that what I had gained was independence, I found that I had entered a state of non-existence. I no longer went out with Paul, Alice did. My friends no longer missed me because Alice so effectively slipped into my place that I began to wonder why I still remained around at all. Then the dream came back and I began to understand a little more. In its reappearance the dream took a different form; I recognized it as the same dream, only a continuation. This time, after I left the house and rushed out into the street, I found myself alone on a dark road where I passed several houses, all of which were similar to the one I had just rushed out of. The problem which confronted me was what to do next? I had a growing sense of alarm because although I knew it was good to be free from the house I had previously inhabited, I realized I would have to make a decision to get indoors again to a place of safety before nightfall. Time was running out on me and I knew I would have to make up my mind soon. While I understood the nature of the dream in relation to my own struggle into independent life with Paul, the answer to the puzzle evaded me: if I am to escape, I thought, how am I to escape in such a way that I don't end up on the path leading to the same places as when I started out? I had given up teaching art and rebelled against the confines of my relationship with Paul precisely because I felt confined. But my break for freedom had actually resulted in a greater confinement: I had no place. Escape had become withdrawal instead of liberation.

Then, one morning in February, I woke in alarm to find the space in bed beside me empty. He had only begun to do this recently; to rise without waking me. I always hated that. In the early years he wakened me with kisses, or we woke together. But on this morning when I woke from the dream, I was alone. In the dream I had been talking to a woman who stood at the entrance to one of the houses in the road, indicating that she lived there. I told her all my inner thoughts for the sort of house I needed to return to. Suddenly I found that the woman, in listening to me, was growing more like me, the more I talked to her. She had taken my colours. We didn't actually change places. What happened was that the more I talked the less of me I became, the more of me she became. I did not become her in return, on the contrary I became no one.

It was as though I was giving my identity away. It was from this dream that I awoke in mental fright to find him gone.

Disturbed, I got out of bed and looked into the mirror, where I noticed for the first time that I had become very fat. My face was swollen almost unrecognizably. Because of my size I could no longer wear the coloured clothes I had been wearing at Christmas. I fished from the wardrobe a large black dress which I used as an overall for artwork at school. I fitted it easily. On reflection, I realized that Alice had begun to dress in the way I had previously. It was not the first time in my life that a dream had drawn my attention to something I consistently refused to acknowledge the existence of in waking life. In the old Hebrew stories or myths of ancient Greece and Ireland, people interpret dreams and act on them – or don't and are proved wrong. I am always too overwhelmed by the meaning of my dreams ever to do anything about them. The only course of action seemed to be to tremble uneasily and wait for disaster to strike. And it did. That evening I waited for their return. I knew that if the dream meant anything, something would happen soon. Paul came home alone and said: 'Alice isn't coming back; she has found somewhere else to live.' I sat down and cried with relief. 'Oh, I'm so glad, my love. I'm so glad. You have no idea what a struggle it's been for me, her being here.' But I looked at his face and saw that his eyes did not mirror my relief. Then he said, 'You don't understand. There's something else I should tell you.'

There was a high-pitched whistle and then the sound went. I felt myself drifting away from his words. His lips moved but nothing came out. Afterwards, still in silence, I watched him leave the house. It's been silent for a long time now. I like it this way. It only gets noisy in here when Alice comes and that isn't often. But it's growing dark now and the nurses will soon come to put on the lights. I can't sleep in the dark in the silence. It frightens me, so they leave the light on. I still take photographs these days, but of houses, not of people: they're quieter.

To Live Or Die

Linda Anderson

I had a doll once. Its hair had been pulled off. It was not a boy or a girl. It looked straight past me as if startled by some frightening thing behind my back.

Sometimes when I catch myself in mirrors, I have that same paralysed look. Or I resemble some other woman older than I remember myself to be. A stranger, yet familiar like one of my sisters living bitter in rooms in New York or in Paris.

It surprises me to think of how the world teems with people and I have so much love inside me and it just sits there like jewels too good and heavy for daily use.

I was brought up in a large family but my memories are of being alone. There were brothers and sisters, squabbling and shouting. The usual harnessed pair of adults, speaking to each other harshly or not at all. I was always off on my own hunting for fairies and ghosts, my ideal companions, who never rewarded my passionate belief in them by manifesting. I've learned since that they appear only to those who do not want them. On one of my doomed investigations of woods near my home, I saw a man. He froze at the sight of me the way an animal does when you trespass on its lair. Then he approached slowly, baring his teeth so as not to scare me. He kneeled down and kept his eyes on my face, asking me what I was doing, who I was with.

I knew he was thinking about me the whole time. I knew he wouldn't turn away in a moment and forget me like my mother did. If I told him my name he wouldn't get it mixed up with someone else's.

"You're all dirty," he said and he wiped grass stains off my knees with his spit. He asked if my dad ever hit me and he said I should never be hit.

His chin was hairy but his breath was not full of smoke and old meat like other grown-ups.

Suddenly he shoved my face against his jacket and I started to cry in case he stole me from my real daddy.

"I never touched you! I never did you no harm!" he yelled after me as I fled.

My parents screamed at me when I got home. My father beat me because my mother cried. They said I could never go outside the garden again.

Later they brought me out of bed and gave me hot milk. My dad had red eyes like before my last sister was born. He said there were bad men who wanted to hurt children. There were also good men like my dad, but you could not tell the difference by looking. Sometimes even good men could turn bad without warning.

I listened and understood that in some mysterious way I was responsible for this ungovernable badness.

This brush with evil was the start of my indoors life and my infant piety.

An image of torture dominated my childhood, the crucified Jesus. This was Ireland, you see, where the grass grows reddest. Our heroes are all dead or aspiring to be. My pin-up was Jesus, a pewter dummy with neat wounds like broken zips and no genitals. When I reached sixteen, my mind revolted. I knew Christ was defeated. He smelt sour, broiling away under the sun, flies feasting on his sticky blood. He died to save the world and I was surrounded by his mimics, men who would die and kill for Ireland, the most precious bit of the world, as everyone knows.

I despised Jesus and I despised Job even more, the snivelling sycophant. The people I loved were the ones who said 'NO!', who would not submit. Daniel, the conqueror of lions, Queen Esther who defied her tyrant husband, and Job's wife, especially Job's wife. I imagined her turning to her whining husband, distaste visible in her features as she looked at him a flogged servant devising new ways to prostrate himself before the great Sadist. "Curse God and die she told him."

My parents and teachers were tame, cautious, mediocre, bills paid, sins expiated, but her voice was thrilling in my head.

The next part of my life was stupid. I made a bad marriage and I made it worse than it had to be. I sought revenge upon myself. I remember a lot of men climbing on and off. Plenty of fish in the sea, they say, plenty of pebbles on the beach. Cold average fish. Hard average pebbles.

I was always dressing up and waiting for the moment when some sly eye would wink at me, some unchaste foot would tap mine, and then it would be my move/his move all the short way to the perfumed acrobatic event, the meeting of mucous membranes. I wanted to have a child, to feel a heart beating beneath mine. I wanted to slit open my hand and someone else's and mingle our blood.

But I loved no man, no one, nothing. You can live like this for a long time and no one will think you are insane.

My life changed. No, that's not accurate. I changed my life. I chose... But wait.

Picture me on a dreary London street on a summer's day full of traffic noise, sunglare, dust. I'm a woman of twenty eight, dressed in the fuctional sombre clothes I have come to favour. I've given up cosmetics but still wear a violent scent I've loved for years.

I refuse to meet anyone's glance. I look guarded and tired although I do not often work. I look like someone with no hunger for experience but that is a lie.

Listen. On the street, I saw him. I had to stop and watch. It was his air of being absolutely free and of doing no harm, no harm.

He was beautiful and I followed him.

He hesitated in front of a shop and I studied his profile. There was nothing frivolous about that face. He would not dole out smiles, lies...

He glanced at me as I entered the cafe after him. I started to spread my newspapers in my efficient way.

"Job-hunting?" he asked.

"How do you know?"

"Five newspapers of differing political viewpoints!" He gave me a sad appraising look: "What would you do if you had unlimited choice?"

I felt the heat in my face. I wanted to touch him everywhere. I wanted to kiss his bones. "Have a huge breakfast," I said. "And I'd like to talk to you."

He looked straight into my eyes and I let him.

"I don't want to be compared with anyone," I said.

"Neither do I."

Paul had no detailed repertoire of bedroom tricks, no changing menu of exhausting ingenuities. He made sex the relief I wanted. He had the mystery of an orphan or an amnesiac. There was no reworked biography. He did not surround me with the ghosts of other women I must dazzle or pay for. He despised the things that other men take seriously. He would not take orders, he didn't own a suit. He worked when he was desperate for cash, but the impulse for flight soon seized him. He was more truly himself than anyone I had ever met. He had power over me not because he was a man, but because he was much older than me and more honourable. There were things that irritated me as well, his incorruptibility, his coercive goodness, but that was later.

I lay in my room for days when I realized I was pregnant. The memory of Paul's body sickened me. I hated him for everything I had previously loved. Saw him with the world's eyes: a determined vagrant with no anchors, no ties. A man of no substance. Well, something substantial was growing inside me and I would have to kill it, make it dead.

But he came to see me. He said that we must not let poverty dictate our choices, that freedom can't be achieved by crushing another life. He begged me not to plant death inside me. He made me see the embryo as a helpless creature who had burrowed inside me for protection. He made me feel strong.

"What if it's twins?" I said finally, and he knew he had won.

And so our daughter Sophie was born under Scorpio. And died twelve years later under car wheels. But I'm jumping ahead again. Our life together was no idyll. Virtue is its own punishment. When Sophie was two years old we were given a council flat, a tacky vandalised box on a penal colony three miles from the nearest shop.

Paul and I were often unemployed and when we worked it was shit work. Our economies were brutal. He was more austere than me. Sometimes I was spendthrift with my money and energy and had to endure his cold reproaches. There were the usual marital howlings and complaints. I loved him but there was no money in it. Sometimes I wept and wondered why some people have so much more freedom than others. Sophie was beautiful with a dear solemn face like Paul's. It was bitter not to have time with her, not to give her good clothes, holidays... Paul's body kept me alive. During the times when we made our assuaging defiant love and the many other times when we just lay together slumped and speechless, premature invalids, I used to watch him. His face inexorably aging, and I wondered if his life and his toil were futile, apart from the love they inspired in me?

Sophie, I have to come to this death, this murder.

The trouble started when she joined the local comprehensive. She was a bright and curious child but she became sullen and began to fail. We blamed puberty and the shock of the school. But when I went to a parents' evening and met her teachers, I heard a relentless chorus: "Shows no interest"/"never speaks"/ "very withdrawn"... I had the feeling that some of them did not know her at all. Sophie told me that her teachers never addressed her by name. She was one of The Girls. What do The Girls think? Have The Girls finished?

It also came out that the girls were milk monitors, never the boys. Paul told her to refuse but that made her cry. She did not want any "attention."

Some weeks later she became sickly and we had to let her stay in bed. On the day she was to return to school she vomited. She begged to stay home and told us everything, choking with shame. There were a group of boys who called the girls slags and cunts. They were waylaying girls on their way home and stripping them: "debagging" was the name of the game. She said there were no teachers who would do anything about it. Her own class teacher said the girls were asking for it with their see-through blouses and short dresses. Sophie said that if a girl sat beside one of the black boys, the teacher called her a "groundsheet for the darkies" in front of the whole class.

We kept her at home for two more weeks before the headmaster granted us an interview. He was one of those fat prim men in whom indignation looks absurdly alarming. He kept us waiting perched on vulgar velvet chairs. I felt shabby, as if dust had settled on my eyelids, in my hair. I glanced at Paul. I realized that we looked like people who have lost all chance in life. We could not protect Sophie. My hands started to sweat. I remembered my poor father's helpless rage against the child molesters.

I cheered up when my Paul started to speak. He had the advantages of being right and determined and of speaking good English. He challenged the head first about the milkmaid system. Told him his daughter was not to serve the boys.

"But we're all servants, aren't we?" the head slimed at us. "The teachers serve the pupils. Is not the Queen the highest servant in the realm?"

Paul asked if he would appoint all the black kids as milk monitors? If he would permit Jewbaiting in his classrooms? He went on to the extra-curricular sex education that was going on and the insults heaped on the girls by boys and male teachers alike. The headmaster spread his hands. "It's a stage boys go through. You wouldn't want to shelter your girl, would you, Mister ah... would you? We have to prepare them for life, for the... somewhat abrasive flirtations in the adult world..."

"No", I said, "I don't want to prepare her for that. That's the last thing I want to prepare her for..."

He looked at me as if I was mad. How to explain to this imbecile? I did not want to prepare Sophie for that hateful dissonance between men and women. I did not want her to see her body as a commodity, an obscenity, a piece of barter. But the school, the television, every hoarding was screaming a different message. I felt guilty for bringing her into a world that would not prize her. I heard Paul say the school was not good enough and he was withdrawing Sophie!

"It's a very serious offence to deny your daughter education."

"I'm glad you realize that, for that's precisely what you're doing." Stalemate. We promised Sophie she would never go back. We would fight to get her a place in a girls' school that was several miles away. She was elated and did not mind that there would be a journey. We won.

"Winner loses" my grandmother always used to say with savage religious glee.

One day my Sophie was late for the coach home. She must have panicked and dashed into the road without looking.

No one was ever caught for it. I lie awake and imagine her murderer. Some careless youth? Some permed and furred lady? Sometimes the murderer has my face.

Paul blamed himself. For being poor, ineffectual. For having no gardens and high walls to protect her. No car to ferry her back and forth. For belonging to a class whose children can be killed with impunity. My Paul. I have never seen anyone so destroyed. I should never have enticed him into this ordinary life.

He would not let me touch him.

The morning before I never saw him again there was no farewell in his eyes.

My life is sleepy and formless. I make tea all day and flick through the magazines my neighbour leaves outside the door. I see pictures of my black sisters in the colour supplement.

They are separated from their men. Their children are starving. They stare at the camera, blaming no one.

"Curse God and die!" I whisper to them.

And suddenly I have a vision of Paul lying in a hospital ward. He is dying without me, not even a credit card to identify him. I start to yell and beat my fists on the table:

"I exist! Don't I exist? Don't I?"

I go to the mirror and see again the face of the doll who looks past you.

To the danger behind you.

Trailing close behind you.

The danger that will engulf us.

would not give me. I heard Paul say the school was not good enough and he was withdrawing Sophie.

[illegible]

Life Drawing

Bernard MacLaverty

After darkness fell and he could no longer watch the landscape from the train window, Liam Diamond began reading his book. He had to take his feet off the seat opposite and make do with a less comfortable position to let a woman sit down. She was equine and fifty and he didn't give her a second glance. To take his mind off what was to come, he tried to concentrate. The book was a study of the Viennese painter Egon Schiele who, it seemed, had become so involved with his thirteen-year-old girl models that he ended up in jail. Augustus John came to mind: "To paint someone you must first sleep with them," and he smiled. Schiele's portraits - mostly of himself - exploded off the page beside the text, distracting him. All sinew and gristle and distortion. There was something decadent about them, like Soutine's pictures of hanging sides of beef.

Occasionally he would look up to see if he knew where he was but saw only the darkness and himself reflected from it. The streetlights of small towns showed more and more snow on the roads the farther north he got. To stretch, he went to the toilet and noticed the faces as he passed between the seats. Like animals being transported. On his way back he saw a completely different set of faces, but he knew they looked the same. He hated train journeys, seeing so many people, so many houses. It made him realise he was part of things whether he liked it or not. Seeing so many unknown people through their back windows, standing outside shops, walking the streets, moronically waving from level crossings, they grew amorphous and repulsive. They were going about their static lives while he had a sense of being on the move. And yet he knew he was not. At some stage any one of those people might travel past his flat on a train and see him in the act of pulling his curtains. The thought depressed him so much that he could no longer read. He leaned his head against the window and although he had his eyes closed he did not sleep.

The snow, thawed to slush and refrozen quickly, crackled under his feet and made walking difficult. For a moment he was not sure which was the house. In the dark he had to remember it by number and shade his eyes against the yellow glare of the sodium street lights to make out the figures on the small terrace doors. He saw fifty-six and walked three houses farther along. The heavy wrought-iron knocker echoed in the hallway as it had always done. He waited, looking up at the semicircular fan-light. Snow was beginning to fall, tiny flakes swirling in the corona of light. He was about to knock again or look to see if they had got a bell when he heard shuffling from the other side of the door. It opened a few inches and a white-haired old woman peered out. Her hair was held in place by a net a shade different from her own hair colour. It was one of the Miss Harts but for the life of him he couldn't remember which. She looked at him, not understanding.

"Yes?"

"I'm Liam," he said.

"Oh, thanks be to goodness for that. We're glad you could come."

Then she shouted over her shoulder, "It's Liam."

She shuffled backwards, opening the door and admitting him. Inside she tremulously shook his hand, then took his bag and set it on the ground. Like a servant, she took his coat and hung it on the hall stand. It was still in the same place and the hallway was still a dark electric yellow.

"Bertha's up with him now. You'll forgive us sending the telegram to the College but we thought you would like to know," said Miss Hart. If Bertha was up the stairs then she must be Maisie.

"Yes, yes, you did the right thing," said Liam. "How is he?"

"Poorly. The doctor has just left - he had another call. He says he'll not last the night."

"That's too bad."

By now they were standing in the kitchen. The fireplace was black and empty. One bar of the dished electric fire took the chill off the room and no more.

"You must be tired," said Miss Hart, "it's such a journey. Would you like a cup of tea? I tell you what, just you go up now and I'll bring you your tea when it's ready. All right?"

"Yes, thank you."

When he reached the head of the stairs she called after him.

"And send Bertha down."

Bertha met him on the landing. She was small and withered and her head reached to his chest. When she saw him she started to cry and reached out her arms to him saying, "Liam, poor Liam."

She nuzzled against him, weeping, "The poor old soul" she kept repeating. Liam was embarrassed feeling the thin arms of this old woman he hardly knew about his hips.

"Maisie says you have to go down now," he said, separating himself from her and patting her crooked back. He watched her go down the stairs, one tottering step at a time, gripping the banister, her rheumatic knuckles standing out like limpets.

He paused at the bedroom door and for some reason flexed his hands before he went in. He was shocked to see the state his father was in. He was now almost completely bald except for some fluffy hair above his ears. His cheeks were sunken, his mouth hanging open. His head was back on the pillow so that the strings of his neck stood out.

"Hello, it's me, Liam," he said when he was at the bed. The old man opened his eyes flickeringly. He tried to speak. Liam had to lean over but failed to decipher what was said. He reached out and lifted his father's hand in a kind of wrong handshake.

"Want anything?"

His father signalled by a slight movement of his thumb that he needed something. A drink? Liam poured some water and put the glass to the old man's lips. Arcs of scum had formed at the corners of his sagging mouth. Some of the water spilled on to the sheet. It remained for a while in droplets before sinking into dark circles.

"Was that what you wanted?" The old man shook his head. Liam looked around the room trying to see what his father could want. It was exactly as he had remembered it. In twenty years he hadn't changed the wallpaper, yellow roses looping on an umber trellis. He lifted a straight-backed chair and drew it up close to the bed. He sat with his elbows on his knees, leaning forward.

"How do you feel?"

The old man made no response and the questions echoed around and around the silence in Liam's head.

Maisie brought in tea on a tray, closing the door behind her with her elbow. Liam noticed that two red spots had come up on her cheeks. She spoke quickly in an embarrassed whisper, looking back and forth between the dying man and his son.

"We couldn't find where he kept the teapot so it's just a tea-bag in a cup. Is that all right? Will that be enough for you to eat? We sent out for a tin of ham, just in case. He had nothing in the house at all, God love him."

"You've done very well," said Liam,. "You shouldn't have gone to all this trouble."

"If you couldn't do it for a neighbour like Mr Diamond -well? Forty-two years and there was never a cross word between us. A gentleman we always called him, Bertha and I. He kept himself to himself. Do you think can he hear us?" The old man did not move.

"How long has he been like this?" said Liam.

"Just three days. He didn't bring in his milk one day and that's not like him, y'know. He'd left a key with Mrs Rankin, in case he'd ever lock himself out again - he did once, the wind blew the door shut - and she came in found him like this in the chair downstairs. He was frozen, God love him. The doctor said it was a stroke."

Liam nodded, looking at his father. He stood up and began edging the woman towards the bedroom door.

"I don't know how to thank you, Miss Hart. You've been more than good."

"We got your address from your brother. Mrs Rankin phoned America on Tuesday."

"Is he coming home?"

"He said he'd try. She said the line was clear as a bell. It was like talking to next door. Yes, he said he'd try but he doubted it very much." She had her hand on the door knob. "Is that enough sandwiches?"

"Yes thanks, that's fine." They stood looking at one another awkwardly. Liam fumbled in his pocket. "Can I pay you for the ham... and the telegram?"

"I wouldn't dream of it," she said, "Don't insult me now, Liam."

He withdrew his hand from his pocket and smiled his thanks to her.

"It's late," he said, "perhaps you should go now and I'll sit up with him."

"Very good. The priest was here earlier and gave him..." she groped for the word with her hands.

"Extreme Unction?"

"Yes. That's twice he has been in three days. Very attentive. Sometimes I think if our ministers were half as good..."

"Yes, but he wasn't what you could call gospel greedy."

"He was lately," she said.

"Changed times."

She half turned to go and said, almost coyly, "I'd hardly have known you with the beard." She looked up at him, shaking her head in disbelief. He was trying to make her go, standing close to her but she skirted round him and went over to the bed.

She touched the old man's shoulder.

"I'm away now Mr Diamond. Liam is here. I'll see you in the morning," she shouted into his ear. Then she was away.

Liam heard the old ladies' voices in the hallway below, then the slam of the front door. He heard the crackling of their feet over the frozen slush beneath the window. He lifted the tray off the chest of drawers and on to his knees. He hadn't realised it, but he was hungry. He ate the sandwiches and the piece of fruit cake, conscious of the chewing noise he was making with his mouth in the silence of the bedroom. There was little his father could do about it now. They used to have the most terrible rows about it. You'd have thought it was a matter of life and death. At table he had sometimes trembled with rage at the boys' eating habits, at their greed as he called it. At the noises they made, "like cows getting out of muck". After their mother had left them he took over the responsibility for everything. One night, as he served sausages from the pan Liam, not realising the filthy mood he was in, made a grab. His father in a sudden downward thrust jabbed the fork he had been using to cook the sausages into the back of Liam's hand.

"Control yourself."

Four bright beads of blood appeared as Liam stared at them in disbelief.

"They'll remind you to use your fork in future."

He was sixteen at the time.

The bedroom was cold and when he finally got round to drinking his tea it was tepid. He was annoyed that he couldn't heat it by pouring more. His feet were numb and felt damp. He went downstairs and put on his overcoat and brought the electric fire up to the bedroom, switching on both bars. He sat huddled over it, his fingers fanned out, trying to get warm. When the second bar was switched on there was a clicking noise and the smell of burning dust. He looked over at the bed but there was no movement.

"How do you feel?" he said again, not expecting an answer. For a long time he sat staring at the old man, whose breathing was audible but quiet - a kind of soft whistling in his nose.

The alarm clock, its face bisected with a crack, said twelve-thirty. Liam checked it against the red figures of his digital watch. He stood up and went to the window. Outside the roofs tilted at white snow-covered angles. A faulty gutter hung spikes of icicles. There was no sound in the street, but from the main road came the distant hum of a late car that faded into silence.

He went out on to the landing and into what was his own bedroom. There was no bulb when he switched the light on so he took one from the hall and screwed it into the shadeless socket. The bed was there in the corner with its mattress of blue stripes. The lino was the same, with it's square pock-marks showing other places the bed had been. The cheap green curtains that never quite met on their cord still did not meet.

He moved to the wall cupboard by the small fireplace and had to tug at the handle to get it open. Inside, the surface of everything had done opaque with dust. Two old radios, one with a fretwork face, the other more modern with a tuning dial showing such places as Hilversum, Luxembourg, Athlone; a Dansette record player with its lid missing and its arm bent back, showing wires like severed nerves and blood vessels; the empty frame of the smashed glass picture was still there; several umbrellas, all broken. And there was his box of poster paints. He lifted it out and blew off the dust.

It was a large Quality Street tin and he eased the lid off, bracing it against his stomach muscles. The colours in the jars had shrunk to hard discs. Viridian green vermilion, jonquil yellow. At the bottom of the box he found several sticks of charcoal, light in his fingers when he lifted them, warped. He dropped them into his pocket and put the tin back into the cupboard. There was a pile of magazines and papers and beneath that again he saw his large Winsor and Newton sketchbook. He eased it out and began to look through the work in it. Embarrassment was what he felt most, turning the pages, looking at the work of this schoolboy. He could see little talent in it, yet he realised he must have been good. There were several drawings of hands in red pastel which had promise. The rest of the pages were blank. He set the sketchbook aside to take with him and closed the door.

Looking round the room, it had to him the appearance of nakedness. He crouched and looked under the bed, but there was nothing there. His fingers coming in contact with the freezing lino made him aware how cold he was. His jaw was tight and he knew that if he relaxed he would shiver. He went back to his father's bedroom and sat down.

The old man had not changed his position. He had wanted him to be a lawyer or a doctor but Liam had insisted, although he had won a scholarship to the university, on going to art college. All that summer his father tried everything he knew to stop him. He tried to reason with him.

"Be something. And you can carry on doing your art. Art is o.k. as a sideline."

But mostly he shouted at him. "I've heard about these art students and what they get up to. Shameless bitches prancing about with nothing on. And what sort of a job are you going to get? Drawing on pavements?" He nagged him every moment they were together about other things. Lying late in bed, the length of his hair, his outrageous appearance. Why hadn't he been like the other lads and got himself a job for the summer? It wasn't too late because he would willingly pay him if he came in and helped out in the shop.

One night, just as he was going to bed, Liam found the old framed print of cattle drinking. He had taken out the glass and had begun to paint on the glass itself with small tins of Humbrol enamel paints left over from aeroplane kits he had never finished. They produced a strange and exciting texture which was even better when the paint was viewed from the other side of the pane of glass. He sat stripped to the waist in his pyjama trousers painting a self portrait reflected from the mirror on the wardrobe door. The creamy opaque nature of the paint excited him. It slid on to the glass, it built up, in places it ran scalloping like cinema curtains, and yet he could control it. He lost all track of time as he sat with his eyes focused on the face staring back at him and the painting he was trying to make of it. It became a face he had not known, the holes, the lines, the spots. He was in a new geography.

His brother and he used to play a game looking at each other's faces upside down. One lay on his back across the bed, his head flopped over the edge, reddening as the blood flooded into it. The other sat in a chair and stared at him. After a time the horror of seeing the eyes where the mouth should be, the inverted nose, the forehead gashed with red lips, would drive him to cover his eyes with his hands, "It's your turn now," he would say, and they would change places. It was like familiar words said over and over again until they became meaningless, and once he ceased to have purchase on the meaning of a word it became terrifying, an incantation. In adolescence he had come to hate his brother, could not stand the physical presence of him, just as when he was lying upside down on the bed. It was the same with his father. He could not bear to touch him and yet for one whole winter when he had a bad shoulder he had to stay up late to rub him with oil of wintergreen. The old boy would sit with one hip on the bed and Liam would stand behind him, massaging the stinking stuff into the white flesh of his back. The smell, the way the blubbery skin moved under his fingers, made him want to be sick. No matter how many times he washed his hands, at school the next day he would still reek of oil of wintergreen.

It might have been the smell of the Humbrol paints or the strip of light under Liam's door - whatever it was, his father came in and yelled that it was half-past three in the morning and what the hell did he think he was doing, sitting half-naked drawing at this hour of the morning? He had smacked him full force with the flat of his hand on his bare back and, stung by the pain of it, Liam had leapt to retaliate. Then his father had started to laugh, a cold snickering laugh. "Would you? Would you? Would you indeed?" he kept repeating with a smile pulled on his mouth and his fists bunched to knuckles in front of him. Liam retreated to the bed and his father turned on his heel and left. Thinking the incident over, Liam knotted his fists and cursed his father. He looked over his shoulder into the mirror and saw the primitive daub of his father's hand, splayed fingers outlined across his back. He heard him on the stairs and when he came back into the bedroom with the poker in his hand he felt his insides turn to water. But his father looked away from him with a sneer and smashed the painting to shards with one stroke. As he went out of the door he said, "Watch your feet in the morning."

He had never really "left home." It was more a matter of going to art college in London and not bothering to come back. Almost as soon as he was away from the house his hatred for his father eased. He simply stopped thinking about him. Of late he had wondered if he was alive or dead - if he still had the shop. The only communication they had had over the years was when Liam sent him, not without a touch of vindictiveness, an invitation to some of the openings of his exhibitions.

Liam sat with his fingertips joined, staring at the old man. It was going to be a long night. He looked at his watch and it was only a little after two.

He paced up and down the room, listening to the tick of snow on the window-pane. When he stopped to look down, he saw it flurrying through the haloes of the street lamps. He went into his bedroom and brought back the sketch-book. He moved his chair to the other side of the bed so that the light fell on his page. Balancing the book on his knee, he began to draw his father's head with the stick of charcoal. It made a light hiss each time a line appeared on the cartridge paper. When drawing he always thought of himself as a wary animal drinking, the way he looked up and down, up and down, at the subject. The old man had failed badly. His head scarcely dented the pillows, his cheeks were hollow and he had not been shaved for some days. Earlier, when he had held his hand it had been clean and dry and light like the hand of a girl. The bedside light deepened the shadows of his face and highlighted the rivulets of veins on his temple. It was a long time since he had used charcoal and he became engrossed in the way it had to be handled and the different subtleties of line he could get out of it. He loved to watch a drawing develop before his eyes.

His work had been well received and among the small Dublin art world he was much admired - justly he thought. But some critics had scorned his work as "cold" and "formalist" - one had written, "Like Mondrian except that he can't draw a straight line" - and this annoyed him because it was precisely what he was trying to do. He felt it was unfair to be criticised for succeeding in his aims.

His father began to cough - a low wet bubbling sound. Liam leaned forward and touched the back of his hand gently. Was this man to blame in any way? Or had he only himself to blame for the shambles of his life. He had married once and lived with two other women. At present he was on his own. Each relationship had ended in hate and bitterness, not because of drink or lack of money or any of the usual reasons but because of a mutual nauseating dislike.

He turned the page and began to draw the old man again. The variations in tone from jet black to pale grey, depending on the pressure he used, fascinated him. The hooded lids of the old man's eyes, the fuzz of hair sprouting from the ear next the light, the darkness of the partially open mouth. Liam made several more drawings, absorbed, working slowly, refining the line of each until it was to his satisfaction. He was pleased with what he had done. At art school he had loved the life class better than any other. It never ceased to amaze him how sometimes it could come just right, better than he had hoped for; the feeling that something was working through him to produce a better work than at first envisaged.

Then outside he heard the sound of an engine followed by the clinking of milk bottles. When he looked at his watch he was amazed to see that it was five-thirty. He leaned over to speak to his father,

"Are you alright?"

His breathing was not audible and when Liam touched his arm it was cold. His face was cold as well. He felt for his heart, slipping his hand inside his pyjama jacket, but could feel nothing. He was dead. His father. He was dead and the slackness of his dropped jaw disturbed his son. In the light of the lamp his dead face looked like the open-mouthed moon. Liam wondered if he should tie it up before it set. In a Pasolini film he had seen Herod's jaw being trussed and he wondered if he was capable of doing it for his father.

Then he saw himself in his hesitation, saw the lack of any emotion in his approach to the problem. He was aware of the deadness inside himself and felt helpless to do anything about it. It was why all his women had left him. One of them accused him of making love the way others rodded drains.

He knelt down beside the bed and tried to think of something good from the time he had spent with his father. Anger and sneers and nagging was all that he could picture. He knew he was grateful for his rearing but he could not feel it. If his father had not been there somebody else would have done it. And yet it could not have been easy - a man left with two boys and a business to run. He had worked himself to a sinew in his tobacconist's, opening at seven in the morning to catch the workers and closing at ten at night. Was it for his boys that he worked so hard? The man was in the habit of earning and yet he never spent. He had even opened for three hours on Christmas Day.

Liam stared at the dead drained face and suddenly the mouth held in that shape reminded him of something pleasant. It was the only joke his father had ever told and to make up for the smallness of his repertoire he had told it many times; of two ships passing in mid-Atlantic. He always megaphoned his hands to tell the story.

"Where are you bound for?" shouts one captain.

"Rio - de - Janeir - io. Where are are you bound for?!"

And the other captain, not to be outdone, yells back, "Cork - a lork - alor - io."

When he had finished the joke he always repeated the punchline, laughing and nodding in disbelief that something could be so funny.

"Cork a-lorka-lorio."

Liam found that his eyes had filled with tears. He tried to keep them coming but they would not. In the end he had to close his eyes and a tear spilled from his left eye on to his cheek. It was small and he wiped it away with a crooked index finger.

He stood up from the kneeling position and closed the sketchbook, which was lying open on the bed. He might work on the drawings later. Perhaps a charcoal series. He walked to the window. Dawn would not be up for hours yet. In America it would be daylight and his brother would be in shirtsleeves. He would have to wait until Mrs Rankin was up before he could phone him - and the doctor would be needed for a death certicate. There was nothing he could do at the moment, except perhaps tie up the jaw. The Miss Harts when they arrived would know everything that ought to be done.

De Rerum Natura

John Banville

The old man was hosing the garden when the acrobats appeared. They were unexpected, to say the least. Elves, now, would not have surprised him, or goblins. But acrobats! Still, he got used to them, and in the last weeks came to value them above all else the world could offer. Glorious weeks, the best of the year, sweltering dog days drenched with sun and the singing of skylarks. He spent them in the garden, thrashing about in the waist-high grass, delirious with the heat and a suffocating sense of the countless lives throbbing all around him, the swarming ants, the birds in the trees, glittering bright blue flies, the lizards and spiders, his beloved bees; not to mention the things called inanimate, the earth itself, all these, breeding and bursting and killing. Sometimes it all became too much, and then he would take the hose and saturate the garden, howling in a rapture of mad glee and disgust. It was at the end of one of these galas that he first saw the acrobats.

George and Lucy hardly recognised him. If they had met him in the garden they might have taken him for a tree, burned mahogany as he was, with that long beard like grizzled ivy. He had stopped using the cutthroat for fear that it would live up to its name some morning, and he had no intention of giving them by accident an excuse for an orgy of mourning. Anyway, at that time it looked as if he would soon starve to death. Then he discovered that the garden was rich with food, cabbages and rhubarb, potatoes, raspberries; all manner of things flourishing under the weeds. There were even roses, heavy bloodred blooms, unsettling. His fits of fury with the hose helped all this growth. What a silence there was after the deluge, and in the silence the stealthy drip of water slipping from leaf to limb to root, into the parched earth.

The acrobats appeared through a mist of sparkling light, a troupe of short stout fellows in black striped leotards, with furred bandy legs and leather straps on their arms and incongruously dainty black dancing pumps. An hallucination, he said, sure that in a moment they would vanish, leaving nothing behind but a faintly reverberating ping! But he was wrong. They set up their trampoline and parallel bars in the clearing at the bottom of the orchard and began to leap and prance about, clapping their hands and urging each other on with enthusiastic squeaks and cries. Allez up! There was one woman only, fat, with hot dark eyes, who managed to be the undisputed centre of the show even though she did nothing more than pose, and toss her hair, and flash those brimming eyes. The first performance was brief, and they went away puffing and sweating.

Next day they were back. He was tending the hives when he saw through the trees a figure sailing up and down with leisurely grace on the trampoline. Already he detected a distinct improvement in their act. They rounded it off with a human pyramid, a wobbly edifice fraught with unacknowledged hilarity. He sat in the shade of an apple tree and watched them bouncing and tumbling, wondering if he was expected to applaud. To the third show he brought along a saucepan and a pair of forks, with which he produced a tattoo as of a snare drum during those moments of stillness and suspense before the last daring splendour of a stunt was attempted. The woman waddled forward, smiling haughtily, and swept him a low bow.

He poured rapturous accounts of their antics into crazed messianic letters which he stuffed stampless in the post-box in the village at dead of night, laughing in the dark at the thought of the storm and panic they would precipitate on the breakfast tables of his family and friends. No replies came, which surprised and annoyed him, until he realised that all to whom he had written were dead, save his son and daughter-in-law, who arrived in the heart of the country one burning noon and laid siege to his sanctuary.

"He must be really bad this time," said George.

"No stamp," said Lucy. "Typical."

The house was silent, the windows blind, the doors barricaded against them. They hammered on it with their fists, and heard within the sound of muffled laughter. They called to him, pleaded, and were turning away when suddenly there erupted a plangent discord of piano music, followed by a shriek of castors rolling on stone. The door collapsed slowly into the hall, and there was the old man grinning at them from behind the piano, his little blue eyes glinting in the gloom. His clothes were in tatters, his feet bare and crusted with grime. He looked more than anything like a baby, the bald dome and bandy legs, the eyes, the gums an ancient mischievous baby.

"My God," Lucy murmured, appalled.

"That's right! That's me!" the old man cried. He executed a brief dance on the flagstones, capering and gesticulating, then stopped and glared at them.

"What do you want?"

George stepped forward, stumbled over the fallen door, and blushed.

"Hello there!" he yelled. "How are you...?"

The heartiness fell sickeningly flat, and he blanched. Although well into middle age, George had the air of a gawky, overgrown schoolboy. His long thin frame gave an impression first of all of paleness, pale eyes and hands, pale dusty hair. When he smiled, the tip of a startlingly red tongue appeared between his teeth. There was an eggstain like a bilious sunburst on his tie. The old man eyed him unenthusiastically and said with heavy sarcasm:

"Rakish as ever, eh Georgie? Well come on, get in here, get in."

Lucy did not stir, rooted by her fury to the spot. How dare this decrepit madman order her George about! A hot flush blossomed on her forehead. The old man smiled at her mockingly, and led his son away down the hall.

He conducted them on a tour of his kingdom as though they were strangers. The house was a shambles. There were pigeons in the bedrooms, rats in the kitchen. That was fine with him, he said. Life everywhere. He told them how he locked himself out one day and broke the door off its hinges to get in again, then had to jam the piano against it to hold it up. The old woman from the farms in the hills who took care of him fled after that episode. He lived in the drawing-room, in a lair of old blankets and newspapers and cobwebs, yet he felt that his presence penetrated every nook and corner of the house like a sustained note of music. Even the mice in the attic were aware of him, he knew it.

In a corridor upstairs Lucy grabbed her husband's arm and whispered fiercely:

"How long are we going to stay fooling around here?"

George ducked his head as though avoiding a blow. He glanced nervously at the old man shambling ahead of them and muttered:

"It's all right now, don't fuss, we've plenty of time."

Lucy sighed wearily, and closed her eyes. She was a plump woman, still pretty, with large expressive breasts which trembled when she was angry. There was a damp sheen on her nose and chin, and she exuded a faint whiff of sweat. Summer did not agree with her.

"Tell him we're taking him away," she said. "Tell him about the home."

"Lucy, he's my father."

He turned his face resolutely away from her and quickened his step. Once again he noticed how odd this house was, with its turrets and towers and pink and white timbering, like an enormous birthday cake set down in the midst of the fields. Only his father had felt at home here, while the rest of the family dreamt vague fitful dreams of escape into a world free of his malevolent, insidious gaiety. George remembered, with a shudder, his childhood, the genteel penury, the mockery of the village, the friends in whose homes he sat with his hands pressed between his bony knees, inwardly wailing in envy of the simple, dull normalcy of lives where fathers in suits and ties returned at evening, scowling and tired, to newspapers and slippers and huge fried teas. A door at the end of a corridor led into one of the turrets, a tiny eyrie of glass and white wood, capped by an unexpectedly graceful little spire. Here, suspended and insulated in this bubble of light, the old man had spent his days working out with meticulous logic the details of his crazy schemes, oblivious of his wife's slow dying, the children's despair. George felt stirring within his the first tendrils of confused rage, and he retreated into the corridor. His father came trotting after him.

"Wait there, I want to show you my plans for the distillery."

George halted.

"Distillery?"

"Aye. With potatoes. The place is full of them out there."

Lucy, behind them, let fall a shrill gulp of laughter.

They had lunch in the ruined dining-room, raw carrots, beans, mounds of raspberries, honey. Lucy found knives and forks and three cracked plates, but the old man would have none of these niceties.

"Do animals use forks?" he asked, leaning across the table, his eyes wide. He had put in his dentures. They lent his face an odd look, both comical and savage.

"Well, do they?"

"We're not animals," she said sullenly.

He grinned. That was the answer he had wanted.

"O yes we are, my girl, yes we are, poor forked animals."

Lucy's chest began to surge, and her forehead darkened, and George, his legs twisted under the table in a knot of anxiety, searched frantically for a way to head off the argument he could see approaching.

"Well listen, why, why don't you tell us about these fellows in the garden that you see, these acrobats?"

The old man's eyes grew shifty, and he munched on a carrot and mumbled to himself. Then he sat upright suddenly.

"They dance, you know. They have this little dance when they're flying in that tells the ones coming out where the source is, how far, what direction, precisely. You don't believe me? I'll show you. O aye, they dance all right."

Lucy looked blankly from the old man to George and back again, and in her bafflement forgot herself and ate a handful of beans off the bare boards.

"Who?" she asked.

The old man glared.

"Who what? Bees, of course. Haven't I just told you? Snails too."

"Snails!" George cried, trying desperately to sound astounded and intrigued, and fired off a nervous laugh like a rapid volley of hiccups.

"Yuck," Lucy grunted softly in disgust.

The old man was offended.

"What's wrong? Snails, what's wrong with snails? They dance. Everything dances."

He picked up the honeycomb. The thick amber syrup dripped unnoticed into his lap. His lips moved mutely for a moment, striving painfully to find the words. Grime gathered at the corners of his mouth.

"It takes six hundred bees to gather a pound of honey. Six hundred, you'll say, that's not bad, but do you know how much flying it takes? Twenty-five thousand miles. Did you know that, did you?"

They shook their heads slowly, gazing at him with open mouths. He was trembling, and all at once tears started from his eyes.

"Think of all that work, thousands of miles, on the flowers, that labour, the queen getting fat, the eggs hatching, then the frost, thousands dead, another world. Another world! You'll say it's blind instinct, cruel, like a machine, nature's slaves, and you're right, you're right, but listen to me, what is it at the centre, how do they keep it all going? They dance."

Suddenly he leaped from his chair and began to zoom about the room, bowing and gliding, crooning and laughing, the tears flowing, waving the comb aloft and scattering honey on the chairs, the table, until at last he tripped on the fender and fell into the fireplace in a storm of dust and soot and cobwebs, out of which his voice rose like the tolling of a bell.

"Poor forked animals, and they dance."

Days passed. Lucy and George cleared the spiders and the mousedirt out of the big front bedroom, and there they spent the hot nights, waking up at all hours to engage in one-sided arguments. George dithered, lapsed into a kind of moral catatonia, smiled a chilling smile, giggled sometimes inexplicably. Once he interrupted her in full flight by saying dreamily:

"Did you know that whales sing? O yes, in the depths of the oceans, songs. So he says."

"George! Get a grip of yourself."

"Yes, yes. But still."

After the first day the old man ceased to acknowledge their presence, and went back to his life in the garden. Often they saw the water cascading in the orchard, and heard his howls. When he met them in the house he would glance at them furtively and smile to himself, like a man recognising familiar, harmless phantoms. Lucy's rage turned into despair. She confronted her husband with final, unavoidable decisions, which somehow he always managed to avoid. The weather held, sun all day, breathless nights. She became obsessed with herself, her sweat, damp hair, scalding flesh. The taps in the bathroom did not work. She smelled, she was sure of it. This could not go on.

"George, it's him or me, I mean it, make your choice."

His head sank between his shoulders, and he cracked his knuckles. That noise made her want to scream. He said:

"What do you mean, you or him? I don't understand."

"You do!"

"Do I? Well, I don't know about that."

She looked at him closely. Was he making fun of her? His pale eyes slid away from her gaze. She changed course.

"George, please, I can't stand it here. Can you not see that? I'll go mad, I'll be like him, worse."

He looked at her directly then, for the first time, it seemed, since they had arrived, and she saw in his face the realisation dawning that she was indeed in pain. She smiled, and touched his hand. The door burst open and the old man came bounding in, waving his arms.

"They're swarming, they're swarming! Come on!"

She held George's arm. He smirked at her in a travesty of appeasement, and wriggled out of her grasp. The old man disappeared from the doorway. George raced after him. When he reached the garden it was empty. The air throbbed with a deep, malevolent hum. He stumbled through the briars and the tangled grass, into the orchard, ducking under the branches. The old man lay on his back among the hives, eyes wide, the hose clutched in his hands, the water rising straight up and splashing back on his face. George knelt by his side, under the spray. The orchard quivered around him. Under the sun all was gloom and growth, green things, stalks, lichen, rot and wrack. He stared into thorns and sodden mould, drenched leaves, the purple hearts of roses. His flesh crawled. Then he saw the snails. They were everywhere in the wet, on the leaves, the trees, glued along slender stalks of grass, gleaming silver and black brutes straining out of their shells as though in ecstasy, their moist horns erect and weaving. It was a dance. The snails were dancing. A black cloud of bees rose from the hives and spun away into the sky, thrumming. The old man was dead.

George stood in the bedroom.

"I had better stay here for a day or two," he said. "Clear things up. You know."

She nodded absently, wandering about the room, picking up things, a newspaper, clothes, a tube of lipstick. She seemed hardly to notice him, and avoided meeting his eyes. He stood in the drawing-room and watched her clatter away down the drive, stumbling in her high heels, and then he went down and pushed the piano against the door.

Glorious weather, days drenched with sun and the singing of larks, a lavender haze over the sweltering meadows, the silence trembling on the upper airs of evening, and then the nights, the glossy black and the pale radiance, Sirius ascending, a smokewhite breeze at dawn. He spent his time in the garden, tending the roses, the vegetables, the hives. Sometimes he took the hose and sprayed the parched plants, the trees, the earth, and then sat for hours studying the surging life around him, the spiders, the birds and flies, his beloved bees. A swarm of them settled in a corner of the drawing room, under the ceiling. That was fine with him. Life everywhere.

Forgiveness

Edna O'Brien

The sun gave to the bare fields the lustre of ripened hay. It is why people go, for the sun and the scenery – ranges of mountains, their peaks sparkling, an almost cloudless sky, the sea a variety of blue, flickering ceaselessly like a tray of precious jewels. Yet Eileen wants to go home to be more precise, she wishes that she had never come. Her son Mark and his girlfriend Penny have become strangers to her and though they talk and go to the beach and go to dinner, there is between them a tautness. She sees her age and her separateness much more painfully here than when at home, and she is lost without the props of work and friends. She sees faults in Penny that she had not noticed before. She is irked that a girl of twenty can be so self-assured, irked at the slow, languid, painstaking way that Penny applies her suntan oil, making sure that it covers every inch of her body, then rolling onto her stomach and ordering Mark to cover her back completely. At other times Penny is moody, her face buried in a large paperback book with a picture of a girl in a gauze bonnet on the cover. There are other things too: When they go out to dinner Penny fiddles with the cutlery or the salt and pepper shakers, is ridiculously squeamish about the food and offers Mark tastes of things, as if he were still a baby.

On the third night Eileen cannot sleep. On impulse she gets out of bed, dons a cardigan and goes out on the terrace to decide a strategy. A mist has descended, a mist so thick and so opaque that she cannot see the pillars and has to move like a sleepwalker to make her way to the balustrade. Somewhere in this sphere of milky white the gulls are screaming and their screams seem all the more ominous because she cannot see them. A few hours earlier the heavens were a deep hushed blue, studded with stars, and the place was calm, enchanting, gentle. Penny and Mark sat on the canvas chairs and pointed to different constellations while they watched for a falling star, hoping they could see one together and make a wish. Eileen had sat a little apart, wondering if she had ever been that young or carefree. Now out on the terrace again, staring into the thicket of mist and unnerved by the screaming gulls, she is unable to make any decision about leaving and so gropes her way back to bed.

The next day they lie there on that crowded beach yielding themselves to a merciless sun. In the late afternoon they drive back to their villa and discuss where they should go for dinner. Penny decides to cut her bangs and stations herself at the kitchen table wielding a huge pair of scissors while Mark takes a small, shell-framed mirror from the wall and holds it directly in front of her. Sometimes in jest she puts the point of the scissors to his temple or nips a little hair from above his ear and they joke as to who has the bluest blood. Afterward the cut blond hairs lie on the table but Penny makes no attempt to sweep them up. Eileen does eventually, resenting it even as she does it.

When they arrive at the hotel for dinner they are bundled out onto a terrace and told they must wait.

"Aspetta ... Aspetta," the waiter keeps saying, although his meaning is already clear. Sitting there Eileen notices everything with frightful clarity – the metal-framed chairs glint like dentists' chairs, a pipe protruding from underneath the terrace disgorges sewage into the sea while a little mongrel dog barks at this with untoward glee. The waiter brings three tall glasses filled with red Campari and soda.

"Just like mouthwash," Eileen says and regrets it. She is doing everything to control herself. She is counting backward from one hundred: she is mindful of her exhalations: she is taking a sip from her glass while wondering to herself if they, too, are aware of the estrangement. She means to tell them that she will go home earlier than planned but each time she is about to, there is some distraction.

As they drive back to the villa after dinner it happens. Its suddenness is meteoric. She does not understand how it happens, except that it does: an eruption, one word leading to another, and her son with eyes the colour of freshly shed blood, passing hateful sentence on her.

"Are you all right there in the back?" Marks asks.

"Fine," Eileen says.

"We're not going to fast for you?" he asks.

"If Penny were driving too fast, I'd tell her to slow down," Eileen says.

"Huh! I'm driving as fast as I did this morning, when you complained," Penny says. Eileen bristles. She infers in Penny's voice insolence, audacity. Suddenly she is speaking rapidly, gracelessly, and she hears herself saying cruel things, mentioning their moodiness, cut hairs, the cost of the villa, the cost of the very car they are driving in, and even as she says these things she is appalled. In contrast, they are utterly still and the only noticeable gesture is that Mark puts his arm around Penny's shoulder to protect her from his mother's assault. Eventually her splurge of speech has finished and they drive for the rest of the journey in silence.

When they arrive home they stagger out of the car and she sees Mark and Penny walk toward the villa with an air of exhaustion and defeat. She realises what she has done and hurries inside to try to salvage things.

"We can't go on like this," she says to her son. She tries to touch the sleeve of his jacket. He flings her hand off as if it were vermin. Now he starts to explode. His rage is savage and she realises that a boy who has been mild and utterly gentle all his life is now cursing her. Penny clings to his side, is sobbing deeply and quietly and there is such a terrible contrast between the sweet appeal of her sobs and the rabid denunciation in his voice. As he shouts, a thousand memories pass through his mother's brain and she realises at that precise moment that she has lost him and that the cord is being savagely cut. She begs to explain herself but he will not hear it. When he finishes his exhortation he leads Penny toward the open door and they go out, down the steps and up the path to the gateway. Eileen knows that to call after them is useless and yet she does. They disappear from sight, and turning round in the kitchen she does something that she knows to be absurd. She dons an apron and goes to the sink to wash the glasses that have been there since before they went out. She washes them in soapy water, rinses them under the hot tap, then under the cold tap, and dries them until they are so dry that she can hear the whish of the cloth on the dry glass.

The kitchen is utterly silent and all she can hear is the lap of water through the open window and the clatter from the rigging of the few boats that bob back and forth in the breeze. She is both waiting for the sound of the car to start up and for their return. She combs her hair, walks around her bedroom, consults her bedside clock and listens for them. After an hour she undresses and turns out her light in the belief that the dark house and the knowledge that she has gone to bed are what will bring them back. Lying there, praying - a thing she has not done for years - she hears them come in on tiptoe, and without any premeditation she rushes out to the passage and in one burst apologises and says some madness possessed her. Idiotically she mentions sunstroke, and they look at each other with blanched and mortified faces.

In the morning they all rise earlier than usual and she can see that, like her, they did not sleep. They are quiet; they are utterly thoughtful and polite but they are embarrassed. She asks a favour of them. She reminds them that for days they had planned to go sailing and she wonders if they could go today, as she would welcome the day to herself. They are relieved and, as she can see, quite glad, and without even touching their breakfast they get up and start to gather a few things - towels, bathing suits, suntan oil and bottled water in case, as Mark says, they are marooned! She waves good-bye to them as they drive off. When they have gone she comes back into the house, makes another pot of tea and sits by the table, moping. Later she makes her bed and then closes the door of their bedroom, not daring, or wanting, to venture in. The floor of their room is strewn with clothes - a pink chiffon dress, silver shoes, a sun hat and, most wrenching of all, a threadbare teddy bear belonging to Penny. Eileen gathers up the large bottles that had contained seltzer water and walks to the little local supermarket with them to collect a refund. She is carrying a dictionary in order to make the transaction easier. In the little harbour a few children are bathing and paddling while their mothers sit on large brightly coloured towels, talking loudly and occasionally yelling at their children. It is not a beach proper, just a harbour with a few fishing boats and a pathetically small strip of sand. After she has exchanged the bottles she comes and sits next to the other mothers, not understanding a word of what they are saying. Everywhere there are children, children darting into the water, children coming out and begging to be dried, children with plastic bubbles like eggs strapped to their backs to enable them to swim, children wet and slippery like eels, their teeth chattering. Two small boys in red seersucker bathing suits are arguing over a piece of string and as she follows the line of the string with her eyes she sees a kite. The kite looks so free up there fluttering in the air, it reminds her of an assured swimmer. The fine thread rising upward and holding the kite suggests to her that thin thread between mother and child. Although not a swimmer, she decides to go in the water. She thinks that it will calm her, that her agitation is only caused by the heat. She rushes home to fetch a bathing suit and towel and on the way there convinces herself that Mark and Penny have come back.

"Yoo-hoo," she says as she enters the kitchen, and then goes toward their bedroom door and knocks cautiously. As there is no answer, she goes inside and starts to make their bed. She pulls the covers off in one rough gesture, pummels the mattress and then very slowly and patiently makes the bed, making sure to fold back the top sheet the way it is done in hotels. She then picks up the various garments from the floor and starts to hang them in the already crammed closet. She notices that Mark has brought two dark suits, a cream suit, sports jackets and endless pairs of leather shoes. She wonders what kind of vacation he had envisioned and suddenly realises that for them too the holiday must seem a fiasco. Her mood alters from shame to anger. They should have understood, should have apologised, should have been more sympathetic. She is alone, she has recently been jilted, she has dreamed of her lover on a swing with his wife, both of them moving through the air like charmed, giddy creatures. Great copious tears run down her face onto her neck and as they fall down her breastbone she shivers. These tears blind her so that the red tiles of the floor appear to be curving, the roses on the bedspread float as if on a pond, and the beaded eyes of the teddy bear look at her with disdain. She will swim – she will try to swim; she will dispel this frenzy.

At the harbour she lifts her dress off shyly and then with considerable shame she reaches for her water wings. They are blue plastic and they carry a flagrant advertisement for suntan lotion. Standing in the water is a boy of about eighteen holding a football and letting out the most unseemly and guttural sounds. He is a simpleton. She can tell by the way he stares. She tries to ignore him but sees the ball come toward her as she makes her intrepid passage through the water. The ball hits her shoulder so that she loses her balance, wobbles and takes a second to stand up straight again. The simpleton is staring at her and trying to say something. There is spittle on his lips as he speaks. Drawing off her wings she looks into the distance, pretending that she is not aware of him. He moves toward her, puts a hand out and tries in vain to catch hold of her but she is too quick. She hurries out of the water, positions herself against a rock and cowers inside a huge brown, fleecy towel.

He follows. He is wearing a chain around his neck and attached to it is a silver medal with a blue engraving of the Virgin Mary. His skin is mahogany colour. He comes close up to her and is trying to say something or suggest something and, trembling inside the big brown towel, she tells him in his language to go away, to get lost *"Vamoose,"* she says and flicks the back of her hand to confirm that she is serious. Then one of the local women yells abuse to him and he goes off silently into the water, tossing the ball to no one in particular.

At home, forcing herself to have lunch. Eileen begins to admit the gravity of things. She realises now that Mark and Penny have left. She pictures them looking at a cheap room on some other part of the island or perhaps buying a tent and deciding to sleep on the beach. On her plate colonies of ants are plundering the shreds of yellow and pink flesh that have adhered to a peach pit, and their application is so great that she has to turn away. She hurries out, takes a shortcut across a field, through some scrubland to the little white church on the hill. It is like a beehive and she thinks, as she goes toward it, that somehow her anguish will lessen once she gets inside, once she kneels down and prostrates herself before her Maker. The door is locked and the black iron knob does not yield as she turns it in every direction. She walks around to find that the side door is also locked and then, attempting to climb the pebble wall in order to look in the window, she loses her grip halfway and grazes her knee. She looks around apologetically in case she has been seen but there is no one there. There is simply a ragged rosemary bush and some broken bottles – the relics of a recent binge. She breaks off a few sprigs of rosemary to put in their bedroom.

"I am doing things as if they are coming back," she says as she searches for a few wildflowers. Walking down from the chapel she is again assailed by the sight of children, children refreshed from their siestas, pedalling furiously on tricycles and bicycles, children on a rampage through the street, followed by a second gang with feathers in their hair, wielding bows and arrows. Mindlessly she walks and her steps carry her away from the town toward a wood. It is a young wood and the pine trees have not grown to any heroic height, but their smell is pleasant and so is the rustle of their long needles. She listens from time to time for a chorus of birds but realises that there are none and hears instead the distant sigh of the sea. Some trees have withered and are merely gray, shorn stumps. They remind her of her anger and once again she recalls last night's scene. It is like a snapshot stitched to her brain forever.

Three youths on motorcycles enter the wood and come bounding across as if intent on destroying themselves and every growing thing. They are like a clan in a film sequence and they shout as they come toward her. She runs into a thicket and, crouching, hides under the trees out of their sight. She can hear them shouting and she thinks that they are calling to her and now on hands and knees she starts to crawl through the underbrush and make her way by a hidden route back to the town. Scratches do not matter. Neither does the fact that her blouse is ripped; her only concern is to get back among people, to be relatively safe.

It is while she is making her way back that the light changes and the young trees are swaying like pliant branches. A wind has risen and in the town itself the houses are no longer a bristling white but gray and cement-colour, like houses robbed of their light. Trash-can lids are rolling along the street and not a child or an adult is in sight: all have gone indoors to avoid the storm. The wind keens like some menacing creature and on the water itself the boats are like baubles, defenceless against the elements. On her terrace, the canvas chairs have fallen over, and so too has her little wooden clotheshorse with its towels. As she crosses to retrieve them the umbrella table keels forward and clouts her. Her mind can only jump to one conclusion. She sees Mark and Penny in a sailboat, suddenly looking up, realising their predicament. She hears Penny exclaim, she sees Mark jumping and tugging at the sails as he tries in vain to steer them to some safety. She realises that though she knows Penny's second name she does not know where her parents live and at once runs to their bedroom to look for Penny's passport. The beautiful childlike face that looks out at her from the passport photograph seems to be speaking to her, begging of her, asking for her aid. She sees them in the middle of the ocean, flung apart by waves and now they are like lovers, ill-starred lovers in a mythological tale, torn apart by fate. The next moment she tells herself that her son is capable, sensible; that somehow he would lead them to safety. Then she asks aloud where she should bury them and then realises with gruesome clarity that if they are lost at sea, she will not have to bury them.

"Nonsense, nonsense," she says and comes up with a sensible thought that people who know the island and every whim of the wind and weather would not hire out sailboats on such a day. Then she asks how long it will be before the authorities call on her to deliver the bad news. And so she runs from room to room closing doors and windows to keep out the beast that is likely to stalk through stone walls so relentless is it, and so powerful. Suddenly she hears a knock. Putting on a semblance of composure she opens the door only to find that there is no one there. She looks out into the pitch-black air and thinks that this indeed is the signal, the knock that yields nothing, not even a spectre. The knock that is the warning before death. And so she goes back in to wait.

The hours drag on and in those hours, she knows every degree of doubt, of rallying, of terror and eventually of despair. She remembers a million things, moments of her son's childhood, his wanting to pluck his beautiful eyelashes and give them to her, a little painted xylophone he had had, stamps that he collected and displayed so beautifully under single flaps of yellow transparent paper. She sees Penny tall and stalklike in her tight jeans and pink T-shirt with little pearl droplets stitched to the front; sees her smile, the smile that disarms everyone and has made other men tell Mark what a lucky man he is. She is already calmer and more focused, realising that there are many practical things she will have to do.

She thinks of Ireland, her native land, and how quickly and fearfully the news of drownings spread there and how the details and the memory of these disasters are told again and again and how each one revives the memory of the one before and the one before that, way back into antiquity. Worse being in this strange place without a single friend and yet she knows that the local people will be helpful, will be sorry.

A car slows down and she waits with bated breath. There is a beam of the headlights in her drive and immediately she concludes that it is the police. As she rises she hears a small friendly hoot that is their signal and also conveys their clemency. All of a sudden she feels awkward and foolish. They come in bright, tousled and brimming with news. They tell her how they met an Englishman with a metal detector who took them on a tour of the island and showed them old ruins and burial grounds and how later they went to a hotel and swam in the pool but had to hide underwater if a waiter went by.

"Did you sail?" she asks.

"We did, but it got a bit dangerous," Mark says. Together they tell her of a beautiful restaurant where they've been. They describe the table tucked away in the corner, the pink cloth, a vase of flowers and they vie with each other as they describe the food.

"We're going to take you tomorrow night," Penny says and smiles. It is the first time that they have looked at each other since the outburst, and Eileen feels that now she is the younger of the two and by far the more gauche.

"We've booked a table for eight o'clock," Mark says and wags a finger to indicate that they are taking her, that it is to be their treat. Then he goes on to tell of the sweet mutton, the vegetables that came in separate dishes and the potatoes tossed in mint and butter.

"Butter, not oil, just the way you do them," he says.

"I think I should go home," she says.

"Don't be silly," he says and looks at her with the most profound insight and now she realises that she is breaking down. Words and tears tumble out of her mouth; she recounts bits of the day, the scrubland, the youths, the umbrella table clouting her, the abortive swim, not knowing Penny's home address, and suddenly all three of them are crying and they hurry to one another and clasp in a foolish and clumsy embrace.

"I'm sorry, I'm sorry," she keeps saying as they try to comfort her, try to tell her the worst has passed. It is at once one of the saddest and sweetest moments of her life. They have forgiven her, she who could never find it in her heart to forgive herself, or another.

Childbirth

Emma Cooke

This story is set in a time when we had Irish dancing on Radio Eireann, and nobody thought the enterprise either strange or comical. We were an island people. There was a World War in progress, but we weren't on anyone's side, because Mr De Valera had said so. In the town in which I was growing up some people were glad that England was in trouble, and hoped that a bomb would drop on Buckingham Palace while the King and the Queen and the two princesses were all tucked in bed; but most of us read English papers and comics and cried at films like "Mrs Miniver."

There wasn't much money about, and a lot of things were scarce, and when people smiled they often showed mouthfuls of bad teeth. Whenever someone died in the town a crepe scarf of frightening blackness was nailed to the door of their house. It was my mother who provided the scarf for Nan Lynch when Gretchen died. She found it in the attic. Details concerning the funeral arrangement were written on a black-bordered envelope. I suppose Gretchen's age was also mentioned. She was seventeen.

The town had only one proper hotel with a bar, and a room

where the commercial travellers could sit in the evenings, writing up their order books. There was a good deal of genuine back-alley poverty, and coveys of barefooted children. The biggest house in the town was owned by a man who spent most of the year elsewhere. There was an organization formed called the Local Defence Force. They wore heavy uniforms and marched out along the country roads in the evenings, and practiced presenting arms and standing to attention. We vaguely believed that their function, when the Germans arrived, would be to defend the big house.

"Oh, Oh, Antonio - " we sang in the summer evenings, pushing each other on the garden swing; and, "The boys are all mad about Nelly, the daugher of Officer Kelly...."

"The Huns," Lizzie Browne cackled, stretching her scrawny hen's neck out from under her fringed black shawl, "go home to your Mammy or the Huns will cut your ears off."

Gretchen was a Hun - a German. She worked as our maid from the time she was fourteen years old. She lived in Nan Lynch's house and when she was seventeen she married Nan Lynch's son - Danno. She was going to have a baby, but even so she continued to work for us. Father O'Keeffe married them. Father O'Keeffe married all the Catholics. In between times he walked up and down the town and along the river bank, peeping at people from behind the screen of his fat black breviary. He was grave and gentle and never threw bicycles which people left leaning against the church railings into the middle of the road.

The walls of the hall and stairway and upstairs landing of our house were painted in two colours - the top half mustardy yellow, the lower half wine red. Oil paint that grew clammy or dull on rainy days. Greta spent most of her time in the kitchen. She was nearly as small as I was, and usually cranky. Sometimes she said things about men; the things they did, the things they wanted. Or about Danno - and how, after a quarrel, she made him sleep with his head down at the foot of the bed until she was ready to start speaking to him again. Even so, she hoped that her baby was going to be a boy; because she, as well as everyone else, liked boys much better than girls. She'd put her tongue out at me. "You be careful, Teresa," she'd say, wringing out the wash-up rag, "you just watch it."

My cousin Lee thought that he was Roy Rogers. Every day he came clippety-clopping up the road on his sandalled feet; he thought he was Roy Rogers and Trigger combined; a seven year old centaur. He was the cleverest child in our small school. By the time he was six he was able to read the newspaper backwards. We sat on wooden benches and learnt our sums from large wall charts, and discovered where our town was marked on the huge map of Ireland with its pinks, and blues, and pale green, and yellow; and its web of twisty lines. Lee was always planning to run away to Hollywood but he never did.

It was I who told Lee where babies came from - I had learnt it from a book of medicine which my mother kept on her bookshelf. After I had told him he wouldn't speak to me for a week. Then he told me he had asked his mother, Aunt Dorothy, if it was true, and she had said I was a dirty girl and not to be believed, and that an angel had flown in the window and dropped Lee on her bed one beautiful summer's morning. I expected her to complain to my mother about me, but I don't think she did.

When Lee asked our school teacher, Miss Solen, what "adultery" meant, she wrinkled her face and said, "Oh, little children needn't bother about a thing like that. Just remember not to tell lies, and not to steal; and you must never take Our Dear Saviour's name in vain."

We had one doctor in the town and he was supposed to be almost ninety years old, Doctor Arnold. He believed in liquid paraffin, and Sloane's liniment, and cheerful society, early rising, exercise in the open air - particularly on horse back, and his own special pills which were taken rolled up in a mixture of butter and brown sugar. He also believed in cold baths, and that army life was the making of a man. When Danno Lynch hopped it to England to become a soldier, leaving his young pregnant bride and his mother in the cottage, Doctor Arnold said he'd always known Danno had it in him and that Gretchen must take exercise and plenty of cold spongings so that the child would be a credit to its father.

There were a great many public houses in the town; almost as many public houses as shops. Women were not welcome in them - except for a queer hawk like Lizzie Browne. And she often ended up by being thrown out at the end of the night. After Danno left, Lizzie took up with Nan Lynch. She'd park her old ass and cart outside Nan's cottage and spend long hours in Nan's company while Gretchen was cleaning up for us. Carrying out slop buckets. There was no bathroom; none of the houses at our end of the town - not even ones where the hall and landings were painted in fashionable tones of yellow and wine red - had bathrooms or flush toilets. We washed our faces in basins in our bedrooms, and did whatever we had to do in our chamber pots, and poured everything into our slop buckets so that Gretchen could carry them down to the ash pit in the yard. Baths were affairs involving cauldrons of hot water and a tub in the kitchen. We thought that our round tins of Gibbs toothpaste, with their red or green or blue lids, were the last word in smartness.

On fine mornings my mother sat in the sun reading library books. Nan had fallen out with Gretchen. She thought it was Gretchen's fault that Danno had gone away. Lizzie Browne said that Gretchen had egged him on because she was a Hun. Gretchen gave the impression that she didn't give a damn. She scrubbed the wooden kitchen table, then took a Woodbine from her apron pocket and smoked it while keeping a wary eye out of the window at my mother and her book. We had a code for talking about Nan Lynch. "What's the weather like?." I'd ask. "Thundery," Gretchen would say - meaning that Nan was in a roaring temper. "Raining," Gretchen would say - meaning that Nan was bawling again. It was an idea I had got from a spy story.

I also played a spy game with Lee. We left written messages for each other in secret places. One of Lee's reported that Aunt Dorothy had said, "I won't mind if I don't see Teresa again from a very long time."

One day a carrier pigeon with a broken wing landed in the field beside our school. It had a plastic ring on its ankle and Miss Solen thought that the ring might conceal a secret message. The guards came with a cardboard box to collect the bird. Nobody could decide what nationality it was.

The weather got so hot that we spent every afternoon after school down on the river bank; and when holiday time came we spent the whole day there. When I told Gretchen about the pigeon she said that it had probably been bringing her a message from Danno and now we had ruined it. My mother had gone to an auction, and Gretchen was sitting with her swollen feet soaking in a zinc basin.

On Sunday, Gretchen's day off, she spent the whole day in bed. Father O'Keeffe called to ask why she hadn't been to Mass. Gretchen said she was too tired. Nan Lynch had been to first Mass even though she had taken to going to the pubs with Lizzie Browne on Saturday nights. Father O'Keeffe assumed that Nan would make Gretchen fulfill her duties in future. Gretchen said she had stopped believing in God. Nan began to scream and said it was worse than living in a house with a murderess. Gretchen repeated the incident to me, and - against my better judgement - I confided in my mother.

My mother suggested that Gretchen might like to move up and sleep in our house until after the baby was born. "It can't be easy for a girl with her husband miles away," she said to my father.

"We can't very well give her the spare room," my father said practically.

"She could always move in with Teresa," my mother said doubtfully. When my father said "Humph!", she added quickly -

"Over in England lots of people are taking in refugees."

"German refugees?" my father asked. Argument over. I felt very fond of him.

Things continued as they were except that Gretchen grew fatter. "He's Nan's only child - all she's got," my mother said about Danno. I thought it was a silly thing to say. I thought that things were sadder for Gretchen, and that if I was her I'd never forgive Herr Hitler for starting the war. Looking back, I remembered that Gretchen had been more excited than any of us, charging into the house on that wet Sunday morning, shouting, "There's a war on, Missus."

"Gretchen is sick," my mother said. She looked worried.

We had to empty our slop buckets ourselves. I kept checking in case I had let anything spill on to the stair carpet. One day Gretchen came up to the house, but she didn't do anything, just stood in the kitchen and stared. Her face looked huge and red.

"Teresa's becoming a great little helper," my mother said.

"Don't be afraid, Teresa. It will be alright," my mother said chummily in the silence that was left after the door slammed.

"Old Doctor Arnold," my mother said suddenly at teatime.

"He's a good man," my father said.

My mother jumped up from the table and went and looked out of the window. No one said anything. After a while, "Only seventeen years old. A mere child," my mother said in a voice that sounded phoney.

Lee and I watched the funeral from the upstairs landing, through a chink in the blind. It was the first really grey autumn day. The summer holidays were truly finished. Nan Lynch walked with the men behind the coffin. Danno was still in some foreign place. Sometime the day before yesterday Nan Lynch had come hammering at our door. She stood looking at my mother, snorting and shuddering like a pig on its way to extinction.

Everything else in the world suddenly seemed of secondary importance. I wanted to giggle and at the same time I was terrified. I experienced the same conflicting sensations as I watched the hearse pulled by plumed horses, and the two men in their crepe swathed top hats, moving slowly up the hill towards the graveyard. I looked back, and saw my mother as she had stared into Nan's bellowing face. She had seemed unsurprised but worried.

There was Miss Solen's mother. Miss Solen's mother had been one of the best people that Miss Solen had ever known. "So full of goodness," Miss Solen trilled. When she was dying she said happily to Miss Solen, and the other people around her bed, "Oh, they're all working up here!" This story gave Miss Solen much comfort.

"Gretchen Lynch is safe in the arms of Jesus," Miss Solen had said to me. I continued to snuffle into my handkerchief. It wasn't just Gretchen. I didn't even know if the baby had been a boy or a girl.

"Teresa is being silly," Miss Solen said sternly. She was right. I cried harder, panic-stricken because my bluff was being called.

After the funeral procession had passed by everything became very quiet. Lee and I went to my bedroom and started a game of draughts. Aunt Dorothy and his father had gone on a trip to

Cork and he was sleeping in our spare room. I was glad he was there although he was such a pest. It was better than sitting on my own, listening to the soft trembling sound of my mother playing the piano in the room beneath us.

"I'm getting a horse for my birthday," Lee said. He was always going to get a horse for his birthday.

"Oh yeah!" I said. "And you'll call it Trigger." Lee was the silliest kid I had ever known.

The day before yesterday my mother had stood pressing her hands against her stomach, shaking her head. We were Protestants, we didn't own a crucifix. "These R.C.s," she had said after Nan had rushed off to someplace else. "What did she expect?" she said to my father when he came in. My father said nothing. For the past few days all their conversations had been very one-sided affairs. "They were counting on Dr Arnold," my mother said. And, "Gretchen has lived with Nan Lynch since she was four years old." And, "She said said it was a sacrament." And, "Gretchen's real mother is in Germany. She used to live next door to Nan."

All my father said was, "I know. I know."

That was part of it; the dead bell tolling was another part.

"What happened to the baby?" I asked my mother.

"Nothing. - Oh, Teresa." Her voice was tight and absent-minded.

And she couldn't find anything. She could't find matches, or an empty bottlc for water, or our old brass candlesticks. It was as if Nan Lynch was posing her a fresh unsolvable problem everytime she called to our door. Nan was very quiet and white-faced. Her voice came out in huge heaving sighs. "Sure it was God's will," she said every now and then.

The worst thing of all that happened was that my mother picked a special ruby glass vase off the mantlepiece and let it fall on purpose. The more I thought about it the worse it seemed.

I took the draught board from Lee and tried to remember some of the games that Gretchen and I had played. There hadn't been many; she was usually too busy or too impatient. If the rules did not immediately become apparent to me she had no interest in persevering. All I could think of was the colour game. You named four colours and matched the initials of certain people to them. You then asked the other person to decide which of the colours they loved, liked, hated, adored.

Lee thought that the game was silly but I told him that if he didn't play he would have to go home and sleep in his house by himself and that Gretchen's ghost would probably haunt him. I made out my list, giving Gretchen's initials the best chance possible.

I wrote down "white," and "grey" and "purple" and "red" and gave "red" to Gretchen. It didn't mean anything. All I could see was an old black scarf that must have belonged to my grandmother; a long floating thing that clung to my mother's hands as she gave it to Nan Lynch. There was nothing but blackness - the thick blackness of Lizzie Browne's shawl; the glossy blackness of Father O'Keeffe's breviary. "Are you going to be a Christian when you grow up? - that's the important thing, Teresa," Miss Solen said. I thought of Gretchen lying in bed and telling Nan Lynch that she didn't believe in God. Now she knew. I began to shake.

Lee was busy picking a scab off his knee. Then my mother was standing at the door in her spotty dress, clapping her hands and crying, "Suppertime, children." She looked perfectly normal.

Ruth

Maeve Kelly

A picture of Ruth standing in a cornfield hung over the kitchen door. Long ago a battered Sacred Heart badge had acted as talisman. Guard this house against all evil was part of their evening prayer. Now the picture of Ruth cut from a child's Bible and framed in black conveniently covered the crack in the plaster.

At the kitchen table the two women seemed to dream over their coffee, floating contentedly, each one embalmed, cocooned in a haze of forgetfulness. An onlooker might have supposed them to be drug takers of a more deliberate kind, smoking pot or sniffing cocaine to induce the same euphoria. The younger of the women pondered on the picture they must have made and for a brief second stepped in imagination outside of her skin to observe the scene. A tableau of mother and daughter. She was conscious of a prickling at the back of her neck and hurriedly retreated to full self-possession. A second's extension might induce trance and precipitate death. For a moment it seemed just that easy.

"It's peaceful here. Such a relief to get away from the children for a few hours."

"You should do it more often."

"It's not easy."

"Ah well. You know best."

The words were breathed out on a sigh. Like an echo, Eithne sighed also. They shared the odd habit of holding their breath too long, as if afraid of disturbing something, some delicate balance, as if they walked always on a cobweb tightrope which might shatter at some rough exclamation and plunge them into too great awareness. When eventually they exhaled, they sounded bored or despairing. But one could not hold one's breath forever. Purpled skin and certain asphyxiation the result, since the brain was the last to be deprived of oxygen, hanging onto it desperately to the bitter end. Poor brain.

"I read a most extraordinary thing yesterday", her mother remarked, "some nineteenth century Frenchman quoting Darwin to the effect that womens' brains are smaller than mens' and cannot be expected to conclude thought processes as effectively as men. And Parisian women have the added disadvantage of having large feet. He appeared to be quite serious. Can you see the connection?"

"Perhaps that's the missing link. Parisian women's large feet and small brains. I think you picked my brain that time."

"Did I? Are you sure it wasn't the other way around?"

Eithne wasn't sure. She could never decide if it was one powerful impulse shooting across to the other that created the contact, an electrical charge, or if one spy invaded the other's privacy. Her first husband had also been telepathic. At times it was inconvenient, even irritating, especially when they shared dreams. But he was dead a long time, almost ten years.

"Perhaps it was a mistake marrying a widower." Her mother's words floated across the table. They were not offensive. Still, she wished them unsaid. "Two families is a lot for one woman. One family is a lot for one woman."

"He's a good man, and they're good children."

"Good? Good? A very relative word."

"Please don't."

"Very well then, I won't."

At the bottom of her cup the coffee sediments settled. She inhaled their fragrance. Peter, her stepson, had hair that colour.

Coffee brown. "Just before you came in," her mother went on, "I was sitting here thinking of the time when you were a baby, before the others were born, I was about twenty-five then, I sat here with my eyes closed thinking about the day I climbed the rickety stairs to the new dressmaker's flat and I went into the wrong room. An old white-haired woman lay in bed. I cried for her when I went outside, she so old, I so young, she with her white hair, I with my golden hair. Your father used to take out a sovereign and hold it against my head to compare the colour. Just as I opened my eyes I was thinking I suppose I'm like that old creature now, and there you were standing there smiling at me. You came in very quietly."

"You are funny," Eithne said lovingly.

"My mother used to say that to me too."

"It's a long time since even I was in my twenties."

"And your hair was never as bright as mine. None of you had hair like mine."

It was not a reproach, or a boast. It was said neither with regret nor complacency. It was simply the truth.

Bright sunshine poured through the window. The yellow coffee mugs beamed it back. On the clothes line outside pink underwear fluttered. On the lawn underneath a thrush picked a foolhardy worm. Scenario for spring. But there were clouds and sudden squally showers.

Her mother poured more coffee.

"Young Peter's at a difficult age. Look out for squalls."

"He called me an old nag yesterday."

"Hag, nag or bag. It has to be one of them."

It was said knowledgeably. What wisdom, what treasures of experience were locked in that knowledge. If only it could all be released to float around in the ether so that everyone could benefit. Not just the studious and the eager to learn, but the indifferent and the callous. Knowledge and wisdom would filter through by osmosis, impossible to escape. There was, after all, only a quantum of knowledge in the biosphere and it had to be rehashed constantly, like yesterday's roast. How could you explain that to a stepson who might reply, "You aren't really my mother. Your knowledge and mine don't even have the same chemical base." She wouldn't dare contradict his mixture of matter and abstraction. He could pluck works out of the air as if he were a conjuror performing for a credulous audience. His sentences quivered and flurried with the startled consciousness of birds. Then he let them fly off, careless of their freedom.

"At that age," her mother continued relentlessly, "a boy needs freedom. You have to let him off."

Had she been let off, long ago when she was a child and her mother still a golden girl? They had shared more joyous celebration then, or at least, more vibrant. The pleasant ease with which they sipped their coffee had been previewed forty years earlier with a glass of milk or lemonade. Only the colours of memory were different. All those other days were golden, all of them extravagant. They had moved through a haze of happiness, making daisy chains by the river in summer, picking blackberries in September, chanting "I saw the sea first" as they cycled over the brow of the last hill before speeding down. Were there no warning cries? No shouts of "Be careful." She could not remember any. Not even for torn summer dresses. She could barely remember the dressmaker.

"The dressmaker was very poor." Her mother's voice was reflective, with an uncharacteristic touch of sadness. Yet was it uncharacteristic? Crowding into her memory were faint echoes of melancholy, trailing comments of wistfulness which seemed to tinge the golden haze with grey.

"Did you know her well?"

"No. But she was wonderful at turning clothes."

"Turning clothes? What do you mean?"

"Have you forgotten the Foxford tweeds? When one of you grew out of yours, Miss Martin would unpick all the seams, turn it and restitch it for one of the younger ones. Those French seams were tedious. I often pitied her, but she was glad of the work and I was glad to have it done. Her eyesight was fading and she would crouch over the cloth. She always sat by the window so that she got the last shred of daylight."

The bony hands were what Eithne suddenly remembered. The bony hands plying the needle, not deftly and elegantly, but painfully, clumsily as if the needle had to be forced into the cloth against its will, as if every stitch unpicked shrieked in rebellion and wailed again when locked into the resisting cloth.

"The stitches tore the cloth, and the cloth suffocated the stitches."

"You remember her saying that? I didn't think you noticed. Poor Miss Martin. She had a very sad life."

"It was the truth."

Eithne warmed her hands around the mug of coffee. Its heat eased the twinges of arthritis in her fingers.

Later, driving home, she made a detour through the narrow back streets of town to avoid the jammed main streets. Every day the bulldozers were at work, tearing down old houses and shops to make way for brighter and better buildings. For months, even years, the gaunt remains exposed themselves to the sky. Chimney breasts and mantelpieces clung for survival to the remaining walls before crashing into dust. For weeks on end patterned wall papers were displayed, violated by the weather, until like tattered flags they, too fell.

The tattered flags were another memory as she drove across the bridge. Under the parapets the river struggled against its corsets of stone and mud, its restricted energy, unchannelled, ever present. Her grandmother wore high whale-boned corsets. Laid across the chair in her bedroom they retained her shape as her body kept the imprint of their bondage. As a child viewing them with alarm, she had hoped for such a suitable compromise, one which her mother had less successfully made.

"Dissipation and waste," her grandmother had said once, scornfully, when Eithne's mother had talked of lost visions, of her wish that she might have been something else, done something else. If-if-if. If only. "You do what you must." For grandmother it had been duty, conscientiously, even, at times, lovingly performed. Certainly the tree planting and the tending of animals had never seemed much of a chore. But one never knew with grandmother. She had learned to live with the constraints of her time, had rebelled only at the age of eighty four when she denied she had ever married, or ever borne children. Calmly disclaiming responsibility for the lives she had created, she lived her last few years insisting that she was Winifred Morgan, spinster. It was hard to know if she had loved the man whose bed she shared for fifty years. Could any woman love any man for so long? Could anyone love anyone for so long? A few years of treasured freedom, which unaccustomed, soured to loneliness before death was a high price to pay for - what? For not being Miss Martin with her bony fingers?

Passing the boat house she looked down the boat slip and glimpsed a canoe being launched by two youths. Every day someone fought the river, plotted and planned its course, devised ways of outwitting its tidal tricks, its strong undercurrents. Often there were casualties, bobbing bodies grasping at an oar as they swept under the parapet before being rescued further up. Occasionally a bloated body drifted to the bank or lodged in one of the reedy islands. An inquest was held and a bland verdict pronounced.

Considering the inadequacies of such verdicts she did not allow for the indifference of two girls sauntering across the road. Heart lurching, she braked. The tyres screeched in protest at her brutality. The girls glared as she passed and she had a glimpse of tight denim-clad bottoms and unrestrained tops. She wondered what she might symbolise for them. Neat, costume-clad car driver versus blue-jeaned liberated pedestrian. Yet their symbols were no less repressive than hers.

By one o'clock she had reached home. The reassuringly normal smell of casseroled beef and vegetables conveniently cooking in their own juices, reminded her to thank God for science and automatic ovens. By ten-past one she was ready for the first arrival. By half past, all seven of them were either fed or feeding. The two youngest quarrelled and gossiped. The three middles read, their books propped up against sauce bottles and sugar bowl. She tried feeble protest and was smiled at innocently and ignored. The two eldest, her stepchildren Peter and Alison, seemed to drown in their own thoughts, polite but remote.

Watching them as she tended their needs she was fllied with love for them all, a painful, tender, protective love. It reached out to them, anxiously yearning to fight their battles with them or for them. Surely they would sense it. Surely one of them would respond with just a small sign. She closed her eyes and concentrated.

The sauce bottle fell with a clatter and cracked a side plate. There were oohs of alarm and reproval from the youngest, silent disapproval from the elders. The middles read on and fed on.

She removed the cracked plate and righted the sauce bottle.

"Why don't you dye your hair, like Mrs O'Callaghan?" Maureen asked. "It would make you much younger looking and no one would ever know."

"I would know, so what use would that be." Her shock at the question was quickly covered.

"You are funny," Maureen said lovingly.

Warmth spread through her veins. Even her toes tingled. Her inner eye, like a concealed lens, caught them, suspended in time, photographed forever on the screen of her mind. Their voices receded and faded. This fact of their existence was the supreme consolation. For one second they were poised, all of them, at the very centre of time, in the very core of the universe. Everything else revolved around them. Their existence illuminated even the dark corners of her soul. Separate and distinct as they were, she became their unifying force, their common bond. Other achievements were as nothing compared with this. God-like, self-satisfied, she lingered.

The fading voices advanced again to become small cries of alarm. He head jerked violently and she became aware of seven pairs of eyes fixed anxiously on her. "I was just day-dreaming. Did I startle you?"

"You looked sick." The youngest rushed to hug her. "Are you alright?"

"You looked," Peter paused for the right word, "disorientated."

"Disoriented," she corrected. "It is the destiny of mothers."

"You are only my stepmother," he reminded her, cruelly polite, rejecting excuses.

She had an urge to slap his face, very hard.

"You shouldn't say only," Alison reproved him, "I never think of you as only, or even step." She looked kindly at Eithne.

"You're only a silly girl," Peter said scornfully.

"And you're a male chauvinist pig, junior grade."

"Enough," Eithne said sternly. "You'll be late back."

"School is sick," Thomas said sadly. "I hate it. Can I take a half-day off?" He whined a little.

"Cry baby," Peter jeered. "Mama's pet."

Thomas lashed out with his feet. Peter side-stepped smartly, grinning at his adroitness and the other's rage.

Boys are cruel, Eithne thought passionately, cruel little beasts.

"Get off to school, all of you. Shoo. Shoo." She waved the tea towel at them.

The young ones laughed and scuttled off, blowing kisses back as they went. The middles followed, a little anxiously. Peter and Alison cycled, Peter thrusting the handlebars slightly ahead of Alison. They left the drive, Alison pretending not to notice, but pressing harder on her pedals. They would pass and re-pass each other before they reached the crossroads where they parted for their separate schools.

Her head ached slightly, the creases between her brow becoming furrows. For no good reason she was exhausted and regretted the wasted morning. Mother was never lovely after all, and needed no visits from dutiful daughters. You need them her inner voice was insistent. You need to be reminded of your existence. You also were born. Once a long time ago you inherited the earth too.

The greasy dinner plates stared menacingly at her from the table. To have to wash them yet again was like permitting new torture. Waste, waste, she cried aloud, dissipation and waste. Flashing in quick succession came images of the dressmaker with the bony fingers, her mother, white-haired, staring at her reflection, white-haired propped up in a bed in a strange room, the two girls straddling the road defiantly, the river thrashing, the houses crumbling all around and somewhere, in the distance, a field of bright corn, and Ruth, alien, weeping amid it.

Will You Please Go Now

Julia O'Faolain

Lost among the demonstrators was a rain-sodden dog. Up and down it ran, rubbing against anonymous trousers and collecting the odd kick. It was a well-fed animal with a leather collar but was quickly taking on the characteristics of the stray: that festive cringe and the way such dogs hoop their spines in panic while they wag their shabby tails.

"Here boy! Come - ugh, he's all muddy. Down, sir, get away! Scram! Tss!"

People threw chocolate wrappers and potato-crisp packets which the dog acknowledged from an old habit of optimism while knowing the things were no good. It was tired and its teeth showed in a dampish pant as though it were laughing at its own dilemma.

Jenny Middleton, a mother of two, recognised the crowd's mood from children's parties.

"Don't tease him," she said sharply to a dark-skinned young man who had taken the animal's forepaws in his hands and was forcing it to dance. The dog's dazed gash of teeth was like a reflection of the man's laugh. "Here," she said, more gently, "let me see his tag. There's a loudspeaker system. It shouldn't be hard to find his owner."

"I'll take him," said the man at once, as though, like the dog, he had been obedience-trained and only awaited direction. "I will ask them to announce that he has been found." Off he hared on his errand, like a boy-scout eager for merit. One hand on the dog's collar, he sliced through the crowd behind a nimbly raised shoulder. "I'll be back," he called to Jenny, turning to impress this on her with a sharp glance from yellowish, slightly bloodshot eyes.

He was the sort of man whom she would have avoided in an empty street - and, to be sure, she might have been wrong. He was friendly. Everyone at the rally was. Strangers cracked jokes and a group carrying an embroidered trade-union banner kept up a confident, comic patter. The one thing she wasn't sure she liked were the radical tunes which a bald old man was playing on his accordion. They seemed to her divisive, having nothing to do with the rally's purpose. When the musician's mate brought round the hat, she refused to contribute. "Sorry," she told him when he shook it in front of her. "I've no change." Turning, she was caught by the ambush of the dusky young man's grin. He was back, breathing hard and shaking rain from his hair.

"The dog will be OK," he assured her. "The authorities are in control."

This confidence in hierarchy amused her. The next thing he said showed that it was selective.

"They," he nodded furtively at the musicians, "come to all rallies. I am thinking maybe they are the police? Musicians, buskers: a good disguise?" He had a shrill, excited giggle.

"There are plenty of ordinary police here," she remarked, wondering whether he was making fun of her. She felt shy at having come here alone in her Burberry hat and mac. The hat was to protect her hair from torch drippings and was sensible gear for a torch-light procession. But then, might not sense be a middle-class trait and mark her out?

"Bobbies," he said, "are not the danger. I am speaking of the undercover police. The Special Branch. They have hidden cameras."

"Oh."

She eased her attention off him and began to read the graffiti on the struts of the bridge beneath which their section of the procession was sheltering. It was raining and there was a delay up front. Rumours or joke-rumours had provided explanations for this. The levity was so sustained as to suggest that many marchers were embarrassed at having taken to the streets. Old jokes scratched in concrete went back to her schooldays: My mother made me homosexual, she read. Did she? goes the answer, conventionally written in a different hand. If I get her some wool will she make me one too? There was the usual Persian - or was it Arabic - slogan which she had been told meant.

Stop killings in Iraq! The man beside her could be an Arab. No.

More likely an Indian.

"I know them," he was saying of the secret police. "We know each other. You see I myself come to all rallies. Every one in London."

"Are you a journalist?"

"No. I come because I am lonely. Only at rallies are people speaking to me."

Snap! She saw the trap-click of his strategy close in on her: his victim for the occasion. It was her hat, she thought and watched his eyes coax and flinch. It had singled her out. Damn! A soft-hearted woman, she had learned, reluctantly, that you disappointed people less if you could avoid raising their hopes. Something about him suggested that a rejection would fill him with triumph. He did not want handouts, conversational or otherwise, but must solicit them if he was to savour a refusal.

A graffito on the wall behind him said: I thought Wanking was a town in China until I discovered Smirnov. Don't laugh, she warned herself - yet, if she could think of a joke to tell him, mightn't it get her off his hook? Would Chinese laugh at the Smirnov joke, she wondered. Probably they wouldn't, nor Indians either. Wankers might. They were solitary and the solitary use jokes to keep people at bay.

"You see," he was saying, "I am a factory worker but also an intellectual. In my own country I was working for a newspaper but here in the factory I meet nobody to whom I can talk. Intellectuals in London are not inviting working men to their homes. I am starved for exchange of stimulating ideas." His eye nailed a magazine she was carrying. "You, I see, are an intellectual?"

"Goodness, no." But the denial was a matter of style, almost a game which it was cruel to play with someone like him. She had never known an English person who would admit to being an intellectual. In India - Pakistan? - wherever he came from it would be a category which deserved honour and imposed duties. Denying membership must strike him as an effort to shirk such duties towards a fellow member in distress.

Her attempts to keep seeing things his way were making her nervous and she had twisted her sheaf of fliers and pamphlets into a wad. Am I worrying about him, she wondered, or myself? Perhaps even asking herself such a question was narcissistic? Objectivity too might be a middle-class luxury. How could a man like this afford it? He was a refugee, he was telling her now, a Marxist whose comrades back home were in prison, tortured or dead. Perhaps his party would take power again soon. Then he would go home and have a position in the new government. Then English intellectuals could meet him as an equal. He said this with what must have been intended as a teasing grin. She hadn't caught the name of his country and was embarrassed to ask lest it turn out to be unfamiliar. It would have to be a quite small nation, she reasoned, if he was hoping to be in its government. Or had that been a joke?

"We're moving." She was relieved at the diversion.

The trade-union group started roaring the Red Flag with comic gusto and the procession ambled off. He was holding her elbow. Well, that, she supposed, must be solidarity. The rally was connected with an issue she cared about. She did not normally take to the streets and the etiquette of the occasion was foreign to her.

"Let cowards mock," came the jovial Greater London bellow from up front, "And traitors sneer..."

"I'm as foreign here as he is," she decided and bore with the downward tug at her elbow. He was small: a shrivelled man with a face like a tan shoe which hasn't seen polish in years. Dusky, dusty, a bit scuffed, he could be any age between thirty and forty-five. His fingers, clutching at her elbow bone, made the torch she had bought tilt and shed hot grease on their shoulders. She put up her left hand to steady it.

"You're married." He nodded at her ring. "Children?"

"Yes: two. Melanie and Robin. Melanie's twelve."

The embankment was glazed and oozy. Outlines were smudged by a cheesy bloom of mist, and reflections from street-lights smeary in the mud for it was December and grew dark about four. Across the river, the South Bank complex was visible still. He remarked that you could sit all day in its cafeteria if you wanted and not be expected to buy anything. His room, out in the suburbs, depressed him so much that on Sundays he journeyed in just to be among the gallery - and theatre-goers, although he never visited such places himself.

"But galleries are cheap on Sundays," she remonstrated. "Maybe even free?"

He shrugged. Art - bourgeois art - didn't interest him. It was - he smiled in shame at the confession - the opulence of the cafeteria which he craved. "Opulence," he said, stressing the wrong syllable so that she guessed that he had never heard the word pronounced. "It is warm there," he explained. "Soft seats. Nice view of the river. Some of the women are wearing scent."

On impulse and because it was two weeks to Christmas, she invited him to join her family for lunch on the 25th.

When the day came, she almost forgot him and had to tell Melanie to lay an extra place just before he was due to arrive. His name - he had phoned to test the firmness of her invitation - was Mr Rao. He called her Mrs Middleton and she found the formality odd after the mateyness of the rally when he had surely called her Jenny? Their procession, headed for Downing Street, had been turned back to circle through darkening streets. Mounted police, came the word, had charged people in front. Several had been trampled. Maimed perhaps? No, that was rumour: a load of old rubbish. Just some Trots trying to provoke an incident. Keep calm. Then someone heard an ambulance. An old working man gibbered with four-letter fury but the banner-bearers were unfazed.

"Can't believe all you hear, Dad," they told him.

Mr Rao tugged at Jenny's arm as though he had taken her into custody: the custody of the Revolution. "You see," he hissed, "it is the system you must attack, root and branch, not just one anomaly. There are no anomalies. All are symptoms." He was galvanized. Coils of rusty hair reared like antennae off his forehead. "Social Democrats," he shouted, "sell the pass. They are running dogs of Capitalism. I could tell you things I have seen..." Fury restored him and she guessed that he came to rallies to revive a flame in himself which risked being doused by the grind of his working existence. He laughed and his eyes flicked whitely in the glow from the torches as he twitted the young men with the trade-union banner in their split allegiance. A Labour Government was loosing its police on the workers. "Aha!" he hooted at their discomfiture. "Do you see? Do you?" His laughter flew high and quavered like an exotic birdcall through the moist London night.

"You remember that demo I went to?" she reminded Melanie.

"Well, I met him there. He's a refugee and lonely at Christmas. A political refugee."

"Sinister?" inquired her husband who'd come into the kitchen to get ice cubes, "with a guerillero grin and a bandit's moustache? Did he flirt with you?"

This sort of banter was irritating when one was trying to degrease a hot roasting pan to make sauce. She'd just remembered too that her mother-in-law, who was staying with them, was on a salt-free diet. Special vegetables should have been prepared. "Did you lay the place for him?" she asked Melanie.

The girl nodded and rolled back her sleeve to admire the bracelet she'd got for Christmas. Posing, she considered her parents with amusement.

Jenny's husband was looking for something in the deep freeze. "He did, didn't he?" he crowed. "He flirted with you?"

She should have primed him, she realized. James was sensitive enough when things were pointed out to him but slow to imagine that other people might feel differently to the way he did. Mr Rao would be hoping for a serious exchange of ideas between men. Stress serious. He had been impressed when she told him that James, a senior civil servant, was chairman of a national committee on education. But now here was James wearing his sky-blue jogging suit with the greyhound on its chest - a Christmas present - all set to be festive and familial. He was a nimble, boyish man who prided himself on his youthfulness.

"Will Mr Rao disapprove of us?" he asked puckishly and tossed his lock of grey-blond hair off his forehead.

"Listen, he's a poor thing." Jenny was peeved at being made to say this. "Be careful with him, James. Can anyone see the soy sauce? I've burnt my hand. Thanks." She spread it on the burn then went back to her roasting pan. "Melanie, darling, could you do some quick, unsalted carrots for your grandmother? Please."

"Better do plenty," James warned. "He may be a vegetarian. Lots of Indians are."

"God, do you think so? At Christmas."

"Why not at Christmas? You'd think we celebrated it by drinking the blood of the Lamb."

"People do," said Melanie. "Communion. There's the doorbell."

"I'll go. Keep an eye on my pan."

In the hall Jenny just missed putting her foot on a model engine which James had bought for five-year-old Robin and himself. An entire Southern Region of bright rails, switches, turntables and sidings was laid out and there was no sign of Robin. Did James dream of being an engine-driver, an aerial bomber or God? Or was it some sexual thing like everything else? Through the Art Nouveau glass of the door, she deduced that the blob in Mr Rao's purple hand must be daffodils, and wished that there was time to hide her own floral display which must minimize his gift.

"You were mean, horrible, appalling."

"He is appalling."

"Shsh! Listen, please, James, be nice. Try. Look, go back now, will you? They'll know we're whispering."

"I'm not whispering."

"Well you should be. He'll hear."

"Jenny, you invited him. Try and control him. He has a chip a mile high on his..."

"Well, allow for it."

"Why should I?"

"You're his host."

"He's my guest."

"God! Look, get the plum pud alight and take it in. I'll get the brandy butter."

"If he suggests Robin eat this with his fingers, I'll..."

"Shush, will you? He doesn't understand children."

"What does he understand? How to cadge money?"

"He didn't mean it that way."

"He bloody did. Thinks the world owes him a living."

"Well, doesn't it? Owe everyone I mean."

"My dear Jenny..."

"Oh, all right. Here."

She put a match to the brandy-soaked pudding so that blue flames sprang over its globe making it look like a scorched, transfigured human head. "Go on. Take it while it's alight." She pushed her husband in the direction of the dining-room and stood for a moment pulling faces at the impassive blankness of the kitchen fridge. Then she followed with the brandy butter.

Later, she came back to the kitchen to clean up. Vengefully, she let the men and her mother-in-law cope with each other over the coffee which their guest had at least not refused. He had refused sherry, also wine, also the pudding because it had brandy on it and had seemed to feel that it was his duty to explain why he did so and to point out the relativity of cultural values at the very moment when Robin's grandmother was telling the child how to pick fowl high.

"Only two fingers, Robin," she'd been demonstrating daintily, "never you whole hand and only pick up a neat bone."

"We," Mr Rao scooped up mashed chestnuts with a piece of bread, "eat everything with our hands." He laughed. "There are millions of us."

The anarchy of this so undermined Robin's sense of what might and might not be done on such an extraordinary day as Christmas that he threw mashed chestnuts at his grandmother and had to be exiled from the table. The older Mrs Middleton was unamused. Mr Rao bared his humourless, raking teeth.

"You are strict with your children," he said, "in imparting your class rituals. This is because as a people you still have confidence and prize cohesion. Maybe now you must relax?"

Nobody chose to discuss this. Doggedly, the family helped each other to sauce and stuffing and Mr Rao began to use his knife and fork like everyone else. A diffidence in him plucked at Jenny who saw that the incident with Robin had been meant as a joke: a humorous overture to the member of the family whom he had judged least likely to reject him. But now Robin himself was rejected, exiled to his room and disapproval of Mr Rao hung unvoiced and irrefutable in the air. Seen by daylight, he was younger than she had supposed at the rally. His was a hurt, young face, puffy and unformed with bloodshot eyes and a soft, bluish, twitching mouth. He wanted to plead for Robin but could only talk in his magazine jargon. Perhaps he never spoke to people and knew no ordinary English at all? She imagined him sitting endlessly in the South Bank cafeteria reading political magazines and staring at the river.

"Pedagogical theory, you see..." he started and James, to deviate him - Robin's exile had to last at least ten minutes to placate his grandmother, interrupted with some remark about a scheme for facilitating adult education with which he was concerned.

"It's designed for people who didn't get a chance to go to university in the first instance," said James. "We give scholarships to deserving..."

"Could you give me one?" Mr Rao leaned across the table. "Please. Could you? I am needing time to think and that factory work is destroying my brain. Have you worked ever on an assembly line?"

"You may certainly apply," James told him. "It's open to all applicants."

"No." Mr Rao spoke excitedly and a small particle of mashed chestnut flew from his mouth and landed on James's jogging suit. His words, spattering after it, seemed almost as tangible. "No, no," he denied, nervous with hope. "You see I apply before for such things and never get them. Inferior candidates pass me by. Here in England, there is a mode, a ritual, you see. It is like the way you educate your son." Mr Rao's mouth twisted like a spider on a pin. "You teach him to give signals," he accused. "To eat the chicken so - and then his own kind will recognize and reward him. I give the wrong signals so I am always rejected." He laughed sadly. "Merit is not noted. In intellectual matters this is even more true. Examiners will take a working-class man only if they think he can be absorbed into their class. I cannot."

"Then perhaps," said James, "you are an unsuitable candidate?"

"But the university," pleaded Mr Rao, "is not a caste system? Not tribal surely? You cannot afford to exclude people with other ways of being than your own. Even capitalism must innoculate itself with a little of the virus it fears. Intellectual life" - Mr Rao swung his fork like a pendulum - "is a dialectical process. You must violate your rules," he begged. "Isn't that how change comes? Even in English law? First someone breaks a bad old law; then a judge condones the breaking and creates a precedent. I have read this. Now you," Mr Rao pointed his fork at James, "must break your bureaucratic rule. Give me a scholarship. Be brave," he pleaded. The fork fell with a clatter but Mr Rao was too absorbed to care. "Give," he repeated, fixing James with feverish eyes as if he hoped to mesmerize him. The eyes, thought Jenny, looked molten and scorched like lumps of caramel when you burned a pudding. The fork was again swinging to and fro and it struck her that Mr Rao might not be above using hypnotism to try and make James acquiesce to his will.

She leaned over and took the fork from his fingers. He let it go. His energies were focused on James. The eyes were leeches now: animate, obscene. Melanie and her grandmother were collecting plates. They were outside the electric connection between the two men. Murmuring together, they seemed unaware of it. James's mouth tightened. Mr Rao, Jenny saw, was in for a rocket. But the man was conscious only of his own need. It was naked now. He was frightened, visibly sweating, his nails scratched at the table cloth. He wiped his face with a napkin.

"Men in lower positions must obey rules," he told James. "They will not let me through. Only you can make an exception. Is not the spirit of your scheme to let the alienated back into society? I am such a man," he said with dramatic intonation. "I," he said proudly, "am needy, alienated, hard working and well read. Do you not believe I am intelligent? I could get references, but my referees," he laughed his unhappy laugh, "are tending to be in gaol: a minister of my country, the rector of my university. Oh, we had an establishment once."

"Then perhaps," said James, "you understand about the need to eliminate personal appeals? Nepotism: the approach which corrupts a system. Did you," asked James with contempt, "pick my wife up at that rally because you knew who she was? Wait!" He held Jenny's hand to stop her talking. "I'm quite well known. A number of people there could have recognized and pointed her out to you. A man like you is ruthless, isn't he? For a higher aim, to be sure." James spoke with derision. "No doubt you feel you matter more than other people?"

The stuffing had gone out of Mr Rao. His head sank. His mouth, a puffy wound mobile in his face, never settled on an emotion with confidence. Even now there was a twitch of humour in its gloom. "Oh," he said listlessly, "many, many personal appeals are granted in this country. But it's like I said: I don't know the signals. I am an outsider here." He stood up.

"Please!" Jenny wrenched her wrist from her husband's grip.

"Mr Rao! You're not going? There's pudding. The meal isn't over at all."

But he had only stood up to welcome Robin who, released from his room by his grandmother, was returning in a haze of smiles and sulks. For the rest of the meal, attention was gratefully divided between the child and food. It was Christmas, after all.

The dishwasher was on. Its noise drowned his approach and added urgency to the hand she felt landing on her arm.

"Jenny!" Mr Rao's shrewd, nervous face peered into hers. "I go now. I am thanking you and..." Words, having betrayed him all day, seemed to be abandoning him utterly. "Sorry," he said as perfunctorily as Robin might have done. "It is not true what your husband said."

"Of course not. I'm sorry too - but I'm glad you came." She smiled with a guilty mixture of sorrow and relief. After all, what more could she do? She gave him her hand.

He didn't take it. "I appreciated this," he said too eagerly. "Being in a family. You know? Mine is a people who care a lot about family life. I miss it. That was why meeting little Robin, I..."

She thought he was apologizing. "It's not important."

"No, no. I know that with children things are always going wrong and being mended quickly. That is the joy of dealing with them. I miss children so much. Children and women - will you invite me again?"

She was astonished. Unaccountably, she felt a stab of longing to help him, to visit the unmapped regions where he lived: eager, vulnerable and alone, with no sense of what was possible any more than Robin had, or maybe great, mad saints. But how could she? The dishwasher had finished a cycle and begun another. It was so loud now that she could hardly hear what he was saying. He seemed to be repeating his question.

"We're going away for a while in January," she began evasively. "Skiing..." But evasion wouldn't do for this man. She looked him in the eye. "I can't invite you," she said. "James and you didn't hit it off. You must realize that."

"Will you meet me in town? I'll give you my number."

"No."

"Please."

"Mr Rao..."

The wound of his mouth was going through a silent-movie routine: pleading, deriding, angry, all at once. "The poor have no dignity," he said, shocking her by this abrupt irruption of sound. "They must beg for what others take."

Suddenly, he had his arms around her and was slobbering, beseeching and hurting her in the hard grip of his hands. The sounds coming from him were animal: but like those of an animal which could both laugh and weep. One hand had got inside her blouse. "A woman," he seemed to be repeating, " a family... a woman..." Then a different cry got through to her: "Mummy!"

Melanie, looking horrified, stood next to them. The dishwasher, now emptying itself with a loud gurgle, made it impossible to hear whether she had said anything else. Behind her stunned face bobbed her grandmother's which was merely puzzled. The older Mrs Middleton was a timorous lady, slow to grasp situations but constantly fearful of their not being as she would like.

"Mother!" yelled Melanie a second time.

Mr Rao, deafened by lust, loneliness or the noise of the dishwasher, was still clinging to Jenny and muttering incomprehensible, maybe foreign, sounds. She heaved him off and spoke with harsh clarity to his blind, intoxicated face.

"I'm sorry," she said. "I'm sorry. But will you please go now. Just leave."

The Hairdresser

Leland Bardwell

Long ago they had painted the houses. Pale pastel shades - mauves, pinks, greys. The estate had expanded up Trevor's Hill, across the old sheep-field, curling back down like an anvil until it seemed the mountain had grown a second crust. Attempts to divert the streams had failed and water ran freely into the residents' gardens and rotted the foundations of the houses.

Paint cracked, window frames warped: there seemed no wisdom in the continuous building of new dwellings but after the last of the city clearances, the Local Authority brought out their trucks, their cranes, their earth movers and packed them in the road that ran directly through the estate till it could run no more and ended, T-shaped beneath the higher slopes.

Electric wires, pylons blew down in the storms and were seldom repaired so the estate lay mostly in darkness during the winter. There were strange happenings behind those closed doors at night. Many of the middle-aged women, whose husbands had taken off or been goaled took in men - those who roamed the country homeless - with whom they shared their bed and welfare payments. Occasionally a daughter would return with a new brood. Those men came and went; domestic unease, lack of money, young children crowding and squabbling would drive them out after a few months.

The women did their best and it was not unusual to see a middle-aged woman perched on her roof, trying to pin over a piece of plastic or rope up a bit of guttering. Like many another families, Mona and her mother had one of the houses in the higher slopes. Victims of the worst winter weather, they spent hours, plastering, drying, mending window frames and replacing slate. With one difference, however; Mona was the only one in the estate who attended secondary school. A rather plain girl with dry ribbed hair and a boxy figure, she was something of a scholar. Her mother was a gaunt angular woman with fierce energy.

Unlike the other woman she attracted a certain type of man, more chaotic, more unprincipled than the average. She responded passionately to these men and was thrown into despair when they left.

To Mona, her mother gave the recurring excuse that "they were safer with a man about". Mere excuse, of course, because the marauding gangs had "cased" every house and in theirs there was little left to steal. To eke out their dole they had sold their furniture, their television, their kitchen appliances one by one. They now made do with the barest necessities. An old kitchen table, over which hung a thin plastic cloth, a few upright chairs, mattresses and one cupboard sufficed for their basic needs. Only Mona's room was spotless. Her fastidious nature forswore squalor, and to this room, as soon as she had cooked the dinner, she would retire, her lesson books spread before her, a stub of a candle lighting up the immediate circle on the floor and with her stiff hair tied back in a knot she would concentrate on her studies to the exclusion of all else.

For some weeks now a new man had established himself in their household. Although he combined all the complexities and evil ways of his forerunners he was yet an unknown quantity to Mona. Her mother forever alert, listened to his speeches - he made speeches all day long claiming an intellectual monopoly on every subject. This irked Mona who had a fine mathematical brain and disagreed with many of his illogical conclusions. However, for the sake of her mother she held her peace.

Today she had decided to scrub the lino. As she scraped and picked between the cracks she could feel his gaze upon her as if it were a physical thing. She rose in confusion; there were rings on her knees from the muddy floor.

"Why don't you kneel on something," he barked, looking down at her legs as if she were a yearling in the ring.

"Ah shut up," she said; for once she lost her temper. "If you'd shift your arse I'd get on more quickly." He gazed at her angrily, his eyes still as glass; they were his most unsettling feature.

All this time her mother was sitting on the edge of her chair watching him, with the air of one who waits for her child to take its first few steps; she said nothing nervously lighting one cigarette from the tip of another.

Mona went to the sink to wring out her cloth: she looked round at him, sizing him up once again. There was madness there, she felt, in this posture, his teeth grinding, the occasional bouts of pacing; he was leaning over, elbows on knees, his stained overcoat folded back like the open page of an almanac. His hands were gyrating as though he were shuffling a pack of cards. He had strangely delicate hands, his fingers tapered into neat girlish nails yet he had huge tense shoulders. His face was stippled and pocked from long hours spent in the open. Yes, this man was not like the others - ruthless, fighting for survival - there were qualities within him, seams of impatience and rage that were beyond his control. Mona knew it was dangerous to answer him back; she wished she had held her tongue. Yet far from antagonising her mother, his rages seemed to make her more submissive, more carressing, more loving than ever. Or perhaps she, too, sensed danger; Mona wasn't sure.

When they were alone she would try to warn her mother but the latter would touch her own brow with the hand of a lover and with her other hand take Mona's and say, "Don't worry, darling. It will all be over one day."

Winter crawled. Snow came, dried off and fell again. It was no longer possible to patch the roof so they caught the water in buckets placed under the worst of the leaks. On a sleety February afternoon, Mona returning from her long journey back from school - it was dole day and they had bought cider - she found them both slightly drunk. They sat by the fire - one more chair had been burnt - and there was a glow of frivolity between them. But on her entry he addressed her rudely, finishing up by shaking his fists and saying, "you're a nasty piece of work." Mona snapped back, "you're a fucking creep, yourself."

There was silence. The skin on her mother's cheeks darkened with fear but she rose - an animal hoisted from its lair - and slowly picked up the flagon. He automatically held out his glass but she ignored it and poured the cider into his eyes.

The kitchen exploded. Chairs, table, went flying, and they were both on the floor, his fingers, those mobile fingers, closing, closing on her mother's throat and Mona screaming, kicking him from behind till he fell back howling in his effort to wipe his eyes with his sleeve. In a second her mother was up, apologising, begging for "another chance". But he was up too and heading for the door, his large frame bent like a sickle, his arms held stiffly from his body, he banged out of the house. The stricken women stood face to face as though waiting for a message that would never come. But her mother was already straining to go after him.

"Let him, mammy, let him go, for God's sake," Mona grasped the wool of her mother's jersey.

"No, no, I must save him. Save him from the police," and she slipped out of her jumper like a snake shedding its skin and she, too, ran out of the house.

The cold mountain air crept into the hall; gusts ran under the mat and up her legs as she shouldered shut the door. She stood for a while, knowing now that her life was beyond the ken of the two people out there. Who was she now? Mona the lucky one, she used to call herself, the only member of the family to forestall the fate that had swallowed up the rest of them. One brother killed in a hit-and-run, another in Mountjoy Gaol for armed robbery, a sister dead - from medical malpractice, another gone to England for an abortion who never returned. Mona the lucky one who had long ago made a pact with herself: to work and work, to use her ability to study, to use her interests that lay beyond this hinterland, so that one day, one far off day, she could take her mother and herself away from this noman's territory where rats and dogs got a better living than they did.

Along with this pact she'd promised herself that she would never allow her neat parts to be touched by the opposite sex, never succumb to the martyrdom of sexual love. In all the other houses, mile upon mile, children had given birth to children and were already grandmothers in their thirties. But she, Mona, tread a different path. Or did she? Should she not just pack her bags, go, too, into the recondite night, join the packs of boys and girls, small criminals, who got by by "doing cheques" or robbing the rich suburbs on the other side of the city.

She climbed the stairs, the re-lit candle dripping hot wax over her hand. In her room, her books, her friends, all stacked neatly, were suddenly strangers, strangers like the two people who had fled into the unyielding darkness. She went on her knees, taking each book and fondling it. The ones she cared for most, those on quantitive or applied mathematics, she held longingly, opening them, smoothing out the pages. But it was no use; they denied the half of her that was her pride. She threw them from her, went to the window, hoping to see her mother returning alone. But the street was dark, the houses down the hill, derelict as an unused railway station. She left the window open and sank down on the bed.

A little while later she heard them; they came into the hall. They spoke in low tones; the fight had been patched up and Mona knew that once again she'd get up, shop, make the dinner and act as if nothing had happened.

In the shop she would spend the few coins that she had, money that she earned from her better off student friends, the ones she helped with their homework; most of her mother's dole went on cigarettes and drink and lasted for about a day. So it was up to her to keep them from the edge of starvation.

She skirted the heaps of rubble, piles of sand that had been there for years. She used her memory to avoid the worst of the puddles and potholes. Even so her shoes filled up with icy water. The journey to the shop usually took about twenty minutes - it was over a mile away - and as it was nearly six Mona began to run.

The fierce cold of that day was the one thing that stuck in Mona's memory above all else. How dirty papers had flared up in front of her feet as she'd run the last few paces home; how the unending gale had pierced her chest and how she had clasped her inadequate coat collar around her chin. It had always been difficult to fit the yale into the keyhole and it seemed to take longer than usual as her white fingers grappled and twisted. But with the help of the wind the door blew in and a glass fell at the end of the passage - a glass of dead flowers - and water dripped quickly on to the floor. At first she had not seen her mother; the man had gone from the kitchen and Mona assumed they had gone upstairs to continue moments of reparition.

So Mona had begun to unwrap the food before she saw the blood. In fact it was when she was about to throw plastic wrapping into the rubbish bin that her eyes lit on the dark expanding pool. And before the horror had fully struck her her first thought had been that the body contains eight pints of blood - a gallon - and that this is what will now run over the floor, sink into the cracks of the lino, make everything black and slimy. He had slit her throat with the kitchen knife and left the body curled up half hidden by the piece of plastic cloth that hung down over the back of the table.

But the years had now passed. That murder had just become another legend in the estate, one of the many legends of killings and rapings. The football pitch, which had once been the place of recreation, had now become a graveyard for the people who died daily of diseases brought on by malnutrition and were bundled into the ground. There were thousands of dogs who crowded the "funerals" and who, when night came, dug up the corpses and ate them. Soon the people had ceased to care and left the bodies unburied for the scavengers. Everyone pretended they had not eaten human flesh.

And what of Mona?

After her mother's murder the madman had disappeared and was never found - no doubt he had holed up with some other lonely woman. Mona had left school and gone to work in a better off suburb as a hairdresser's assistant. She had continued to live in the same house which was now neat and tidy, the roof neat and patched and the gutters straightened. She had no friends and seldom went out after dark. But as the country fell further and further into the well of poverty, the rich, behind their gun towers and barbed wire, grasping to themselves their utopian "freedom", jobs in the better suburbs folded one by one, so for want of something to do, Mona took over the old hardware shop and turned it into an establishment of her own. Nobody could pay, so she accepted anything they could offer, from watercress, which still proliferated on the hills - to bits of food stolen from the itinerants, who's powers of survival were stronger than theirs.

People would do anything to get their hair fixed by Mona. It was the only entertainment left to them. Men, women and children flocked in, happy to queue for hours, their absent expressions momentarily lit by narcissistic anticipation. There was nothing for them to do. The revolution that once people had hoped for petered out in the nineties. The only way in which they might have expressed themselves would have been to fight the gangs of vigilantes who held the city in a grip of violence. But that would have meant a long trek into town and people were too underfed to face it. So Mona cut and dyed and permed from nine to six; the mathematician in her enjoyed the definition of a pleasant hairdo. She had grown gaunt, like her mother, and her strong brown eyes would survey her "customers", assessing the sweep of their locks with the same fixed gaze as that which her mother had used to pin down her men-friends.

The smell from the football pitch would waft in while people admired their reflections in the mirror; at times the purple fissure enhanced or disguised their grey features, their hollow eye sockets, their sagging skin.

But Mona didn't care about any of this but she cared, oh so deeply about her own expertise. If a person moved his head suddenly she'd get into a stifling rage. One day, she knew, she would kill one of her customers with the scissors, she would murder them as cold bloodedly and as bloodily as her mother had been murdered. She'd clip them inch by inch, first the ears, then she'd shove the scissors up their nostrils and so on and so forth.

Memory And Desire

Val Mulkerns

The television people seemed to like him and that was a new feeling he found exciting. Outside his own work circle he was not liked, on the whole, although he had a couple of lifelong friends he no longer cared for very much. The sort of people he would have wished to be accepted by found him arrogant, unfriendly, and not plain enough to be encouraged as an oddity. His wealth made him attractive only to the types he most despised. He was physically gross and clumsy with none of the social graces except laughter. Sometimes his jokes were good and communicable. More often they were obscure and left him laughing alone as though he were the last remaining inhabitant of an island.

Sometimes, indeed, he wondered if he spoke the same language as most other people, so frequently were they baffled if not positively repelled. He liked people generally, especially physically beautiful people who seemed to him magical as old gods. Sometimes he just looked at such people, not listening or pretending to listen to what they said, and then he saw the familiar expression of dislike and exclusion passing across their faces and he knew he had blundered again. Now for several weeks he had been among a closely knit group who actually seemed to find his company agreeable. When the invitation had first come he had been doubtful. He knew nothing about television and seldom watched it. But because his father's small glassmaking business had blossomed under his hand and become an important element in the export market, the television people thought a programme could be made out of his success story, a then-and-now sort of approach which seemed to him banal in the extreme. He had given his eventual consent because time so often hung on his hands now that expansion had progressed as far as was practicable and delegation had left him with little to do except see his more lucrative contacts in Europe and the United States a couple of times a year.

The only work he would actually have enjoyed doing these days was supervising the first efforts of young glass-blowers. Two of the present half-dozen were grandsons of his father's original men. At a time when traditional crafts were dying out everywhere or falling into strange (and probably passing) hands, this pleased him. He tried to show signs of his approval while keeping the necessary distance right from the boys' first day at work, but this was probably one of the few places left in Ireland where country boys were shy and backward still, and their embarrassment had been so obvious that nowadays he confined himself to reports on them from the foreman. It had been different in his father's time. The single cutter and the couple of blowers had become personal friends of his father and mother, living in the loft above the workshops (kept warm in winter by the kiln) and eating with the family in the manner of medieval apprentice craftsmen. During the holidays from boarding school they had become his friends too, gradually and naturally passing on their skills to him, and so listening without resentment to the new ideas on design he had in due course brought back with him from art school and from working spells in Sweden. Gradually over the years of expansion after his father's death he had grown away from the men. Now since the new factory had been built in Cork he knew very few of them any more.

The odd thing about the television people was that right from the beginning they had been unawed and called him Bernard, accepting that he had things to learn about their business and that he would stay with them in the same guest house, drink and live with them during the shooting of the film, almost as though they were his family and he an ordinary member of theirs. It had irritated and amused and baffled and pleased him in rapid progression and now he even found it hard to remember what his life had been like before he knew them or how his days had been filled in. Their youth too had shocked him in the beginning; they seemed like children at play with dangerous and expensive toys. The director in particular (who was also the producer and therefore responsible for the whole idea) had in addition to a good-humoured boy's face an almost fatherly air of concern for his odd and not always biddable family. What was more remarkable, he could discipline them. The assistant cameraman who had got drunk and couldn't be wakened on the third day of shooting had not done it again. When Eithne, the production assistant, had come down to breakfast one morning with a streaming cold and a raised temperature, Martin had stuffed a handful of her notes into the pocket of his jeans and sent her back up to bed, weeping and protesting that she was perfectly all right and not even her mother would dare to treat her like that.

Martin was very good with uncooperative fishermen, and with the farmer on whose land the original workshop still hung over the sea. A nearby hilly field had recently been sown with oats, and the farmer began with the strongest objection to a jeep laden with gear coming anywhere near it. He had agreed to it during preliminary negotiation, but shooting had in fact been delayed (delayed until more money became available) and that field, the farmer said, was in a delicate condition now. If they'd only come at the right time - Martin it was who finally talked him around with a guarantee against loss which would probably land him in trouble back in Dublin. But Martin (the Marvellous Boy was Bernard's private label for him) would worry about that one when he came to it and he advised Bernard to do the same about his fear of appearing ridiculous in some sequences. Not even half the stuff they were shooting would eventually be used, Martin said, and anyhow he'd give Bernard a preview at the earliest possible moment. Bernard stopped worrying again. Most of the time he had the intoxicating illusion of drifting with a strong tide in the company of excellent seamen and a captain who seemed to know his business.

The actual process of remembering was occasionally painful, of course. His only brother Tom had been swept away by a spring tide while fishing down on the rocks one day after school, and at first Bernard hadn't believed any reference to it would be possible when the script finally came to be written. Martin had come back to it casually again and again however, and finally one day of sharp March winds and flying patches of blue sky he had stood with Bernard on the headland near the roofless house.

"Let me show you what I have in mind," Martin said gently, the south Kerry accent soft as butter. "It will be very impressionistic, what I've in mind, a mere flash. A spin of sky and running tides, a moment. If you'd prefer, it won't need anything specific in the script. Just a reference to this friendly big brother mad about fishing, who knew about sea birds and seals and liked to be out by himself for hours on end. Maybe then, a single sentence about the nature of spring tides. The viewers generally won't know that spring tides have nothing to do with spring. You may say we're telling them about a successful glass industry, not about the sea, but the sea takes up a large part of your own early background and this piece is about you too. I'd write you a single sentence myself for your approval if you wouldn't mind - just to show you what I think would work - o.k.?"

"'These are pearls that were his eyes' - you could end like that, couldn't you?" Bernard heard himself sneering and almost at once regretted it. The director actually blushed and changed the subject. In a few seconds it was as if the moment had never happened, but it seemed to Bernard that a kind of bond had been perversely established.

Two days later a spring tide was running and he watched a few sequences being shot that might well be used for the passage he knew now he was going to write. He walked away from the crew when he found he could no longer watch the sort of sling from which the chief cameraman had been suspended above the cliffs to get some of the necessary angles. The whole thing could have been done better and more safely by helicopter but Martin had explained about the problems he had encountered after overrunning the budget for the last production. It wasn't of course that he wanted necessarily to make Bernard's backward look a cheaper affair; you often got a better end result (in his own experience) by using more ingenuity and less money: he thought he knew exactly how to do it. The somewhat unconvincing argument amused and didn't displease Bernard, who thought it more than likely that something less conventional might finally emerge. The last he saw of the crew was that crazy young man, clad as always when working in a cotton plaid shirt, suspending himself without benefit of the cameraman's sling to try to see exactly what the lens saw.

A fit of nervousness that had in it something of the paternal and something else not paternal at all made him walk the seven miles around to the next headland. He hadn't thought like a father for five years. For half of that isolated time he hadn't brought home casual male encounters either because nothing stable had ever emerged from them and more often than not he was put off by the jungle whiff of the predator and managed to change direction just in time. Now he tried to resist looking back at the pair of boys busy with their games which they apparently regarded as serious. The head cameraman was even younger than Martin. He had a fair freckled face and red hair so long that it would surely have been safer to tie it back in a girl's ponytail before swinging him out in that perilous contraption. Bernard turned his face again into the stiff wind and looked back at the receding insect wriggling above the foaming tide, man and technology welded together in the blasting sunlight. The weird shape drew back his eyes again and again until a rock they called the Billygoat's Missus cut it off and he was alone for (it seemed) the first time in several weeks.

For the first time as in a camera's framed eye he saw his own room at home. Tidy as a well-kept grave, it was full of spring light from the garden. There were daffodils on his desk. Spangles of light from the rocky pool outside danced on the Yeats canvas that took up most of one wall and struck sparks from the two early balloons which he treasured. Five poplars in a haze of young green marked the end of his garden. Beyond it, the sharp-breasted great Sugarloaf and eventually the sea. The room had been tidy for five years now. No maddening litter of dropped magazines, no hairpins, no shoes kicked off and left where they fell: left for the woman next morning to carry to the appropriate place in the appropriate room because she was born to pick up the litter of other people's lives, paid for it as the only work she knew. One night in a fit of disgust he had kicked into the corner a black leather clog, left dead centre on the dark carpet awaiting the exact moment to catch his shin. Uncontrolled fits of violence he despised. Recovering quickly he had placed the shoes side by side outside the door as though this were an old-fashioned hotel with dutiful boots in residence. She had come in laughing later on, both clogs held up incredulously in her hand, laughing and laughing, tossing them finally up in the air to fall where they might before she left the room. As perhaps she had done last night and would do again tomorrow. Wherever she was.

A rising wind drove before it into the harbour a flock of black clouds that had appeared from nowhere, and when drops of rain the size of old pennies began to lash down he sought refuge in the hotel which had been small and unpretentious in its comfort when he was a child. His father's clients had often stayed here. He had sometimes been sent on messages to them with his brother. Now the place had several stars from an international guide book and was famous both for its seafood and the prices that foreign gourmets were willing to pay for it.

He sat in the little bar full of old coastal maps and looked out at the sea; alone for the first time in two weeks he was no less content than in the casual company of the television people. Their young faces and their voices were still inside his head. As though on cue, Martin suddenly came through into the bar, also alone. The wind had made any more shooting too dangerous for today he said, and the girls had gone off to wash their hair. He had his fishing gear in the boot, but he doubted if he'd do much good today.

"Have lunch with me, then, and eat some fish instead," Bernard invited, and was amused to see a flash of pure pleasure light up the director's face. Beer and a sandwich usually kept them going until they all sat down together at the end of the day.

"This place has got so much above itself even since the last time I was down here that I expect to be asked my business as soon as I set foot inside the door," Martin grinned.

"They wouldn't do that in late March," Bernard assured him. "Neither the swallows nor the tourists have arrived yet, so I fancy even people in your advanced state of sartorial decay would be encouraged."

Martin took an imaginary clothes brush out of the jeans pocket (too tight to hold anything larger than a toothbrush) and began to remove stray hairs from that well-worn garment which had seaweedy stains in several places and looked slightly damp. The boy walked with a sort of spring, like a healthy cat, and there was no trace yet of the flab which his pint-drinking would eventually bring. He ate the bouillabaisse and the fresh baked salmon which followed with the relish of a child brought out from boarding school for the day and determined to take full advantage of it. He praised the Alsace wine which was apparently new to him and Bernard decided that one of the great remaining pleasures of money was never to have to worry about the cost of anything one suddenly wanted to do. Bernard listened abstractedly to a little house politics over the coffee and then at the end of the first cognac he spoke one unwary line about buying all those bandy little boss men for a next birthday present for Martin should he wish it. The sea-reflecting blue eyes opposite him narrowed coldly for a moment before they closed in a bellow of laughter and the moment passed, like the rain outside. The sea was too uneasy, however, in the whipping wind to yield anything, but Bernard remembered one good story about his dead brother on a long-ago trip to Kinsale. Martin made a note in biro on the back of the wrist which held his fishing rod and Bernard knew it would be transferred to the mounting heaps of papers back at the hotel. More and more in the course of the programme he was being his own production assistant.

Mr O'Connor had carried in a mountain of turf for the fire and Eithne rather liked to listen to the rattle of the rain outside by way of contrast. Her hair was dry by now but spread all over the hearthrug and she swung it back in a tickling blanket over the recumbent figure of John D who was still struggling with the Irish Times crossword.

"Give that over and sit up," she said, fetching her eternal dice-throwing version of Scrabble which she had bought somewhere in Holland.

"I was just going to work out another angle for that last shot to put to Martin when he gets back."

"Martin is probably half way to France by now on an ebbing tide. We'll find his pathetic little bits and pieces in the morning."

"Stop that!" John D was superstitious as well as red-haired. He was nervous about things like that. "All right, I'll give you three games and that's it."

"Nice John D. Did you notice Bernard's face today when you were strung up over the cliff, by the way?"

"I had other things to worry about. Is 'cadenza' allowed?"

"It's not English but I supposed it's in the OED like everything else - it's virtually been taken over, after all."

"O.K. it's allowed." John D formed the word.

"But no brio or allegro molto," Eithne warned.

"No brio or allegro molto - I haven't the makings of them anyhow. What sort of look did Bernard have on his unlovely mug?"

"A bit nervous for you, I think. I think that's why he walked away."

"Arrogant bastard a lot of the time." John D swept up the dice after totting his score. "Are capitalists human? You should put that theme to Martin some time."

"More a Neville sort of line, surely? But I think you're wrong. He's shy and he's only just stopped being uneasy with us."

"Just in time to say goodbye then," said John D with satisfaction. "There's hardly a week in it, if the weather lifts a bit."

"If," Eithne said, scooping a single good score. It was her game, her thing, but the others always won. "I think he's lonely, which only goes to show you money isn't everything."

"You can be miserable in much more comfort though. He looks to me like a bod who'd have it off wherever he pleased with one sex or t'other, despite his ugly mug. He has the brazen confidence you only get from too much money."

"I think you're wrong and the death of his brother is still bothering him after all these years. It's something I just have a hunch about. And then of course his wife walked out on him a few years ago. Prime bitch they say she was too. He come home one night and found not as much as a hairclip left behind, and his baby gone too."

" 'Hunch' is not a permissible word all the same. Thirties slang," said John D with finality. "Why wouldn't she walk out on him when he's probably given to buggery?"

"It's much more permissible than 'cadenza'. How about to hunch one's shoulders?"

"Go and ask Mr O'Connor if he has a dictionary then."

"You go. My hair isn't dry yet."

"Your hair is practically on fire, lady," John D said, settling himself comfortably on the hearthrug again. A car crunched in the sandy drive outside and Eithne gave a long sigh.

"Thank God. I couldn't have borne the smell of good country roast beef much longer."

"There'll be frogs' eyes to follow."

"At worst there'll be stewed apples, at best apple pie. Doesn't your nose tell you anything except whether a pint's good or bad?"

In out of the rain and the early dusk, Bernard was touched all over again by the sight of two apparent children playing a game beside the fire. He came over very willingly to join them when Eithne called and Martin went upstairs to look over his notes before dinner. He would call Evelyn on his way down, he said.

Later they all went out in the pouring rain to the pub and listened while a couple of local Carusos rendered songs like "Two Sweethearts" - one with hair of shining gold, the other with hair of grey - or the endless emigrant laments favoured by local taste. Whiskey chasing several pints made John D a bit quarrelsome and he shouted for a song from Bernard just to embarrass him. To everybody's surprise Bernard was not embarrassed. He stood up, supported only by two small Jamesons (the second of which he was still nursing) and gave the company a soft-voiced but not untuneful version of "Carrickfergus" which was vociferously applauded by the locals and earned him delightful approval from the team. Eithne thought they ought maybe incorporate "Carrickfergus" into the soundtrack, and John D wanted to know why they couldn't all move up to Carrickfergus and let Bernard do his party piece with his back against the castle walls. This suggestion was received with the contempt it deserved but Bernard wasn't discomfited.

That happened only when he got back to the guest house and he heard Martin telling Mrs O'Connor that they would almost certainly be finished shooting by the end of the week and would hardly stay over the weekend. The sinking of the heart was like what came long ago with the necessity of facing back to school after the long summer holidays. He felt ashamed of his emotion and unsure how to conceal it, so he went up early to his room. Normally he would hang about for hours yet, reading the newspapers they hadn't had time for during the day, swapping stories, doing crossword puzzles, discussing the next days work. Usually he didn't contribute much to the conversation; like a silent member of a big family he was simply there, part of what was going on, perfectly content to sit up as long as they did.

Now there was something symbolic about hearing the murmur of their voices downstairs. The script still had to be written and there would be consultations in Dublin about it, hopefully with Martin, but (give or take a few days from now) the thing was over. Next week they would all be busy taking somebody else through his mental lumber room. The little family would re-form itself around another fire, and it would have nothing to do with him. And soon it would be April, breeding lilacs out of the dead land, mixing memory and desire. Time perhaps to go away; he had promised himself a few weeks in April. On the other hand, why not stay here?

He let down the small dormer window and looked out over the water. The house echoed, in almost exact detail, the other, roofless house: the murmur of voices, even, was like his sisters' voices before they settled down for the night, all together in the big back bedroom. His own small room above the harbour used to be shared with his brother. The rain had stopped now and there was almost no sound from the sea and he wasn't surprised when Martin came to his door to say the weather forecast had been very good for the south-west and they night get a full day's shooting tomorrow.

"Come in and have a nightcap," he invited, and Martin said he wouldn't stay long but happily didn't refuse the brandy when it was taken from the wardrobe.

"What will you do next?" Bernard asked, just for a moment unsure of how to begin.

"A bit of a break before I join Current Affairs for a short stint," the boy smiled. "Yours is the last programme in the present series. No more now until next season."

"You mean you're going to take a holiday?" He strove to make his voice sound casual, although he was suddenly aware of the beating of his heart.

"Unless something untoward crops up, yes."

"Why not join me in Greece, then, since that's where I'm heading next week or the week after? The place I have on Ios needs to be opened up after the winter and there's plenty of room I assure you. Also two local women waiting to cook and clean for us." Bernard saw the refusal before it came; it was only a question of how it would be framed, how lightly he would be let down.

"It's a tempting offer, and there's nothing I'd enjoy more, all things being equal. Never been further than Corfu as a matter of fact. But my wife has organised a resident babysitter for the two boys and we're off on a busman's holiday to Canada as soon as I'm free. Laura is Canadian you know. I met her when I was training in London with the B.B.C. When we get back, maybe you'd come over for supper with us some evening? Laura's an unpredictable cook, but you'll agree that doesn't matter too much when you meet her. Is it a deal?"

He drained the glass and got off Bernard's bed with the same catspring which was noticeable also in the way he walked.

"It's a deal. Many thanks. And maybe you'll join me some time in Greece?"

Martin made the appropriate noises and didn't go at once, but started talking about a painter called Richard Dadd who (somebody had told him) had probably given Yeats his Crazy Jane themes. He hadn't seen the paintings himself at the Tate but Bernard had, so this kept them going until the door closed behind him, and on his youth, and on the hollow promise of knowing him as one knew every line of one's own hand. There was a lot of the night left and, fortunately, a lot of the brandy too.

The weather behaved as the weathermen said it would and the

rest of the shooting went without a hitch. During this couple of weeks the year had turned imperceptibly towards summer, primroses in the land-facing banks, sea-pinks along the cliffs and an air about the television people that Bernard had seen before and couldn't quite place. Only when he went with them for the final day's shooting did he pin it down; a fairground the day after the circus. The television gear was more easily moved, of course; no long hours were needed for the pull-out. But the feeling was the same. They didn't believe him when he said he was staying on and they seemed shocked, which amused him, when he determinedly heaped presents on them the morning they were going: his Leica for Eithne who (incredibly) had never owned a camera of her own, a sheepskin jacket for John D because his own was in flitters from the rocks, a silver brandy flask (circa 1840), a cigarette lighter and a gold biro scattered apparently at random among the rest. The vulgarity of the largesse amused Bernard himself because such behaviour was not usual and he didn't entirely understand his impulse. But he understood perfectly why he gave Martin his signed first edition of "The Winding Stair", a volume which for a year or more had lived in the right hand door-pocket of his car for no better reason than that he liked to have it there. He had bought it somewhere along the quays in Cork.

"Fair and foul are near of kin
And fair needs foul," I cried
"My friends are gone and that's a truth
Nor grave nor bed denied
Learned in bodily lowliness,
And in the heart's pride."

A former owner had marked that with a small star in the margin, and Martin smiled slightly as he read it aloud in gratitude when the book fell open.

"I often have a disturbing feeling when I finish a job like this that I know -" he searched patiently for the words he wanted and his hesitation seemed to Bernard like comfort consciously-given for some loss he could understand. "That I know almost enough to begin all over again. Properly." He didn't smile at all when they shook hands so that the handgrip seemed warmer. "Until soon, in Dublin," were his last words, a rather childish farewell which would have left a pleasant glow behind if Bernard had not known by now that they would not meet again. The vanful of technology went on ahead of the boy's unreliable little red sports car, and watching from the drive of the guesthouse, Bernard had the feeling of the fairground again after the circus caravans have rolled away. It was peaceful, though, with the blue sea breathing quietly all around him and a few mares' tails of cloud slowly unravelling in the sky.

He was leaning over the wall considering how he would fill his remaining time when the guesthouse owner strolled by, indicating the blue boat which bobbed at the end of its mooring rope below them. "You could take the aul' boat out fishing any day you had a fancy for it, Mr Golden. You're more than welcome to her any time though I wouldn't recommend today, mind you."

"I'm much obliged to you, Stephen. I have all the gear I need in the boot of the car so I might do just that. But why not today?"

"She'll rise again from the south-west long before evening," his host said positively. "And she'll blow herself out if I'm not mistaken. 'Twould be a dangerous thing to go fishing out there today."

"The weather men last night didn't mention any gales blowing up."

"The weather men don't live around this Hook either," O'Connor said drily. "I've caught those same gentlemen out once or twice, and will again with the help of God."

"You might be right at that, I suppose. But if I do go out, I'll only fish for a short while, I promise you."

A pleasant man, Stephen O'Connor, a retired Civic Guard with an efficient wife to make a business out of the beautiful location of their house and her own hard work. Bernard remembered him vaguely from childhood, pedalling wet and fine around the coast roads, stopping here and there for a chat, missing nothing. It was he who had brought the news that Tom's body had been washed ashore somewhere near Kinsale. It was he who had in fact identified it. On remembering this Bernard toyed for a moment with the idea of having an actual conversation with this kindly man whose memories touched his own at one black juncture. The moment passed however, and Stephen made a little more chat, lingering with natural courtesy just long enough for a guest to make up his mind whether or not further company would be welcome, and then he ambled contentedly in the direction of the greenhouse for the day's pottering. Old man, old man, if you never looked down again at a drowned face of my father's house it would be time enough for you. Forgive me, Stephen O'Connor.

The first warm sun of the year touched Bernard's eyes and he smiled, sitting up on the sea wall. No more Aprils, no more lilacs breeding out of the dead land, no more carnal awakenings. He felt peaceful, then a little surprised that the image behind his closed eyelids was not of his brother or of the young Martin or even of the caravans pulling out. It was the small wilful face of his daughter in the act of breaking away when one tried to hold her. He didn't know where she was, or even how she looked now, whether she still mirrored her mother in every gesture. He had a perfect right to know for the mere trouble of enforcing it. He hadn't done that, at first put off by the refusal of maintenance, by the eternal sound of the phone ringing in an empty flat and by two or three unanswered letters. He hadn't made a very energetic effort to keep in touch. As one year became two or three and now five, it had always seemed too late, but it would be untrue to pretend he greatly cared. It was just that, not being able to understand why the child's face should be so vivid in his mind, he was bothered by it as by some minor irritation, a door that slammed somewhere out of sight, a dripping tap. It wasn't until he was actually aboard the boat starting up the engine in a freshening breeze that he realised why he couldn't rid himself of his daughter's face today, of all days.

Autumn Sunshine

William Trevor

The rectory was in Co. Wexford, eight miles from Enniscorthy. It was a handsome eighteenth century house, with virginia creeper covering three sides and a tangled garden full of buddleia and struggling japonica which had always been too much for it's incumbents. It stood alone, seeming lonely even, approximately at the centre of the country parish it served.

It's church - St. Michael's Church of Ireland - was two miles away, in the village of Boharbawn.

For twenty years the Morans had lived there, not wishing to live anywhere else. Canon Moran had never been an ambitious man; his wife, Frances, had found contentment easy to attain in her lifetime. Their four girls had been born in the rectory, and had become a happy family there. They were grown up now, Frances's death was still recent: like the rectory itself, its remaining occupant was alone in the countryside. The death had occurred in the spring of the year, and the summer had somehow been bearable. The clergyman's eldest daughter had spent May and part of June at the rectory with her children. Another one had brought her family for most of August, and a third was to bring her newly married husband in the winter. At

Christmas nearly all of them would gather at the rectory and some would come at Easter. But that September, as the days drew in, the season was melancholy.

Then, one Tuesday morning, Slattery brought a letter from Canon Moran's youngest daughter. There were two other letters as well, in unsealed buff envelopes which meant they were either bills or receipts. Frail and grey haired in his elderliness, Canon Moran had been wondering if he should give the lawn in front of the house a last cut when he heard the approach of Slattery's van. The lawnmower was the kind that had to be pushed, and in the spring the job was always easier if the grass had been cropped close at the end of the previous summer.

"Isn't that a great bit of weather, Canon?" Slattery remarked, winding down the window of the van and passed out three envelopes. "We're set for a while, would you say."

"I hope so, certainly."

"Ah, we surely are, sir."

The conversation continued a few moments longer, as it did whenever Slattery came to the rectory. The postman was young and easy-going, not long the successor to old Mr O'Brien, who'd been making the round on a bicycle when the Morans first came to the rectory in 1952. Mr O'Brien used to talk about his garden, Slattery talked about fishing and often brought a share of his catch to the rectory.

"It's a great time of year for it," he said now, "except for the darkness coming in."

Canon Moran smiled and nodded, the van turned round on the gravel, dust rising behind it as it moved swiftly down the avenue to the road. Everyone said Slattery drove too fast.

He carried the letters to a wooden seat on the edge of the lawn he'd been wondering about cutting. Deirdre's handwriting hadn't changed since she'd been a child; it was round and neat, not at all a reflection of the girl she was. The blue English stamp, the Queen in profile blotched a bit by the London postmark, wasn't on it's side or half upside down, as you might expect with Deirdre. Of all the Moran children, she'd grown up to be the only difficult one. She hadn't come to the funeral and hadn't written about her mother's death. She hadn't been to the rectory for three years.

I'm sorry, she wrote now. I couldn't stop crying actually. I've never known anyone as nice or as generous as she was. For ages I didn't even want to believe she was dead. I went on imagining her in the rectory and doing the flowers in church and shopping in Enniscorthy.

Deirdre was twenty-one now. He and Frances had hoped she'd go to Trinity and settle down, but although at school she'd seemed to be the cleverest of their children, she'd had no desire to become a student. She'd taken the Rosslare boat to Fishguard one night, having said she was going to spend a week with her friend Maeve Coles in Cork. They hadn't known she'd gone to England until they received a picture postcard from London telling them not to worry, saying she'd found work in an egg-packing factory.

Well I'm coming back for a little while now, she wrote, if you could put up with me and if you wouldn't find it too much. I'll cross over to Rosslare on the 29th, the morning crossing, and then I'll come on to Enniscorthy on the bus. I don't know what time it will be but there's a pub just by where the bus drops you so could we meet in the small bar there at six o'clock and then I won't have to lug my cases too far? I hope you won't mind going into such a place. If you can't make it or don't want to see me, it's understandable, so if you don't turn up by half six I'll see if I can get a bus on up to Dublin. Only I need to get back to Ireland for a while.

It was, as he and Slattery had agreed, a lovely autumn. Gentle sunshine mellowed the old garden, casting an extra sheen of gold on the leaves that were gold already. Roses that had been ebullient in June and July, blossomed modestly now. Michaelmas daisies were just beginning to bud. Already the crab apples were falling, hydrangeas had a forgotten look. Canon Moran carried the letter from his daughter into the walled vegetable garden and leant against the side of a greenhouse, half sitting on a protruding ledge, reading the letter again. Panes of glass were broken in the greenhouse, while paint and putty needed to be renewed, but inside a vine still thrived, and was heavy now with black, ripe fruit. Later that morning he would pick some and drive into Enniscorthy, to sell the grapes to Mrs Roche in Slaney Street.

Love, Deirdre: the letter was marvellous. Beyond the rectory the fields of wheat had been harvested, and the remaining stubble had the same tinge of gold in the autumn light; the beech trees and chestnuts were triumphantly magnificent. But decay and rotting were only weeks away, and the letter from Deirdre was full of life. Love, Deirdre, were words more beautiful than all the seasons glories. He prayed as he leant against the sunny greenhouse, thanking God for this salvation.

For all the years of their marriage Frances had been a help. As a younger man, Canon Moran often hadn't known quite what to do. He'd been at a loss amongst his parishioners, hesitating in the face of this weakness or that: the pregnancy of Alice Pratt in 1954, the argument about grazing rights between Mr Willoughby and Eugene Ryan in 1960, the theft of an altar cloth from St. Michael's and reports that Mrs Tobin had been seen wearing it as a skirt. Alice Pratt had been going out with a Catholic boy, one of Father Hayes's flock, which had made the matter more difficult than ever. Eugene Ryan was one of Father Hayes's also, and so was Mrs Ryan.

"Father Hayes and I had a chat," Frances had said, and she'd had a chat as well with Alice Pratt who married the Catholic boy, but to this day attended St. Michael's every Sunday, the children going to Father Hayes. Mrs Tobin was given Hail Marys to say by the priest; Mr Willoughby agreed that his father had years ago granted Eugene Ryan the grazing rights. Everything, in these cases and many others, had come out all right in the end: order emerged from the confusion that Canon Moran so disliked and it was Frances who had always begun the process, though no one ever said in the rectory that she understood the mystery of people as well as he understood the teachings of the New Testament. She'd been a freckle-faced girl when he'd married her, pretty in her way. He was the one with the brains.

Frances had seen human frailty everywhere: it was a weakness in people, she said, that made her own share of such frailty, falling short in all sorts of ways of the God's image her husband preached about. With the small amount of housekeeping money she could be allowed she was a spendthrift, and she said she was lazy. She loved clothes and often over reached herself on visits to

Dublin; she sat in the sun while the rectory gathered dust and the garden became rank; it was only where people were conce_ned that she was practical. But for what she was, her husband had loved her with unobtrusive passion for fifty years, appreciating her conversation and the help she'd given him because she could so easily sense the truth. When he'd found her dead in the garden one morning he'd felt he had lost some part of himself.

Though many months had passed since then, the trouble was that Frances hadn't yet become a ghost. Her being alive was still too recent, the shock of her death too raw. He couldn't distance himself, the past refused to be the past. Often he thought that her fingerprints were still in the rectory, and when he picked the grapes or cut the grass of the lawn it was impossible not to pause and remember other years. Autumn had been her favourite time.

"Of course I'd come," he said. "Of course, dear. Of course."

"I haven't treated you very well."

"It's over and done with, Deirdre."

She smiled and it was nice to see her smile again, although it was strange to be sitting in the back bar of a public house in Enniscorthy. He saw her looking at him, her eyes passing over his clerical collar and black clothes, and his thin quiet face. He could feel her thinking that he had aged, and putting it down to the death of the wife he'd been so very fond of.

"I'm sorry I didn't write," she said.

"You explained in your letter, Deirdre."

"It was ages before I knew about it. That was an old address you wrote to."

"I guessed."

In turn he examined her. Years ago she'd had her long hair cut. It was short now, like a neat black cap on her head. And her face had lost its chubbiness; hollows where her cheeks had been, making eyes more dominant, pools of seaweed green. He remembered her child's stocky body, and the uneasy adolescence that had spoilt the family's serenity. Her voice had lost it's Irish intonation.

"I'd have met you off the boat, you know."

"I didn't want to bother you with that."

"Oh now, it isn't far, Deirdre."

She drank Irish whiskey, and smoked a brand of cigarettes called Three Castles. He'd asked for a mineral himself and the woman serving them had brought a bottle of something that looked like water but fizzed up when she poured it. A kind of lemonade he imagined it was and didn't much care for it.

"I have grapes for Mrs Roche," he said.

"Who's that?"

"She has a shop in Slaney Street. We always sold her the grapes. You remember?"

She didn't, and he reminded her of the vine in the greenhouse. A shop surely wouldn't open at this hour of the evening, she said, forgetting that in a country town of course it would be. She asked if the cinema was the same in Enniscorthy, a cement building halfway up a hill. She said she remembered bicycling home from it at night with her sisters, not being able to keep up with them. She asked after her sisters and he told her about the two marriages that had taken place since she'd left: she had in-laws she'd never met, and nephews and a niece.

They left the bar and he drove his dusty black Vauxhall straight to the small shop he'd spoken of. She remained in the car while he carried into the shop two large chip baskets full of grapes. Afterwards Mrs Roche came to the door with him.

"Well, is that Deirdre?" she said as Deirdre wound down the window of the car. "I'd never have known you, Deirdre."

"She's come back for a little while," Canon Moran explained, raising his voice a little because he was walking around the car to the driver's seat as he spoke.

"Well isn't that grand?" said Mrs Roche.

Everyone in Enniscorthy knew Deirdre had just gone off, but it didn't matter now. Mrs Roche's husband, who was a red cheeked man with a cap, much smaller than his wife, appeared beside her in the shop doorway. He inclined his head in greeting, and Deirdre smiled and waved at both of them. Canon Moran thought it was pleasant when she went on waving while he drove off.

In the rectory he lay wakeful that night, his mind excited by Deirdre's presence. He would have loved Frances to know, and guessed that she probably did. He fell asleep at half-past two and dreamed that he and Frances were young again, that Deirdre was still a baby. The freckles on Frances's face were out in profusion, for they were sitting in the sunshine in the garden, tea things spread about them, the children playing some game among the shrubs. It was autumn then also, the last of the September heat. But because he was younger in his dream he didn't feel part of the season himself nor sense its melancholy.

A week went by. The time passed slowly because a lot was happening, or so it seemed. Deirdre insisted on cooking all the meals and on doing the shopping in Boharbawn's single shop or in Enniscorthy. She still smoked her endless cigarettes, but the peakiness there had been in her face when she'd first arrived wasn't quite so pronounced - or perhaps, he thought, he'd become used to it. She told him about the different jobs she'd had in London and the different places she lived in because on the postcards she'd occasionally sent there hadn't been room to go into detail. In the rectory he had always hoped she'd managed to get a training of some sort, though guessing she hadn't. In fact, her jobs had been of the most rudimentary kind: as well as her spell in the egg-packing factory, there'd been a factory that made plastic ear-phones, a cleaning job in a hotel near Euston, and a year working for the Use-Us Office Cleansing Service. "But you can't have liked any of that work, Deirdre?" he suggested, and she agreed that she hadn't.

From the way she spoke he felt that that period of her life was over: adolescence was done with, she had steadied and taken stock. He didn't suggest to her that any of this might be so, not wishing to seem either too anxious or too pleased, but he felt she had returned to the rectory in a very different frame of mind from the one in which she'd left it. He imagined she would remain for quite a while, still taking stock, and in a sense occupying her mother's place. He thought he recognised in her a loneliness that matched his own, and he wondered if it was a feeling that their loneliness might be shared that had brought her back at this particular time. Sitting in the drawing-room while she cooked or washed up, or gathering grapes in the greenhouse while she did the shopping, he warmed delightedly to this theme. It seemed like an act of God that their circumstances should interlace this autumn. By Christmas she would know what she wanted to do with her life and in the spring that followed she would perhaps be ready to set forth again. A year would have passed since the death of Frances.

"I have a friend," Deirdre said when they were having a cup of coffee together in the middle of one morning. "Someone who's been good to me."

She had carried a tray to where he was composing next week's sermon, sitting on the wooden seat by the lawn at the front of the house. He laid aside his exercise book, and a pencil and a rubber.

"Who's that?" he enquired.

"Someone called Harold."

He nodded, stirring sugar into his coffee.

"I want to tell you about Harold, Father. I want you to meet him."

"Yes, of course."

She lit a cigarette. She said:

"We have a lot in common. I mean, he's the only person..."

She faltered and then hesitated. She lifted her cigarette to her lips and drew it. He said:

"Are you fond of him, Deirdre?"

"Yes, I am."

Another silence gathered. She smoked and drank her coffee. He added more sugar to his.

"Of course I'd like to meet him," he said.

"Could he come to stay with us, Father? Would you mind? Would it be all right?"

"Of course I wouldn't mind. I'd be delighted."

Harold was summoned and arrived at Rosslare a few days later. In the meantime Deirdre had explained to her father that her friend was an electrician by trade and had let it fall that he was an intellectual kind of person. She borrowed the old Vauxhall and drove it to Rosslare to meet him, returning to the Rectory in the early evening.

"How d'you do?" Canon Moran said, stretching out a hand in the direction of an excessively thin youth with a birthmark on his face. His mouse-coloured hair was cut very short, cropped almost. He was wearing a black leather jacket.

"I'm fine," Harold said.

"You've had a good journey?"

"Lousy, 's matter of fact, Mr Moran."

Harold's voice was strongly Cockney, and Canon Moran wondered if Deirdre had perhaps picked up some of her English vowel sounds from it. But then he realised that most people in London would speak like that, as people did on the television and the wireless. It was just a little surprising that Harold and Deirdre should have so much in common, as they clearly had from the affectionate way they held one another's hands. None of the other Moran girls had gone in so much for holding hands in front of the family.

He was to sit in the drawing-room, they insisted, while they made supper in the kitchen, so he picked up the Irish Times and did as he was bidden. Half an hour later Harold appeared and said that the meal was ready: fried eggs and sausages and bacon, and some tinned beans. Canon Moran said Grace.

Having stated that County Wexford looked great, Harold didn't say much else. He didn't smile much either. His afflicted face bore an edgy look, as if he'd never become wholly reconciled to his birthmark. It was like a scarlet map on his left cheek, a shape that reminded Canon Moran of the toe of Italy. Poor fellow, he thought. And yet a birthmark was so much less to bear than other afflictions there could be.

"Harold's fascinated actually," Deirdre said, "by Ireland."

Her friend didn't add anything to that remark for a moment, even though Canon Moran smiled and nodded interestedly. Eventually Harold said: "The struggle of the Irish people."

"I didn't know a thing about Irish history," Deirdre said. "I mean, not anything that made sense."

The conversation lapsed at this point, leaving Canon Moran greatly puzzled. He began to say that Irish history had always been of considerable interest to him also, that it had a good story to it, its tragedy uncomplicated. But the other two didn't appear to understand what he was talking about and so he changed the subject. It was a particularly splendid autumn, he pointed out.

"Harold doesn't go in for anything like that," Deirdre replied.

During the days that followed Harold began to talk more, surprising Canon Moran with almost everything he said. Deirdre had been right to say he was fascinated by Ireland, and it wasn't just a tourist's fascination. Harold had read widely: he spoke of ancient battles, and of the plantations of James I and Elizabeth, of Robert Emmet and the Mitchelstown martyrs, of Pearse and de Valera. "The struggle of the Irish people" was the expression he most regularly employed. It seemed to Canon Moran that the relationship between Harold and Deirdre had a lot to do with Harold's fascination, as though his interest in Deirdre's native land had somehow caused him to become interested in Deirdre herself.

There was something else as well. Fascinated by Ireland, Harold hated his own country. A sneer whispered through his voice when he spoke of England: a degenerate place, he called it, destroyed by class-consciousness and the unjust distribution of wealth. He described in detail the city of Nottingham, to which he appeared to have a particular aversion. He spoke of unnecessary motorways and the stupidity of bureaucracy, the stifling presence of a Royal Family. "You could keep an Indian village," he claimed, "on what those corgis eat. You could house five hundred homeless in Buckingham Palace." There was brainwashing by television and the newspaper barons. No ordinary person had a chance because pap was fed to the ordinary person, a deliberate policy going back into Victorian times when education and religion had been geared to the enslavement of minds. The English people had brought it on themselves, having lost their spunk, settling instead for consumer durables.

"What better can you expect," Harold demanded, "after the hypocrisy of that empire the bosses ran?"

Deirdre didn't appear to find anything specious in this line of talk, which surprised her father. "Oh, I wonder about that," he said himself from time to time, but he said it mildly, not wishing to cause an argument, and in any case his interjections were not acknowledged. Quite a few of the criticisms Harold levelled at his own country could be levelled at Ireland also, and Canon Moran guessed at many countries throughout the world. It was strange that the two neighbouring islands had been so picked out, although once Germany was mentioned and the point made that developments beneath the surface there were a hopeful sign, that a big upset was on the way.

"We're taking a walk," Harold said one afternoon. "She's going to show me Kinsella's Barn."

Canon Moran nodded, saying to himself that he disliked Harold. It was the first time he had admitted it, but the feeling was familiar. The less generous side of his nature had always emerged when his daughters brought to the rectory the men they'd become friendly with or even proposed to marry. Emma, the eldest girl, had brought several before settling in the end for Thomas. Linda had brought only John, already engaged to him. Una had married Carley not long after the death, and Carley had not yet visited the rectory: Canon Moran had met him in Dublin, where the wedding had taken place, for in the circumstances Una had not been married from home. Carley was an older man, an importer of tea and wine, stout and flushed, certainly not someone Canon Moran would have chosen for his second youngest daughter. But then he had thought the same about Emma's Thomas and about Linda's John.

Thomas was a farmer, sharing a sizeable acreage with his father in Co. Meath. He always brought to mind the sarcasm of an old schoolmaster who in Canon Moran's distant schooldays used to refer to a gang of boys at the back of the classroom as "farmer's sons", meaning that not much could be expected of them. It was an inaccurate assumption but even now, whenever Canon Moran found himself in the company of Thomas, he couldn't help recalling it: Thomas was mostly silent, with a good-natured smile that came slowly and lingered too long. According to his father, and there was no reason to doubt the claim, he was a good judge of beef cattle.

Linda's John was the opposite. Wiry and suave, he was making his way in the Bank of Ireland, at present stationed at Waterford. He had a tiny orange-coloured moustache and was good at golf. Linda's ambition for him was that he should become the Bank of Ireland's manager in Limerick or Galway, where the insurances that went with the position were particularly lucrative. Unlike Thomas, John talked all the time, telling jokes and stories about the Bank of Ireland's customers.

"Nothing is perfect," Frances used to say, chiding her husband for an uncharitableness he did his best to combat. He disliked being so particular about the men his daughters chose, and he was aware that other people saw them differently: Thomas would do anything for you, John was fun, the middle-aged Carley laid his success at Una's feet. But whoever the husbands of his daughters had been, Canon Moran knew he'd have felt the same. He was jealous of the husbands because ever since his daughters had been born he had loved them unstintingly. When he had prayed after Frances's death he'd felt jealous of God, who had taken her from him.

"There's nothing much to see," he pointed out when Harold announced that Deirdre was going to show him Kinsella's Barn. "Just the ruin of a wall is all that's left."

"Harold's interested, Father."

They set off on their walk, leaving the old clergyman ashamed that he could not like Harold more. It was just his grimness: there was something sinister about Harold, something furtive about the way he looked at you, peering at you cruelly out of his afflicted face, not meeting your eye. Why was he so fascinated about a country that wasn't his own? Why did he refer so often to "Ireland's struggle" as if that struggle particularly concerned him? He hated walking he had said, yet he'd just set out to walk six miles through woods and fields, to examine a ruined wall.

Canon Moran had wondered as suspiciously about Thomas and John and Carley, privately questioning every statement they made, finding hidden motives everywhere. He'd hated the thought of his daughters being embraced or even touched, and had forced himself not to think about that. He'd prayed, ashamed of himself then too. "It's just a frailty in you," Frances had said, her favourite way of cutting things down to size.

He sat for a while in the afternoon sunshine, letting all of it hang in his mind. It would be nice if they quarrelled on their walk. It would be nice if they didn't speak when they returned, if Harold simply went away. But that wouldn't happen, because they had come to the rectory with a purpose. He didn't know why he thought that, but he knew it was true: they had come for a reason, something that was all tied up with Harold's fascination and with the kind of person Harold was, with his cold eyes and his afflicted face.

In March, 1798, an incident had taken place in Kinsella's Barn, which at that time had been just a barn. Twelve men and women, accused of harbouring insurgents, had been tied together with ropes at the command of Sergeant James. They had been led through he village of Boharbawn, the Sergeant's soldiers on horseback on either side of the procession, the Sergeant himself bringing up the rear. Designed as an act of education, an example of the inhabitants of Baharbawn and the country people around, the twelve had been herded into a barn owned by the farmer Kinsella and there burnt to death. Kinsella, who had played no part in either the harbouring of insurgents or in the execution of the twelve, was afterwards murdered by his own farm labourers.

"Sergeant James was a Nottingham man," Harold said that evening at supper. "A soldier of fortune who didn't care what he did. Did you know he acquired great wealth, Mr Moran?"

"No, I wasn't at all aware of that," Canon Moran replied.

"Harold found out about him," Deirdre said.

"He used to boast he was responsible for the death of a thousand Irish people. It was in Boharbawn that he reached the thousand. They rewarded him well for that."

"Not much is known about Sergeant James locally. Just the legend of Kinsella's Barn."

"No way it's a legend."

Deirdre nodded, Canon Moran did not say anything. They were eating cooked ham and salad. On the table there was a cake which Deirdre had bought at Murphy-Flood's in Enniscorthy, and a pot of tea. There were several bunches of grapes from the greenhouse, and a plate of wafer biscuits. Harold was fond of salad cream, Canon Moran had noticed: he had a way of hitting the base of the jar with his hand, causing large dollops to spurt all over his ham. He didn't place his knife and fork together on his plate when he'd finished, but just left them anyhow. His fingernails were edged with black.

"You'd feel sick," he was saying now, working the salad cream again. "You'd stand there looking at that wall and you'd feel a revulsion in your stomach."

"What I meant," Canon Moran said, "is that it had passed into local legend. No one doubts it took place, there's no question about that. But two centuries have almost passed."

"And nothing has changed," Harold interjected. "The Irish people still share their bondage with the twelve in Kinsella's Barn."

"Round here of course -"

"Its not round here that matters, Mr Moran. The struggle's world wide, the sickness's everywhere actually."

Again Deirdre nodded. She was like a zombie, her father thought. She was being used because she was an Irish girl; she was Harold's Irish connection, and in some almost frightening way she believed herself in love with him. Frances had once said they'd made a mistake with her. She had wondered if Deirdre had perhaps found all the love they'd offered her too much to bear. They were quite old when Deirdre was a child, the last expression of their own love. She was special because of that.

"At least Kinsella got his chips," Harold pursued, his voice relentless. "At least that's something."

Canon Moran protested. The owner of the barn had been an innocent man, he pointed out. The barn had simply been a convenient one, large enough for the purpose, with heavy stones near it that could be piled up against the door before the conflagration. Kinsella, that day, had been miles away, ditching a field.

"It's too long ago to say where he was," Harold retorted swiftly. "And if he was keeping a low profile in a ditch it would have been by arrangement with the imperial forces."

When Harold said that there occurred in Canon Moran's mind a flash of what appeared to be the simple truth. Harold was an Englishman who had espoused a cause because it was one through which the status quo in his own country might be damaged. Similar such Englishmen, read about in newspapers, stirred in the clergyman's mind: men from Ealing and Liverpool and Wolverhampton who had changed their names to Irish names, who had even learned the Irish language, in order to ingratiate themselves with the new Irish revolutionaries. Such men dealt out death and chaos, announcing that their conscience insisted on it.

"Well I'd better wash the dishes," Deirdre said, and Harold rose obediently to help her.

The walk to Kinsella's Barn had taken place on a Saturday afternoon. The following morning Canon Moran had conducted his services in St. Michael's, addressing his small protestant congregation, twelve at Holy Communion, eighteen at morning service. He had prepared a sermon about repentance, taking as his text St. Luke 15,32:... for this thy brother was dead, and is alive again; and was lost and is found. But at the last moment he changed his mind and spoke instead of the incident in Kinsella's Barn nearly two centuries ago. He tried to make the point that one horror should not fuel another, that passing time contained it's own forgiveness. Deirdre and Harold were naturally not in the church, but they'd been present at breakfast, Harold frying eggs on the kitchen stove, Deirdre pouring tea. He had looked at them and tried to think of them as two young people on holiday. He had tried to tell himself they'd come to the rectory for a rest and for his blessing, that he should be grateful instead of fanciful. It was for his blessing that Emma had brought Thomas to the rectory, that Linda had brought John. Una would bring Carley in November. "Now, don't be silly." Frances would have said.

"The man Kinsella was innocent of everything," he heard his voice insisting in the church. "He should never have been murdered also."

Harold would have delighted in the vengeance exacted on an innocent man. Harold wanted to inflict pain, to cause suffering and destruction. The end justified the means for Harold, even if the end was an artificial one, a pettiness grandly dressed up. In his sermon Canon Moran spoke of such matters without mentioning Harold's name. He spoke of how evil drained people of their humour and compassion, how people pretended even to themselves. It was worse that Frances's death, he thought as his voice continued in the church: it was worse that Deirdre should be part of wickedness.

He could tell that his parishioners found his sermon odd and he didn't blame them. He was confused and naturally distressed.

In the rectory Deirdre and Harold would be waiting for him. They would all sit down to Sunday lunch while plans for atrocities filled Harold's mind, while Deirdre loved him.

"Are you well again, Mrs Davis?" he enquired at the church door of a woman who suffered from asthma.

"Not too bad, Canon. Not too bad, thank you."

He spoke to all the others, enquiring about health, remarking on the beautiful autumn. They were farmers mostly and displayed a farmer's gratitude for the satisfactory season. He wondered suddenly who'd replace him among them when he retired or died. Father Hayes had had to give up a year ago. The young man, Father White, was always in a hurry.

"Goodbye so, Canon," Mr Willoughby said, shaking hands as he always did, every Sunday. It was a long time since there'd been the trouble about Eugene Ryan's grazing rights; three years ago Mr Willoughby had been left a widow himself.

"You're managing alright, Canon?" He asked, as he also always did.

"Yes I'm all right thank you, Mr Willoughby."

Someone else enquired if Deirdre was still at the rectory, and he said she was. Heads nodded, the unspoken thought being that that was nice for him, his youngest daughter at home again after all these years. There was forgiveness in several faces, forgiveness of Deirdre, who had been thoughtless to go off to an egg-packing factory. There was the feeling, also unexpressed, that the young were a bit like that.

"Goodbye," he said in a general way. Car doors banged, engines started. In the vestry he removed his surplice and his cassock and hung them in a cupboard.

"We'll probably go tomorrow," Deirdre said during lunch.

"Go?"

"We'll probably take the Dublin bus."

"I'd like to see Dublin," Harold said.

"And then you're returning to London?"

"We're easy about that," Harold interjected before Deirdre could reply. "I'm a tradesman, Mr Moran, an electrician."

"I know you're an electrician, Harold."

"What I mean is I'm on my own, I'm not answerable to the bosses. There's always a bob or two waiting in London."

For some reason Canon Moran felt that Harold was lying. There was a quickness about the way he'd said they were easy about their plans, and it didn't seem quite to make sense, the logic of not being answerable to bosses and a bob or two always waiting for him. Harold was being evasive about their movements, hiding the fact that they would probably remain in Dublin for longer than he implied, meeting other people like himself.

"It was good of you to have us," Deirdre said that evening, all three of them sitting around the fire in the sitting-room because the evenings had just begun to get chilly. Harold was reading a book about Che Guevera and hadn't spoken for several hours. "We've enjoyed it, Father."

"It's been nice having you, Deirdre."

"I'll write to you from London."

It was safe to say that: he knew she wouldn't because she hadn't before, until she'd wanted something. She wouldn't write to thank him for the rectory's hospitality, and that would be quite in keeping. Harold was the same kind of man as Sergeant James had been: it didn't matter that they were on different sides. Sergeant James had maybe borne an affliction also, a humped back or a withered arm. He had ravaged a country that existed then for its spoils, and his most celebrated crime was neatly at hand so that another Englishman could make matters worse by attempting to make amends. In Harold's view the trouble had always been that these acts of war and murder died beneath the weight of print in history books, and were forgotten. But history could be rewritten, and for that Kinsella's Barn was an inspiration: Harold had journeyed to it as people make journeys to holy places.

"Yes?" Deirdre said, for while these reflections had passed through his mind he had spoken her name, wanting to ask her to tell him the truth about her friend.

He shook his head. "I wish you could have seen your mother again," he said instead. "I wish she were here now."

The faces of his three sons-in-law irrelevantly appeared in his mind: Carley's flushed cheeks, Thomas's slow good-natured smile, John's little moustache. It astonished him that he'd ever felt suspicious of their natures, for they would never let his daughters down. But Deirdre had turned her back on the rectory and what could be expected when she came back with a man? She had never been like Emma or Linda or Una, none of whom smoked Three Castles cigarettes and wore clothes that didn't seem quite clean. It was impossible to imagine any of them becoming involved with a revolutionary, a man who wanted to commit atrocities.

"He was just a farmer, you know," he heard himself saying. "Kinsella."

Surprise showed in Deirdre's face. "It was Mother we were talking about," she reminded him, and he could see her trying to connect her mother with a farmer who had died two hundred years ago, and not being able to. Elderliness, he could see her thinking. "Only time he wandered," she would probably say to her friend.

"It was good of you to come, Deirdre."

He looked at her, far into her eyes, admitting to himself that she had always been his favourite. When the other girls were busily growing up she had still wanted to sit on his knee. She'd had a way of interrupting him no matter what he was doing, arriving beside him with a book she wanted him to read to her.

"Goodbye, Father," she said the next morning while they waited in Enniscorthy for the Dublin bus. "Thank you for everything." "Yeah, thanks a ton, Mr Moran," Harold said.

"Good-bye, Harold. Good-bye my dear."

He watched them finding their seats when the bus arrived and then he drove the old Vauxhall back to Boharbawn meeting Slattery in his postman's van and returning his salute. There was shopping he should have done, meat and potatoes, and tins of things to keep him going. But his mind was full of Harold's afflicted face and his black-rimmed fingernails, and Deirdre's hand in his. And then flames burst from the straw that had been packed around living people in Kinsella's Barn. They burnt through the wood of the barn itself, revealing the writhing bodies. On his horse the man called Sergeant James laughed.

Canon Moran drove the car into the rectory's ramshackle garage, and walked around the house to the wooden seat on the front lawn. Frances should come now with two cups of coffee, appearing at the front door with the tray and then crossing the gravel and the lawn. He saw her as she had been when first they came to the rectory, when only Emma had been born; but the grey-haired Frances was there as well, shadowing her youth. "Funny little Deirdre," she said, placing the tray on the seat between them.

It seemed to him that everything that had just happened in the rectory had to do with Frances, with meeting her for the first time when she was eighteen, with loving her and marrying her. He knew it was a trick of the autumn sunshine that again she crossed the gravel and the lawn, no more than pretence that she handed him a cup and saucer. "Harold's just a talker," she said. "Not at all like Sergeant James."

He sat for a while longer on the wooden seat, clinging to these words, knowing they were true. Of course it was cowardice that ran through Harold, inspiring the whisper of his sneer when he spoke of the England he hated so. In the presence of a befuddled girl and an old Irish clergyman England was an easy target, and Ireland's troubles a kind of target too.

Frances laughed, and for the first time her death seemed far away, as her life did too. In the rectory the visitors had blurred her fingerprints to nothing, and had made of her a ghost that could come back. The sunshine warmed him as he sat there, the garden was less melancholy than it had been.

Someone's Coming

Terence de Vere White

"Someone's coming." Joan announces the approach of humans in a voice of dread. I look up, irritated by the threatened interruption, but even more by Joan's churchyard tone. When I'm not at work I welcome visitors, but my good wife, except for a small group - which includes none of my relations - suspects the motives of the world in general, and is delighted when she can demonstrate the soundness of her prejudice by pointing at gates left open and litter lying about. When picnic parties come to our cove she confronts them: "This is private property." (I wish I were quite sure of this). She looks very fierce. Our view is enormously important to us: Dingle Bay and Mount Brandon, with the Blaskets to the furthest west. No more land then till you reach America.

"It may be a visitor for next door."

We live at the end of a cul-de-sac, a road round a hill we call the Mountain. Our bungalow is under the road in a field that slopes down to the cliffs. Underneath is our cove and, round the corner of the rock, the O'Sullivans'.

So here we were in a familiar situation: I at work in my tiny study; someone on the road, dangerously near our gate; and my wife, like Cassandra, in the doorway. I drop the Irish dictionary I am consulting and rise from my chair - Joan gets annoyed on these occasions if I don't, as it were, strip for action; anyhow, one can only see what is happening on the road from the kitchen window.

The local taxi was up there, and a man had got out of it and was handing over a king's ransom in banknotes to Jimmy Cody. The man stood there until the taxi turned and rattled off towards the village. Only then did he raise the latch of our gate. I could feel Joan beside me quivering like a hound on a leash.

"An American."

I cannot convey the horror with which that was said. The stranger, a small square elderly man, was dressed in a lemon and grey checked suit. In his Texan hat he looked like a mushroom. This was most certainly a visitor for next door. I acted on an impulse to save him from more bag-carrying than was necessary by rushing out to divert him. When he saw me coming he dropped his heavy suitcase and waited, his nut-brown face creased with pleasure.

"Well, if it's not Trottie himself."

No one has called me "Trottie" in fifty years.

"John!"

And then we were hugging each other.

John is my second eldest brother, the family black sheep. When he was sacked from the brewery for punching a colleague's head father paid his fare to Canada. None of us had ever heard from him since. I shepherded him indoors, put him in the best chair, whiskey in hand, facing our view. Joan couldn't take her eyes off the checked suit, and he began with apologies. "You must forgive me for landin' on you like this, but I only heard this morning that you lived in these parts and if I had waited to call you up I'd lost the chance of a lift."

He was in Killarney on business and got into conversation with a "nice guy" who, noticing the name John Perry on his luggage, asked him if he was by any chance a relation of Hugh Perry his brother's next-door neighbour, over in Rossbeigh. "I said I had a little brother one time, called Trottie universally, but his proper name was Hugh. "That's him, and he is the spit and image of you." I told him that all the men in our family have legs that look as if they were made for someone else and got fitted on by mistake. I guess that didn't sound respectful enough for a man who is revered hereabouts for his learning. Whatever about the legs, I had the chance to see you again, and if I didn't take it I'd reproach myself for the rest of my life. So I took the cab and landed myself on you."

"For a good long time, we trust," I said, catching Joan's inhospitable eye.

"Could you put up with me for a week?"

"For as long as you like."

"I notice your missus is not committing herself."

"Oh, I'd be delighted." I wish Joan could sound as if she meant it when she is being gracious. John adopted from the start a courtly manner towards her. He used to be the family rebel, despising the Perry tone of anxious respectability. Watching his face when my wife was holding forth, I was reminded of a way he had as a child of driving father mad by paying him the same kind of elaborate attention when he was laying down the law. It was a subtle form of cheek, but father was no fool, and it didn't take him in. Joan revelled in the encouragement to be as insensitive as she pleased. But when we were alone John and I derived huge enjoyment from resurrecting the past. Why had he dropped the family, I wanted to know. We missed him. I had often surprised mother in tears, and I knew the cause of them.

"I felt I had disgraced you all. And there was my stupid pride. I despised the family attitudes, the snobbishness, being ashamed of being Irish. I shall never forget the expression on father's face when he saw me sign my name "Sean", when he had called me "John" after the youngest of the Royal Family at the time, the one who died of haemophilia. I used to tease him by mentioning that. By the way, I'm afraid I have annoyed your good lady just now. I said you were my favourite brother, the only one who wasn't a bloody West Briton. The words were hardly out of my mouth when I realised that she must be English. It was thick of me. Please tell her how sorry I am. I could see she was ruffled."

I didn't say he had certainly finished himself so far as Joan was concerned. It can't be helped. I wanted to hear about his life, driving buses in Canada, working as a builder's labourer in Boston. He was stationed for a time in Northern Ireland when he was in the U.S. Army, he told me.

"Why didn't you get in touch then?"

"Thought about it, but I had gotten myself caught up with a girl."

"Did you marry her?"

"Yep."

That was all I was to learn about my brother's domestic life. I sensed he wanted the subject changed. "What brought you to Killarney?"

"I got into the amusement business after the war. I thought there might be an opening in Killarney."

"What exactly - ?"

"Fairground stuff, merry-go-rounds, dodgem cars, swing-boats, switchback rides, slot machines, peepshows - but I try to keep my business clean. It's for kids as well as adults, I tell my boys."

"But I thought you had retired from business. How old are you, John? You must be -"

"Seventy-two on September twenty-ninth. What is a man to do? I'm bored stiff with television; I was never one for books; since my prostate operation I can't get a proper erection. I have to meddle in business or I'd go out of my lovely mind."

Whatever John had said to my wife, it was irremediable. I knew from the way she kept calling him "your brother", and used me as an intermediary when she had to ask him a question. ("Does your brother like cheese?").

First thing next morning he said he must call on our neighbours, the O'Sullivans. He had heard from Matt's brother that Siobhan liked fruit cake, and he was bringing her the biggest he could find in Killarney.

"Quite unnecessary," Joan said.

John looked taken aback; I could have kicked her. I knew only too well what my wife, born and reared in a London outer suburb, thought of socialising with our neighbours, or calling Mrs O'Sullivan by her Christian name. We had established a friendly relationship. We could count on each other's help in an emergency - Matt was useful in hundreds of ways. I was no use at all. Mrs O'Sullivan was a chronic invalid. Joan gave her a pot-plant at Christmas. My brother's familiar ways were threatening a delicately balanced arrangement. He couldn't understand why Joan wouldn't come along. When she made getting lunch an excuse, he said: "Give yourself a holiday for once. I'll stand us lunch at the hotel. Matt's brother said the cooking there is real classy."

"I don't want to dress up. I'd much rather we ate at home."

John could only stare, and once again I was ashamed of my wife. How could I explain her Wimbledon ways to my rough brother? He might, of course, have taken her measure, with a neat, indecent term to describe it.

"Joan isn't up to the mark at the moment. The troubles in the North get her down. She ought to have a holiday. She thinks, being English, people here don't like her. I tell her she is imagining things." We were at the O'Sullivans' before I had finished. John had said nothing. If he had been disappointed by my wife's welcome, our neighbours made up for it. Because John was my brother, he was treated like a prince. Hitherto I had seen Mrs O'Sullivan as a dim, dying figure in the background - but she was almost flirtatious with John, smiling continually, laughing at his rather laboured jokes, pressing hospitality. "Not at this time of the mornin'." John said, declining poteen. We were given strong tea while Matt proudly showed us examples of his wife's skill with a needle. John admired it so warmly, she insisted he take a grass-green crocheted necktie. Against a sky-blue shirt and the lemon and grey check suit, it struck a resounding blow for Ireland.

We found it hard to get away, and were late for lunch, to Joan's displeasure. She had been listening to the news at mid-day: more killings in the North. "The bastards," she said tight-lipped, "the cruel bastards." I agreed with her, but wished, for John's sake, that she wasn't giving the impression that she was blaming us. It was not surprising that he should look for entertainment outside. We dined as his guests at the hotel a few times, but I saw very little of my brother during his stay. He fished with Matt O'Sullivan, often until late, and sometimes he was out already when we were at breakfast. He hired a car, and he and Matt were away for hours in it. John said he was looking out for business opportunities, but I assumed that the real object was getting around and meeting people for the fun of the chat and the booze. Matt had a wide acquaintance in the country round.

I would have like to be included in the fishing expeditions, but I had made such a song and dance about people interrupting my work that I had only myself to blame. When I mentioned this to Joan, she said: "They don't want you."

"Why not? I used to be quite useful in a boat."

"What do you think that pair is up to?"

"You know. John must have done very well in his amusement business. I never saw anyone slinging money around the way he does."

"I was watching them down at the cove. Your brother was taking photos of everything in sight."

"You know Americans on holiday. Camera-crazy."

She wasn't listening to me. I hate it when she does that.

"I wish for my sake you would try to be nicer to my brother."

"Be your age. Don't tell me you have fallen for that prodigal brother story. The coincidence that has been treated miraculous is not that he has found that you were living so near Killarney, but that you have a well concealed cove."

"What are you saying? I really think you should get away. I'll take you anywhere you like. John will be gone tomorrow. I'm only asking you to be reasonably civil to him until then."

"Are you going to speak to him about all this?"

"Your crazy suspicions you mean? Certainly not."

"I see. Now I know where I am."

The full extent of Joan's mania was now coming home to me. I had, for once, to put our long detente at risk.

"You are to keep your mouth shut about this. Do you hear me?"

I must have sounded as if I meant business, but she gave me no reply because John swept in at that moment, full of plans for a bumper farewell dinner at the hotel. Joan was more gracious than usual. My message must have got home, but her face was a study in amazed horror when John announced casually that he had tried to persuade the O'Sullivans to join us. Siobhan wasn't up to it. "I wish she could get about more. There's a remarkable woman there, going to waste." After that the evening went smoothly enough, if not so hilariously as John would have liked.

I hope he did not misconstrue my anxiety next morning to get him away in good time. Joan managed to be civil at parting. I drove him to the train in half a mind to broach the subject of my wife's crazy suspicions, but the opportunity never arose. He waxed lyrical about the scenery on our way, and put me to shame by his gratitude for what he insisted was one of the best weeks of his life. He hinted at someone back home who would be waiting for him, but as he left it at that, so did I. At parting, he said, "Until next year."

When I got home there was a case of wine in the hall addressed to both of us. I was opening the wine when the damned radio announced the explosions in the London Parks, the blowing up of the Army bandstand, the Guardsmen killed and hideously wounded, the horses.... the horses were what Joan minded most. She could not bring herself to look at me after I switched the radio off. We sat there staring at nothingness. There was no attempt to prepare supper that evening. I went to bed early to escape from the atmosphere in the sitting-room. The birds were singing before Joan came in at last and lay on the very edge of her side of the bed, like a marble effigy on a tomb. I recognised this deployment of herself. It went back to the honeymoon.

After a silent breakfast I said: "Don't take it out on me. You know I am as much disgusted by the Provos as you are."

"I'd like to see some proof of that."

"Oh, for Christ's sake."

"You are all the same, every one of you. Muttering disapproval, never speaking out, helping the bastards to escape. Your brother and the O'Sullivans and you - look at you. The Provos at least are sincere. I hate this bloody country, even the sound of its name. The way you treat animals. It's the way you treat women. You're only half-civilised."

"You pinched our country; you plundered it; you planted it with Protestants; and when you had done your worst, you partitioned it, as you did in India and Cyprus and the other places which God gave you."

I stopped then amazed at myself. I don't know what possessed me. Resentment, deep resentment, kept down for years, coming up at last. Against England? Against Joan, my wife? At that moment I couldn't tell the two apart. Joan stared at me as if she was seeing me for the first time, but said not a word.

Next day we had a lettuce for lunch. Green vegetables are hard to come by in our part of the county. The Garda Sergeant grew some in his front garden, and when we ran out we called on him, or on his wife if the Sergeant was not at home, a splendid woman, she was even prepared to strangle a hen in an emergency, but I preferred not to be privy to her slaughter. That lettuce disturbed me. I had heard Joan go out, but she had other shopping to do in the village. I did no work that afternoon, and was not greatly surprised when the Sergeant called in at the end of the day. Merely a call; he happened to be passing and had dropped in. His manner was apologetic - it was cruel to be troubling me - but as he had, he might as well take the opportunity to ask if I had seen any unusual activity along the coast recently? The trouble with this strip of coast was that it could not be seen from the land, and the way the rocks were formed it was not easy to keep an eye on the shore from the sea. "It's a very nice place you have here, Mr Perry, and I hope you have never regretted your decision to settle in the Kingdom of Kerry. What a powerful view you get from the window. I don't know its match in these parts."

He refused whiskey - which meant he was on duty. But nothing could have sounded more casual than his "I hope your brother enjoyed his stay. Didn't he have the height of luck with the weather? Am I right - he was your brother?"

"Yes. John, the only one now. He lives in America."

"So I heard. You don't happen to have his address on you?"

I started to feel in my pockets. "He lives in Boston," I offered when I realised that I had let John go off without leaving his address. I would get it when he wrote to us. I tried to explain and under the Sergeant's steady gaze felt I was cutting an implausible figure. To help me, he explained that he had heard about schemes to bring business to these parts. That was "great news entirely", but there had been some disappointing experiences recently where the anxiety to encourage anyone who promised employment, people - not to mention Government departments - had been taken in. Not that he had suspicions - of any sort - about a brother of mine. It was routine checking. He would have to be in a position to say he had made it.

He stayed a long time, as if he thought it would look rude to hurry away after doing his business what was not business.

"I'll give you John's address when I get it," I said when at last he pulled himself out of the sofa into which he had sunk.

"Time enough. Don't let it be botherin' you. By the same token I might as well drop in on your neighbour. It's not often my business brings me to this side of the village. The hard cases must like it better at the other end."

The Sergeant made no reference to Joan. She had disappeared when I was letting him in. Now she came back looking as if she had laid an egg. We stood there for I don't know how long. We heard the Sergeant's shoes scrunch on the gravel and the road gate squeal as he opened it and then his feet scrunching on Matt's gravel. I couldn't hear his knock on the cottage door, but there were expressively cordial sounds when Matt opened it. We stood saying nothing until we heard voices again and Matt's cheery "Goodnight, Sergeant." A minute later the police car drove away.

That was more than a year ago. Since then Joan and I have adopted a new manner of elaborate politeness towards each other. I wonder if our acquaintances notice the difference. At home it makes a working solution to our problem. There has been one other change. I moved into the spare bedroom. Our relations with the O'Sullivans have returned to normal, as if they were friendly Indians. Matt is gloomy. The doctor was discouraging after his wife's last visit. He asked me once if I had heard a word from my brother. I said I had not. After that John was never mentioned, not by the O'Sullivans, not by the Sergeant, not by Joan and not by me. For the record: he never wrote.

Bluebell Meadow

Benedict Kiely

When she came home in the evening from reading in the park that was a sort of an island the sergeant who had been trounced by the gypsies was waiting to ask her questions about the bullets. He had two of them in the cupped palm of his right hand, holding the hand low down, secretively. His left elbow was on the edge of the white-scrubbed kitchen table. The golden stripes on his blue-black sleeve, more black than blue, were as bright as the evening sunshine on the old town outside. He was polite, almost apologetic, at first. He said: "I hate to bother yourself and your aunt and uncle. But it would be better for everybody's sake if you told me where you got these things. People aren't supposed to have them. Least of all girls in a convent school."

There had been six of them. The evening Lofty gave them to her she had looked at them for a whole hour, sitting at that table, half-reading a book. Her uncle and aunt were out at the cinema. She spread the bullets on the table and moved them about, making designs and shapes and patterns with them, joining them by imaginary lines, playing with them as if they were draughts or dominoes or precious stones. It just wasn't possible that such harmless mute pieces of metal could be used to kill people. Then she wearied of them, put them away in an old earthenware jug on the mantelpiece and after a while forgot all about them. They were the oddest gifts. God knew, for a boy to give to a girl. Not diamonds again, darling. Say it with bullets.

This is how the park happens to be a sort of an island. The river comes out of deep water, lined and overhung by tall beeches, and round a right-angled bend to burst over a waterfall and a salmon leap. On the right bank and above the fall a sluice-gate regulates the flow of a millrace. A hundred yards downstream the millrace is carried by aqueduct over a rough mountain stream or burn coming down to join the river. Between river and race and mountain stream is a triangular park, five or six acres, seats by the watersides, swings for children, her favourite seat under a tall conifer and close to the corner where the mountain stream meets the river. The place is called Bluebell Meadow. The bluebells grow in the woods on the far side of the millrace.

When the river is not in flow a peninsula of gravel and bright sand guides the mountain stream right out into the heart of the current. Children play on the sand, digging holes, building castles, sending flat pebbles skimming and dancing like wagtails upstream over the smooth water. One day Lofty is suddenly among the children just as if he had come out of the river which is exactly what he has done. His long black waders still drip water. The fishing-rod which he holds in his left hand, while he expertly skims pebbles with the right, dips and twiddles above him like an aerial. The canvas bag on his back is sodden and heavy and has grass, to keep the fish fresh, sticking out of the mouth of it. One of the children is doing rifle-drill with the shaft of his net. She has never spoken to him but she knows who he is.

When she tires of reading she can look at the river and dream, going sailing with the water. Or simply close her eyes. Or lean back and look up into the tall conifer, its branches always restless and making sounds, and going away from her like a complicated sort of spiral stairway. She has been told that it is the easiest tree in the world to climb but no tree is all that easy if you're wearing a leg-splint. She is looking up into the tree, and wondering, when Lofty sits beside her. His waders are now dry and rubbery to smell. The rod, the net and the bag are laid on the grass, the heads of two sad trout protruding, still life that was alive this morning. Her uncle who keeps greyhounds argues that fishing is much more cruel than coursing: somewhere in the happy river are trout that were hooked and got away, hooks now festering in their lovely speckled bodies. She thinks a lot about things like that.

Lofty sits for five minutes, almost, before he says: "I asked Alec Quigley to tell you I was asking for you."

"He told me."

"What did you say?"

"Did he not tell you?"

"He said you said nothing but I didn't believe him."

"Why not?"

"You had to say something."

"If I said anything Alec Quigley would tell the whole town."

"I daresay he would."

"He's the greatest clatter and clashbag from hell to Omagh."

"I didn't know."

"You could have picked a more diplomatic ambassador."

The words impress him. He says: "It's a big name for Alec Quigley. I never thought of him as an ambassador."

"What then? A go-between? A match-maker? A gooseberry?"

They are both laughing. Lofty is blond tall freckled fellow with a pleasant laugh. He asks her would she like a trout.

"I'd love one. Will we cook it here and now?"

"I can roll it in grass for you and get a bit of newspaper in McCaslan's shop up at the waterfall."

"Who will I tell my aunt and uncle gave me the trout?"

"Tell them nothing. Tell them you whistled and a trout jumped out at you. Tell them a black man came out of the river and gave you a trout."

He left his bag and rod where they were and walked from the apex of the triangular park to the shop at the angle by the waterfall. He came back with a sheet of black parcelling paper and wrapped up the trout very gently. He had long delicate hands, so freckled that they were almost totally brown. The trout, bloody mouth gaping, looked sadly up at the two of them. Lofty said: "I'd like to go out with you."

"I'm often out. Here."

So he laughed and handed her the trout and went on upstream towards the falls, casting from the bank at first, then wading knee-deep across a shallow bar of gravel and walking on across a green hill towards the deeps above the falls. She liked his long stride, and the rod dipping and twiddling above him, and the laden bag -even though she knew it was full of dead gaping trout. She knew he was a popular fellow in town. Yet she didn't tell her aunt and uncle who exactly it was had made her a gift of the trout. She said it was an elderly man and she wasn't quite sure of his name, but she described him so that they'd guess he was a well-known fisherman, a jeweller by trade and highly respected in the town. Not that Lofty and his people were disrespectable.

The gypsies who trounced the sergeant hadn't been real romany gypsies but tinkers or travelling people from the west of Ireland, descendants, the theory was, of broken people who went on the roads during the hungry years of the 1840s and hadn't settled down since. Five of them, wild, ragged, rough-headed fellows came roaring drunk out of a pub in Bridge Lane. The pub was owned by a man called Yarrow and the joke among those literate enough to appreciate it was about Yarrow Visited and Yarrow Revisited. There was also an old English pishuoge about girls putting Yarrow, the plant, between two plates and wishing on it and saying: "Good morrow, good Yarrow, thrice good morrow to thee! I hope before this time tomorrow thou wilt show my true love to me."

One of the five fell with a clatter down the three steps from the door of the pub. In their tottering efforts to pick him up two of the others struck their heads together and began to fight. The remaining two joined in and so, when he was able to stand up, did the fellow who had fallen down the steps. The sergeant was walking past and was fool enough to try to stop them. In the west of Ireland the civic guards had more sense and stood as silent spectators until the tinkers had hammered the fight out of each other.

The five of them, united by foreign invasion, gave the sergeant an unmerciful pounding. He had just enough breath left to blow his whistle. More police came running. More tinkers came shouting, men, women and children, out of the pub, out of dark tunnels of entryways between houses, out of holes in the walls. The battle escalated. More police came. The tinkers made off on two flat carts. One old man was so drunk he fell helpless off a cart and was arrested. The police followed in a tender.

At their encampment of caravans a mile outside the town the tinkers abandoned the carts and took, in the darkness, to the fields and the hedgerows and even, it was said, to the tops of the trees. The police wisely did not follow, but set a heavy guard on the camp, caravans, carts, horses, scrap metal and everything the tinkers owned. Sober and sheepishly apologetic they reappeared in the morning and gave themselves up and half a dozen of them went to jail. But for a long time afterwards when the sergeant walked the town the wits at the street-corner would whistle: "Oh, play to me gypsy, the moon's high above."

Thanks to Arthur Tracy, known as the Street Singer, it was a popular song at the time.

In spite of all that, the sergeant remained an amiable sort of man, stout, slow-moving, with a large brown moustache and a son who was a distinguished footballer.

Yarrow is a strong-scented herb related to the daisies. It has white or pink flowers in flat clusters.

One Sunday in the previous June in an excursion train to Bundoran by the western sea she had overheard Lofty's mother telling funny stories. As a rule Protestants didn't go west to Bundoran but north to Portrush. The sea was sectarian. What were the wild waves saying: At Portrush: "Slewter, slaughter, holy water, harry the papishes every one, drive them under the and bate them asunder, the Protestant boys will carry the drum."

Or at Bundoran: "On St. Patrick's day, jolly and gay, we'll kick all the Protestants out of the way, and if that won't do we'll cut them in two and send them to hell with their red, white and blue."

Nursery rhymes.

She sat facing her aunt in the train and her uncle sat beside her. They were quiet, looking at all the long beauty of Lough Erne which has an island, wooded or pastoral, for every day in the year. Her aunt, a timid little woman, said now and again: "Glory be to God for all his goodness."

Her uncle said just once: "You should see Lake Superior. No end to it. As far as the human eye can see."

Then they were all quiet, overhearing Lofty's mother who had no prejudices about the religion of the ocean and who, with three other people, sat across the corridor from them and who had a good-natured carrying voice and really was fun to listen to. She was saying: "I'm a Protestant myself, missus dear, and I mean no disrespect to confession but you must have heard about the young fellow who went to the priest to tell him his sins and told him a story that had more women in it than King Solomon had in the Bible and the goings-on were terrible, and the priest says to him. Young man are you married? And the young fellow says back to him, dead serious and all, Naw father but I was twice in Fintona."

The train dived through a tunnel of tall trees. The lake vanished. Sunlight flashing and flickering through leaves made her close her eyes. Everybody on the train, even her aunt, seemed to be laughing. A man was saying: "Fintona always had a bit of a name. For wild women."

Lofty's mother said: "I was born there myself but I never noticed that it was all that good, nobody ever told me."

She opens her eyes and the sunlight flickers down on her through the spiralling branches of the great conifer. There's a book in the public library that has everything, including pictures, about all the trees of Great Britain and Ireland.

Lofty is on the very tip of the peninsula of sand and gravel, demonstrating fly-casting to half a dozen children who are tailor-squatting around his feet. She is aware that he's showing off to impress her and the thought makes her warm and pleased, ready to laugh at anything. But to pretend that she's unimpressed she leans back and looks up into the tree in which the sunlight is really alive, creeping round the great bole, spots of light leaping like birds from one branch to another. She thinks of the omu tree which grows on the pampas of South America. Its trunk can be anything up to 40 or 50 feet thick. The wood is so soft that when cut it rots like an over-ripe melon and is useless as firewood. The leaves are large, glossy and deep green like laurel leaves - and also poisonous. But they give shade from the bare sun to man and beast, and men mark their way on the endless plains by remembering this or that omu tree. She has read about omu trees. Her own tree is for sure not one of them. She sits up straight when her book is lifted from her lap. Lofty is sitting by her side. The children are pointing and laughing. He must have crept up on hands and knees pretending to be a wild animal, a wolf, a prowling tiger. He's very good at capers of that sort. His rod and net lie by the side of the burn.

It was April when he first sat beside her. It was now mid-June. Her school will close soon for the holidays and she will no longer be compelled to wear the uniform: black stockings, pleated skirt of navy blue serge, blue gansey, blue necktie and saffron stripes, blue blazer with school crest in saffron on breast pocket, blue beret, black flat-heeled shoes. Even Juliet, and she was very young, didn't have to wear a school uniform. If she had had Romeo wouldn't have looked at her.

Not that they are star crossed lovers or Lofty any Romeo. They haven't even crossed the millrace to walk in the bluebell wood as couples of all ages customarily do. She isn't shy of walking slowly because of the leg splint but she knows that Lofty hasn't asked her because he thinks she might be: that makes her feel for him as she might feel, if she had one, for a witless younger brother who's awkward. And a bit wild: for a lot of Lofty's talk doesn't go with the world of school uniforms mostly blue for the mother of God. What the saffron is for, except variety of sort, she can't guess. Lofty's rattling restless talk would lift Mother Teresa out of her frozen black rigidity.

Lofty with great good humour fingers the saffron stripes and says that, in spite of everything, she's a wee bit of an Orange-woman. They hold hands regularly. Lofty can read palms, a variant reading every time. They have kissed occasionally, when the children who are always there have been distracted by a waterhen or rat or leaping fish or a broken branch or an ice-berg of froth from the falls.

"Don't look now," he says one day, "But if you swivel round slowly you'll see my three sisters in action."

Beyond the millrace against the fresh green of woods she can see a flash of coloured frocks, the glint of brass buttons and pipe-clayed belts. In those days it was only the wild ones who went with the soldiers: it wasn't money and security they were after.

"They're hell for soldiers," he says, "between the three of them they'd take on the Germans."

Lofty himself reads a lot of military books, campaigns and generals, Napoleon and Ludendorf, all the way from Blenheim to the Dardanelles. When he doodles as he often does on the writing pad she always carries with her - to make notes on her reading, to transcribe favourite poems - he doodles uniforms, every detail exact. Yet he listens to her when she reads poetry or the splendid prose of a volume of selected English essays, Caxton to Belloc.

"They're advancing on us," he says. "They have us surrounded, enfiladed, debouched and circumnavigated."

"We'll tell Maryanne," the three sisters say, "that you're with another."

Two of them, Mildred and Rosemary, are plump, laughing, blonde girls, and Mildred who is the youngest is as freckled as her brother. Gertie, the eldest, is olive-faced with jet black hair, wrinkles on the forehead and around the eyes like her mother. She is never to see the father of the family but the gossip of the town is to tell her that he's away a lot in Aldershot and India and that Lofty's mother, that merry woman, is friendly with more soldiers than the one she's married to.

The three British soldiers who are with the sisters are, one of them from Sligo, one from Wexford and one actually from Lancashire, England. They all talk a lot and laugh a lot and she likes them. The Lancashire lad climbs right up to the top of the tree and pretends to see everything that's going on in the town and tells them about it: he has a lurid imagination. Then they go away towards the waterfall, still laughing, calling back about telling Maryanne. She asks him who Maryanne is. Lofty who clearly likes his sisters is not in the least embarrassed by the suggestion that he has another woman.

"Oh Maryanne's nobody or nobody much."

"She has a name. She must be somebody."

She's not really jealous, just curious.

"Maryanne's a girl I met one day on the road beyond McCaslan's shop."

"You met nobody on the road?"

"She was wheeling a pram."

"She's married to Mr Nobody?"

"It wasn't her pram. She's nursemaid to the Mooney's, the fancy bread bakery. There was a lovely smell of fresh bread."

"Had you a good appetite, apple-jelly, jam-tart."

But since the rest of that rhyme to which children, Protestant and Catholic, rope-skip on the streets, is tell me the name of your sweetheart, she doesn't finish it and finds herself, to her annoyance, blushing. Lofty doesn't seem to notice.

"There were twins in the pram. I pushed it for her up the hill to the main road. Then she said I bet you wouldn't do that for me if it was in the town on the courthouse hill where everybody could see you. I said why not and she said Christian Brothers' boys are very stuck-up. I've met some that would do anything they could or you'd let them if they had a girl in the woods or in the dark, but that wouldn't be seen talking to her in the street, maids aren't good enough for them. I didn't tell her I was a Presbyterian and went to the academy."

"Why not?"

"She mightn't like a Presbyterian pushing her pram."

They laugh at that until the playing children turn and look and laugh with them. Cheerful voices call from beyond the millrace where the soldiers and sisters are withdrawing to the woods.

"We have girls at the academy, on the house, what Harry Cassidy and Jerry Hurst and the boys don't have at Brothers. Harry and the boys are mad envious when we tell them about the fun we have feeling Daisy Allen under the desk at school. All lies of course."

"I hope Daisy Allen doesn't hear that."

"Och Daisy, she's well handled anyway, she's going about with a bus-driver and he's a married man as well, he ruined a doctor's daughter in Dungannon. Harry and the Catholic boys think the Protestant girls are wilder because they don't have to tell it all in confession. That isn't true either."

One other funny story she heard Lofty's mother telling that day as the train in the evening left Bundoran station and the great romantic flat-topped mountains diminished into the distance. This time the story teller faced her aunt and sat beside her uncle who had been talking about jerry-building a new housing estate. Lofty's mother agreed with him. She had a shopping-bag of sugar to smuggle back into the Six Counties where it cost more. The sugar was tastefully disguised under a top-dressing of dulse. With content and triumph Lofty's mother sang a parody popular at the time: "South of the border down Bundoran way, that's where we get the Free State sugar to sweeten our tay."

She was great fun. She had bright blue eyes and a brown hat with a flaring feather, and a brown crinkly face. She said: "Those houses are everything you say and worse. Fancy fronts and ready to fall. When you flush the lavatory in them the noise is heard all over the town. Only the other day the lady who lives in number three sent down to River Row for old Mr Hill, the chimney sweep, and up he came and put the brush up the chimney and then went out, the way sweeps do, to see if the brush was showing out of the top of the chimney. No brush. In he went and screws on another length of handle on the brush and pushes for dear life, and out again to look, but no brush. In again and screws on the last piece of handle he has, and he's pushing away when the lady from number eleven knocks on the door. Have you the sweep in, missus dear, she says. I have, missus dear, says the lady from number three. Then please ask him to be careful, missus dear, she says, that's twice now he's upset our wee Rosy from the lavatory seat.."

Because of her happy carrying voice passers-by in the corridor stop to join the fun. The three sisters also look as if they'd be good for a lot of laughs.

Her uncle is a tall broad-shouldered man with a good grey suit, a wide brimmed hat, two gold teeth and a drawl. Years ago he was in the building trade in the United States and knows a lot about jerry-building. He gets on very well with Lofty's mother.

It was well on towards the end of August when the black man sat on the bench beside her. She was looking sideways towards the bridge over the millrace, and laughing: because two big rough young fellows were running like hares before

Mr McCaslan's boxer dog. Mr McCaslan who owned the shop was also water bailiff and park-keeper. The rough fellows had been using brutally one of the swings meant for small children, so brutally that the iron stays that supported it were rising out of the ground. Mr McCaslan had mentioned the matter to them. They had been so offensive, even threatening, to the old rheumatic man so he hobbled back to his shop and sent the boxer dog down as his deputy. The pair took off as if all hell were behind them. It was funny because the dog didn't bark growl or show his hostility, didn't even run fast, just loped along with a certain air of quiet determination and wouldn't (as far as she knew) savage anybody. But he was a big dog, even for a boxer and the retreat of the miscreants was faster than the Keystone Cops. She laughed so much that the book fell on the grass. The black man picked it up and sat down beside her.

She thought of him as a black man not because he was a Negro but because her uncle had told her he was a member of the black preceptory which was a special branch of the Orange Order. She had seen him walking last twelfth of July in the big parade in memory of the Battle of Boyne, which happened a long time ago, and in honour of King William of Orange who was a long time dead and had never been in this town. He had worn the black sash, with shining metallic esoteric insignia attached, as had other men who marched beside him. The contingent that followed wore blue sashes and were supposed to be teetotallers but her uncle said that that was not always so. One of the blue men, a red-faced, red-headed fellow was teetering and might have fallen if he hadn't been holding onto one of the poles that supported a banner.

The drums drummed, the banner bellied in the breeze, the pipes and fifes and brass and accordions played:

It is old but it is beautiful
And its colours they are fine
It was worn at Derry, Aughrim,
Enniskillen and the Boyne,
My father wore it in his youth,
In bygone days of yore,
And on the Twelfth I'll always wear
The sash my father wore.

The name of the black man who sat beside her was Samuel McClintock and he was a butcher. It was said about him for laughs that if the market ran out of meat the town could live for a week off McClintock's apron: blue with white stripes. That August day and in the public park he naturally wasn't wearing the apron. He had a black moustache, a heavy blue chin, a check cloth cap, thick-soled boots, thick woolen stockings and whipcord knee breeches. The Fomorians, the monsters from the stormy seas had, each of them, one arm, one leg and three rows of teeth. He said: "The dog gave those ruffians the run"

The way he said it took the fun out of it. She said: "Yes, Mr McClintock."

She wished him elsewhere. She half-looked at the book. She was too well-reared to pick it up from her lap and ostentatiously go on reading. The river was in a brown fresh that day, the peninsula of sand and gravel not to be seen, nor Lofty, nor the children. The black man said: "Plenty water in the river today."

She agreed with him. It was also a public park in a free and easy town and everyone had the right to sit where he pleased. Yet this was her own seat under the tall tree, almost exclusively hers, except when Lofty was there. The black man said: "The Scotchies have a saying the salmon's her ain when there's water but she's oors when it's oot."

He explained: "That means that often they're easier to catch when the water's low."

He filled his pipe and lighted it. The smell of tobacco was welcome. It might have been her imagination but until he pulled and puffed and sent the tobacco smell out around them she had thought that the resinous air under the tree was polluted by the odours of the butcher's shop and the apron. He said that the salmon were a sight to see leaping the falls when they went running upstream. She said that she had often watched them.

"I'm told you're very friendly with a well-known young fisherman of my persuasion."

"Who, for instance?"

"You know well. That's what I want to talk to you about. It's a serious matter."

"Being friendly with a fisherman?"

"Don't play the smartie with me, young lassie. Even if you do go to the convent secondary school. Young people today get more education than's good for them. Lofty at the academy and you at the convent have no call to be chumming it up before the whole town."

"Why not?"

But it occurred to her that they hadn't been chumming-up or anything else before the whole town. What eyes could have spied on them in this enchanted island?"

"His uncle's a tyler, that's why."

"I never knew he had an uncle."

"His mother's brothers a tyler, and very strict."

"What's a tyler?"

"I shouldn't repeat it, lassie. But I will, to impress on you how serious it is. A tyler he is and a strict one. Wasn't it him who spoke up to have Lofty let into the B Specials?"

"Don't ask me. I never knew he was a B Special."

But one day for a joke, she remembered, he had given her a handful of bullets.

"The nuns wouldn't tell you this at school but B Specials were set up by Sir Basil Brooke to hold Ulster against the Pope and the Republic of Ireland."

The nuns, for sure, hadn't told her anything of the sort: Mother Teresa who was very strong on purity and being a lady and not sitting like a man with your legs crossed had never once mentioned the B Specials who, out in country places, went about at night with guns and black uniforms, holding up Catholic neighbours and asking them their names and addresses - which they knew very well to begin with. The Lofty she knew in daylight by this laughing river didn't seem to be cut out for such nocturnal capers.

"If his uncle knew that the two of you and you a Catholic girl were carrying on there'd be hell on earth."

"But we're not carrying-on."

"You were seen kissing here on this bench. What's that but carrying-on?"

"What does he level?"

"What does who level?"

"The uncle who's a leveller or whatever you called him."

"Speak with respect young lassie. A tyler, although I shouldn't tell you the secret, is a big man in the Order at detecting intruders. His obligation is this: I do solemnly declare that I will be faithful to the duties of my office and I will not admit any person into the lodge without having found him first to be in possession of the financial password or without the sanction of the Worshipful Master of the Lodge."

Then after a pause he said with gravity: "And I'm the Worshipful Master."

He was the only one of the kind she had ever met or was ever to meet and she did her best, although it was all very strange there by the river and the rough stream and under the big tree, to appear impressed, yet all she could think of saying was; "But I'm not interfering with his tyling."

Then she was angry and close to tears, although it was also funny: "For all I care he can tile the roofs and floors and walls of every house in this town."

The big man hadn't moved much since he sat down, never raised his voice, but now he shouted: "Lassie, I'll make you care. The B Specials are sworn to uphold Protestant liberty and beat down the Fenians and the IRA."

"I'm not Fenian or IRA."

"You're a Roman Catholic, aren't you? And there isn't any other sort. Sir Basil Brooke says that Roman Catholics are 100 per cent disloyal and he wouldn't have one of them about the house."

"Sir Who's It?"

"No cheek, lassie. Didn't he sit up a tree at Colebrook all night long with a gun waiting for the IRA to attack his house? Didn't he found the B Specials to help the police defend the throne and the Protestant religion?"

What was it to her if Sir Somebody or Other spent all his life up a tree at Colebrook or anywhere else? The Lancashire soldier had climbed her tree and been as comic as a monkey up a stick. The black man calmed himself: "Your own clergy are dead set against mixed marriages."

"We weren't thinking of marriage."

"What of then? Silliness and nonsense. The young have no wit. What would Mother Teresa say if she heard you were keeping company with a Protestant?"

"Who would tell her?"

"I might. For your own good and for Lofty."

He knocked the ash out of his pipe and put it away. The pleasant tobacco smell faded. She smelled blood and dirt and heard screams and knew, with a comical feeling of kindness, that she had been wrongly blaming him for bringing with him the stench of the shambles. There was a piggery at the far end of the field beyond the river and the wind was blowing from that direction.

"That's the piggery," she said. "It's a disgrace."

"Time and again I've said that to the town council. You must have read what I said in the papers. It's a sin, shame and scandal to have a piggery beside a beauty spot. Not that I've anything against pigs, in my business, in their own place."

He stood up and patted her on the shoulder. He was really just a big rough friendly man: "You don't want to put him out of the Specials or the Lodge itself."

"Why should he be?"

"These are deep matters. But they tell me you read a lot. You've the name for being one of the cleverest students in this town, Protestant or Catholic. So I'll talk to you, all for the best, as if you were a grown-up and one of my own. It is possible but very difficult for a convert to be accepted as a member of the Orange Order."

He was as good as standing to attention. He was looking over her head towards the waterfall.

"A convert would have to be of several years standing and his background would have to be carefully screened. His admission would have to be authorised by the Grand Lodge. They'd have to go that high, like Rome for the Catholics. No convert can get into the Black Preceptory if either of his parents is still living, in case the Roman Catholic Church might exert pressure on a parent."

He was reciting. Like the sing-song way in which in school the children learned the Catechism.

Q: What are the seven deadly sins?

A: Pride, covetousness, lust, gluttony, envy, anger and sloth.

Q: What are the four sins that cry to heaven for vengeance?

A: Wilful murder, sodomy, oppression of the poor and defrauding the labourer of his wages.

Dear Sacred heart it was a cheery world. "A convert who was even a Protestant clergyman was blacked-out because one of his parents was still living and there is an automatic expulsion for dishonouring the Institution by marrying a Roman Catholic."

The great tree creaked it's branches above them. The brown water tumbled on towards the town.

"You see what I mean, lassie?"

She supposed she saw. In a way she was grateful. He was trying to help. He shook her hand as if they were friends forever. He went off towards the waterfall so that, without turning around, she could not see him walking away and he could not, thank God, see her face laughing, laughing. For, sweet heart of Jesus fount of love and mercy to thee we come thy blessings to implore, but it was comic to think of him marching up the convent grounds (he should wear his black sash and have a fife and drum before him) holy white statues to left and right a Lourdes grotto as high as mount Errigal, to relate all about the love-life of Lofty and herself to Mother Teresa who had a mouth like a rat-trap - and a mind. A worshipful master and a most worshipful reverend mother and never, or seldom, the twain shall meet. She was an odd sort of girl. She sat around a lot and read too many books. It was funny, also to think of his daughter, Gladys, a fine good-natured brunette with a swinging stride, a bosom like a Viking prow, and a dozen boy-friends of all creeds and classes. Nothing sectarian about Gladys who was one of his own kind and a daughter of a worshipful master. Somebody should tell the tyler to keep an eye on her. But she was too clever to be caught, too fast on her feet, too fast on her feet.

Walking slowly past the Orange Hall on the way home she thought the next time she met him she would have a lot to tell to lazy, freckled, lovable Lofty. The Orange Hall was a two-storeyed brownstone building at a crossroads on the edge of the town. High on it's wall a medallion image of William of Orange on an impossibly white horse rode forever across the Boyne. The two old cannon-guns on the green outside had been captured from the Germans in the Kaiser war. In there, Lofty's lodge met and it was a popular joke that no man could become a member until he rode a buck goat backwards up the stairs. Sometimes in the evenings bands of music played thunderously in there, practising for the day in July when they marched out, banners flying. It was crazy to think that a man on a white horse, riding across a river 200 years ago could now ride between herself and Lofty. Or for that matter - although Mother Teresa would have a fit if she thought that a pupil of hers could think of such things - another man on a chair or something being carried shoulder high in the City of Rome.

All this she meant to mention to Lofty the next time she came to the seat under the tree. But all she could get round to saying was: "Lofty, what's a tyler?"

He had no rod and net and was dressed, not for fishing, in a new navy-blue suit. The children called to him from the gravel but he paid no attention to them. At first he didn't pretend to hear her, so she asked him again. He said that a tyler was a man who laid tiles. That was the end of that. Then it was winter. One whole week the park was flooded. She couldn't remember when it was that Lofty had given her the bullets.

Over the supper table he remembers the time he had been a policeman in Detroit: "Some Negro trouble then and this rookie policeman from Oklahoma was on patrol with a trained man. The rookie has no gun. So they're rushed by twenty black men and the first rock thrown clobbers the trained man unconcious. But the Oklahoma guy he stoops down, takes the pistol out of the other man's holster and shoots six times and kills six black men, one, two, three, four, five, six. He didn't waste a bullet."

"Sacred heart have mercy," says her aunt.

"What did the other black men do, uncle?"

"They took off for home and small blame to them. He was a cool one, that rookie, and a damned good shot. Here in this place they make a helluva fuss over a few bullets. I told them so."

Lofty came never again to the tall tree. They met a few times on the street and spoke a few words. She left the town after a while and went to work in London. Once, home on holidays, she met Lofty and he asked her to go to the pictures, and she meant to but never did. The Hitler war came on. She married an American and went to live in, of all places, Detroit. Her uncle and aunt and the sergeant and worshipful master and the tyler and, I suppose, Lofty's mother and old McCaslan and his dog died.

Remembering her, I walked, the last time I was in the town, to revisit Bluebell Meadow. The bridge over the millrace was broken down to one plank. Rank grass grew a foot high over most of the island. The rest of it was a wide track of sand and gravel where the river in fierce flood had taken everything before it. The children's swings and all the seats were gone, smashed some time before by reluctant young soldiers from the North English cities doing their national service. Repair work had been planned but then the bombings and murders began.

No laughing Lancashire boy in British uniform will ever again climb that tall tree. For one thing the tree is gone. For another the soldiers go about in bands, guns at the ready, in trucks and armoured cars. There are burned-out buildings in the main streets - although the great barracks is unscathed - and barricades and checkpoints at the ends of the town. As a woman said to me: "Nowadays we have gates to the town. Still, other towns are worse. Strabane which was on the border and easy to bomb is a burned out wreck. And Newry, where the people badly needed shops and factories, and not ruins. And Derry is like Dresden on the day after."

When I wrote to her about this she said, among other things, that she had never found out the name of that tall conifer.

It was also crazy to think that Lofty's laughing mother could have a brother who went about spying on people and nosing them out. What eyes had spied on Lofty and herself on the enchanted island? What nosy neighbour had told somebody who told somebody who told the sergeant that she had bullets in the earthenware jug?

"If you don't tell me," the sergeant said, "it will be awkward for all concerned. What would Mother Teresa think if she thought you had live bullets in an earthenware jug?"

It wasn't possible to control the giggles. What, in the holy name of God, would Mother Teresa think, if the sergeant and the worshipful master descended on her simultaneously, what would she say, how would she look? Keeping live bullets in a jug must be one of the few things that she had not warned her girls against.

"You'll have to come down to the barracks with me. I'll walk ahead and you follow just in case the people are passing remarks. They might think I'm arresting you."

"What are you doing?"

"Och, I'd just like you to make a statement. It's not a crime to have bullets. Not for a young lady like you who wouldn't be likely to be using them. But we have a duty to find out where they came from. My son Reggie speaks highly of you. Reggie the footballer you know."

She knew. It was a town joke that the sergeant couldn't speak to anybody for ten minutes without mentioning Reggie who parted his hair up the middle, wore loud scarves and played football very well: it was clear that the sergeant thought that to be thought well of by Reggie was a special distinction.

Old low white houses line the hill that goes up from the brook and the co-operative creamery to the centre of the town. The sergeant plods on, twenty yards ahead of her. The town is very quiet. His black leather belt creaks and strains to hold him together. The butt of his pistol, his black baton case shine. She has never noticed before that Lofty has a stutter. Another sergeant sits behind a desk in the dayroom and makes notes. The young constables are laughing in the background. The blackman comes in and says: "I warned the two of them."

Her own sergeant says: "There wasn't much harm in it."

"Not for the girl," says the man behind the desk. "But for him a breach of discipline."

Lofty has surely never stuttered when he talked to her by the meeting of the waters.

"Did you tell them I gave you the bullets?"

"Dear God, it wasn't a crime to give me the bullets."

"Did you tell them?"

"I did not."

"They say you did."

"So."

Her own sergeant looks ashamed and rubs his moustache.

The other sergeant says: "Case closed."

Then her uncle walks in, and so hopping mad that he seems to have a mouthful of gold teeth. He talks for a long time and they listen respectfully because he's a famous man for keeping running dogs which he feeds on brandy and beef. He says over and over again: "You make a helluva fuss about a few bullets."

"A breach of discipline," says the man behind the desk.

"My ass and yours," says her uncle. "A helluva fuss."

And repeats it many times as they walk home together.

"But all the same they'll put him out of the Specials," he says. "And I dare say he shouldn't have been assing around and giving away government issue."

The Passing Of Billy Condit

Sam McAughtry

Like the city, the street was young, in 1885. It was steep and narrow, running down to the very perimeter of the harbour estate. It overlooked the cranes and gantries, the spars of coastal sailing vessels, and the upperworks of steamers, moored by newly-built wharves.

In mid-morning there were no men to be seen, only the occasional shawled woman walking, head down. The children in the school at the top of the street chanted multiplication tables. The heavy stamp of a draught horse, and the crash of iron-rimmed wheels on cobblestones carried through the kitchen door, to where Mary Condit was on her knees.

Her long, black hair was caught and tied at the back of her neck. When a strand fell out of place she would throw her head back and push the hair away from her eyes with a hand that was guttered from the floor's dirt.

Lizzie was at work in the mill on York Street, and Hugh was at school. The boy would come round the corner in an hour, for his lunch. Through the kitchen window the finished washing could be seen on the line in the yard. Her husband's rough flannel working shirts were pegged alongside long, grey drawers, pummelled and knuckled on the washboard an hour earlier. The tuppenny bone for the supper broth, the vegetables and peeled potatoes, were ready in their pots on the hob.

Rim-high in the bowls, the broth would be served when Billy Condit sat down, shining pink clean, after his wash at the scullery sink. Mary scrubbed the kitchen floor contentedly. The day was going with no fuss. At seven in the evening it would reach its high point when the family, the four of them, sat down to supper.

When Mary was growing up in this street her mother, with eight people packing the tiny kitchen, had eaten on the move, spooning food from a saucer as she stirred and ladled and handed out helpings. But at seven o'clock Mary would sit opposite Billy, with Hugh and Lizzie in between. There would be time for talk. She would see her man's face, newly-shaved, and on the bare chest the breast-curls, and the silken line that ran from broad to narrow: from chest to navel. And when he caught her looking he would wink...

Beside Mary on the floor was a large paint tin. It was half filled with black, soft soap. She scooped some of this on to the tip of the scrubbing brush and scoured the red, rough tiles. The fumes from the soap could bring tears to the eyes. She scrubbed in loops and whirls, rinsed and dried, then stood, wiping her hands on the sacking apron that she wore. Carrying the bucket, she stepped out into the yard.

Opposite the scullery pipe outlet, Mary bent and lifted the hem of her heavy skirt. Pulling her knickers down below the knees, she crouched. Her water ran down the slope of the yard and gurgled into the grating, carrying with it part of the brown-yellow beard of tea leaves that rimmed the gulley's edge. The woman idly watched the course of the water. Her eyes lifted, and, suddenly, with a half scream, she stood, clutching and plucking at her clothing, turning away from the face that watched, just visible over the edge of the wall. Knees together, tucking vest under knickers, she hurtled to the kitchen door, away from the wide, watching eyes.

The face wore a grey moustache that hung wetly down the sides of the mouth: "Ya dirty oul blirt ye, Johnny Millar," Mary yelled, hopping from foot to foot, straightening her clothes. The long, thin face slid down out of sight. A voice that was high and nasal was heard: "I was only looking for my canary that got out."

"I'll canary ye, ya oul get ye. If ya want to look at a woman why the hell don't ya get married." Restored to decency, Mary came back out into the yard, ducking under the clothes line: "By God but when my man comes home the night I'll not be long in telling him about you, ya bloody oul whoremaster."

From the other side of the wall the thin voice was heard: "Dick? Come here, Dick. Where are ye, son?"

Back inside, Mary scrubbed her hands in the scullery. The annoyance gradually died from her face, to be replaced by the twitch of a smile. There was no sense in telling Billy. All the other times, he'd only smiled: "I only wish I was as easily pleased," he'd said, "it's a hell of a cheap way to get your satisfaction, you have to admit it. My appetite costs me my week's wages."

She was drying her arms when there came a sudden knock at the front door. She went into the hall. On the step was a man, a tall stranger. In his fifties, sour-featured, he wore a navy blue, shiny suit, and a black, hard hat. His high, starched collar bit into the undersides of his jowls:

"Are you Missus...?" He paused, peering at a scrap of paper in his hand: "... Condit?" Mary nodded, bowing her head respectfully, for his tone was one of authority.

"Well?" Impatiently, "can I come in, then?"

Pulling the sleeves of her cardigan down over her bare arms, Mary pushed back against the kitchen door, as the man went into the house ahead of her. "I'm just after washing the floor," she said, shyly. Frowning, the visitor's gaze followed hers. Seeing the paint tin, he stooped and lifted it. Dipping a finger into it, he held it close to his nose and sniffed: "Was that soap lifted out of the yard?"

His dentures fitted badly, puffing his upper lip out. His eyes, watching her, were narrowed. Flustered, the woman's face flamed: "No, mister."

It had, in fact, come from the shipyard. Every time a ship was launched the slipways were covered in a mixture of crude soap and engine oil, and after the launch the workmen scooped it into tins and carried it home, with the knowledge of the foremen.

The soap was so strong that it stung the hands. It was fit only for scrubbing floors.

Mary's face paled. She looked from the soap to the man, afraid to meet his gaze, rubbing her hands on the sacking tied round her waist.

"You can get yourself into serious trouble, taking shipyard property," the stranger said, sternly. His voice had the Scots harshness of North Antrim. It was a familiar sound to Mary. Belfast, doubling and redoubling in size, growing in prosperity, was sucking in the coastal people in tens of thousands. Mary herself belonged to a Carrickfergus, Co. Antrim family, only one generation in the city.

The man made to point a finger at Mary, and suddenly noticed the paper in his hand. He cleared his throat: "Is William Condit, hand riveter in the Queen's Island, your man?"

"He's my man, mister, but he never took the soap. My wee girl got it from a woman in the mill."

"For dear sake, missus, I'm not talking about the soap." The man's expression was almost contemptuous: "I'm here to tell you what happened at the White Star boat this morning." He looked again at the paper: "Your man fell off the staging. He fell forty feet."

Mary was still. Her hands fell to her sides.

"He broke his neck." The stranger's eyes were fixed on the wall behind and above Mary's head: "He's dead. He's in the City Morgue."

Her first feeling was one of relief. The man wasn't talking any more about the soap. Then, for the first time since he had come into her house, she looked him full in the face, questioning, searching.

He stood watching her. He kept sucking his teeth, pushing at the dentures with the inside of his lip. Suddenly he turned to the door. Mary followed, her head shaking slightly. At the step he adjusted his hard hat: "You have a boy, they say?" She nodded.

"Usually, when this happens, the first son gets preference. But there's a question here about religion. I can't promise anything." He glanced past Mary through the open door, and saw the tin of soap on the floor. Shaking his head irritably, he walked quickly down the street, buttoning his jacket, not looking back.

Watching him, Mary's hand sought support from the doorpost.

The street was still and quiet, except for the tiny slap of the red, white and blue bunting that hung in rows all the way down to the docks. Immediately outside the Condit's house hung a huge portrait of Queen Victoria. Under it were the words: "God Save Our Queen. No Home Rule."

It was the central feature of the street's Twelfth of July decorations. Ever since Mary and Billy had come to live there, in 1870, fifteen years earlier, they'd hung the Queen's portrait outside their house.

As a reminder.

She had the place to herself. She dug the nose of the scrubbing brush viciously into the pitted scullery tiles, and twisted the cloth so fiercely that it reared in her hands like a snake, until the last drop of water was wrung from it. The scullery didn't need washing. It had been done over half a dozen times since Billy had been taken, in his coffin, to the new cemetery near Glengormley, under the shadow of Ben Madigan. That was a week ago but still the sweet flower scent clung. The whole house was full of the smell of carbolic soap, but still it wasn't enough to drown the camphor from the priest's vestments, the new-varnished pine smell.

Mary stood, rubbing her bare knees to ease the smarting. She opened the yard door and emptied the bucket into the grating. Back in the kitchen she sighed. There was still the fire to be laid.

On the first morning of their married life Billy had laid the fire, and for every day of his life after, he'd made it up for her, leaving the hearth clean and shining for Mary to come down to. She'd never quite grown used to the luxury of it. She was standing, looking at the untidy grate, when there was a light tap on the kitchen door, and Kathleen Johnstone came in.

"You haven't got a wee taste of physic, have you, love?" Kathleen took her usual seat on the sofa, opposite the yard window: "It's wee Tommy," she said, "he's not at himself, and his tongue's all white, like." Her gaze shifted from the window to the dresser by the door, back to the window. She looked down at the ragged, canvas slippers on her feet.

Mary was at the cupboard beside the mantelpiece: "I've some seeney pods left." She handed the other woman a thin, paper bag. As she did so, she glanced shrewdly at her: "What was it you did want, Katie?"

They'd been friends since childhood, working at adjoining looms in the York factory. And one lunch time the two girls had been part of the crowd cheering the Inniskillin Fusiliers, in their brass and regimentals, newly returned from India, marching behind their pipes to Victoria Barracks when, behind them, Billy Condit and Alec Johnstone, on their meal hour from the shipyard, had begun to tease the pair of them.

That had been fifteen years earlier. Now Kathleen, with six children, was Mary's neighbour. Small and stout, with sleeves rolled up and hair in a bun, she could have passed for Mary's sister. In the first years of their married lives the two had many times agreed that they'd been lucky that day on York Street, meeting men who'd brought their pay home, and caused no worry.

Kathleen sighed: "There's more trouble, love."

"What way, trouble?"

The kitchen door from the street opened and Hugh came in. Small, finely built, he had the black hair and brown eyes of his parents. His jersey and knee-length trousers sat neatly on him. The boy sat down beside Kathleen, who gave his ear an affectionate tweak: "There's a wee boy's in for a piece and jam, and then he's wanting straight out again, isn't that right, Hugh?"

Hugh looked from one to the other: "So that's the way of it?" His voice was clear and carrying, like his father's. "That's the way of it," he said, "I've to let yez get on with your talking, have I?"

Kathleen gave the boy a quick hug. "You've a quare wise head on them shoulders," she said.

Mary had cut a thick slice of home-baked bread and was covering it with salted, country butter, bought from farm carts in the street. Hugh came and stood beside her as she spread jam on it, and handed it to him. The boy's eyes sought her's, but she was staring at Kathleen Johnstone a frown on her face. He ran out into the street again.

"It's about Hugh," Kathleen said. "Him going to the Star of the Sea school with the other sort." She was looking down at her hands. "The way you're rearing him, you know?" She stood up and walked to the door. "Alex was told in the shipyard. There's some big man from the Orange coming to see you. I think Alex was told on purpose, with him being a friend of your Billy's. So that it would get to you." She looked down at the senna pods in her hand. "I'll have to be getting back, so I will."

When Hugh came back Mary was still looking at the open door: "Have you finished all your secret talking?" He winked his father's wink. Mary gave a sudden smile and pulled him down on to the sofa. "Are the wee boys in the street leaving you alone?" she asked, tossing his hair, then straightening it.

"Aw they don't bother me," he said, "anyway, they're not annoying me since my daddy died." He squirmed away from her, knelt at the fire. "Do you want me to fix the fire for you?"

He rolled up his sleeves, as tears filled Mary's eyes.

"Excuse me for asking," Mary said, "but how well did you know my man?"

The Orangeman crossed and uncrossed his legs. One leg of his long, white drawers showed, tucked into the top of a thick woollen stocking. He studied his brown boots. "Well," uncomfortably, "I didn't actually know him. Not as a friend, like."

"Do you work in the shipyard, then?"

"No, I'm at the docks, myself. Cross Channel."

He was a well-paid craneman. The Protestants worked the cross-Channel boats, the Catholics did heavier, poorly-paid work at the deep-sea sheds.

"I see. You don't - didn't - know Billy. You didn't work with him, but you're sorry for my trouble. Well, it's very good of you. Mister. Do you live round here?"

"Well, I live down the Shore Road."

"It's very good of you." Mary moved to the door, opened it.

The Orangeman stood. He was angry with himself for feeling awkward, but this woman had taken him by surprise, standing there, quiet and calm. Dignified, even.

She must have been bloody good looking as a girl. It must have been one powerful shock to her people, when she came home and said she was for marrying one of the left footers. He twisted his cap into a crescent, turned it over in his hands: "What I called about was the wee fellow."

This call had been his own idea. To impress the retired colonel who had taken the chair at the District Lodge meeting.

From the Grand Lodge, the colonel was. He'd explained about Gladstone getting in, but needing the 86 Irish Nationalists. So the Government was talking about a Home Rule Bill: "That's if we're stupid enough to let them," the colonel had said. Then he'd explained that it took time for a Bill to become an Act: "It's time we must use," he said.

Later in the meeting the talk had come round to the death of the Catholic hand riveter. Behind hands, it was described as the first Home Rule protest. So, since he'd not known enough to join in the debate about Home Rule, the District Secretary had said that there was a Protestant mother and a Catholic son, and that he'd call and put the mother right on some things. "Sounds like a jolly good idea," the colonel had said.

"Do you not think you should rear the wee fella in your own church?" the Orangeman asked. He was, somehow, standing on the pavement. "I believe your wee girl's Church of Ireland, like yourself. Why not the wee fella, now that...?"

"You mean, now that they've killed his father?"

He unrolled his cap, put it on his head. He was low-set and stocky. His shirt front sat out from his high-buttoned jacket, as though there was an extra garment underneath. "You can't say you weren't warned," he said, and turned to go.

Mary's voice stopped him. "You hadn't the bloody neck to come and say that when my man was alive." Her voice was low, and steady. "You chicken-chested wee blirt ye, he'd have put ye on yer bloody back."

"Go you back and tell the Orange that the whole lot of them put together wouldn't make shitehouse paper for my Billy's arse. Now take yourself off."

Across the street Beeny Mills stood, arms folded high over breasts pushed up by her stays. Beeny's man had been lost when a locally owned ship, half sail, half steam, had foundered with all hands in the North Atlantic two years earlier. Middle-aged, she was childless. After her day in the mill she practically lived at her front door. As the Orangeman walked down the street, mouthing bitter words, Beeny smiled over at Mary. "I don't know what you were saying there, love, but you look as if it was doing you good."

"It was, Beeny, it was," Mary waved as she closed the kitchen door. Once inside, she took the sofa cushions on which the Orangeman had sat, walked with them to the yard, and flung them on to the roof of the shed to air.

Lizzie and Hugh were in the house with Mary when the priest called. It was early evening. Mary had been cutting vegetables for the next day's supper when the knock came. Lizzie, in the long, grey frock run up from cotton remnants that she wore to work, took the scullery duties over from her mother. Hugh was sitting on the sofa, idly drawing on his school slate. He jumped to fetch a chair for the priest, who came straight to the point.

"I was talking to the children in the Star of the Sea today about these Twelfth of July decorations, and pictures of the Queen."

He had the hard, flat vowels of South Armagh. His thighs were thick on the chair. His red neck contrasted with the white of his Roman collar. Dandruff sat on his oily hair, and lay scattered on his shoulders. He glanced to where Mary sat, in a good black dress, by the table. "I see they've honoured you, as usual, with the setpiece of the display." She gave only a dry smile in reply.

"Queen Victoria is described on coins, and on Orange pictures, as the Defender of the Faith. But, as I told the children today - didn't I Hugh? - the Queen doesn't defend the Catholic faith. We must do that for ourselves. That's the reason for my visit, Missus Condit. That's why I'm here. To defend the faith."

There was only the scratching of Hugh's chalk on the slate. In the scullery Lizzie listened, stirring bone and vegetables on the hissing, new-fangled gas stove.

The priest moved irritably. She hadn't even offered a cup of tea. He glanced around the neat room. There wasn't one holy picture, hadn't been, even when Condit had been here. He'd been the independent sort, held his own views on politics, was neither Nationalist nor Loyalist. Went to the Protestant church and took part in the confirmation service for his daughter, knowing that it was against Catholic teaching. There were others like him in Belfast, too. Funny, how the mixing of the two faiths caused this independence of thought in both parties. Odd. It couldn't please the Protestant church, either.

"I've called to make sure that you intend to keep the promise to the Church," the priest said.

"What promise, to what church?"

He sighed: "Your late husband, God be with him, undertook to rear the boy as a Catholic. I'm here to remind you, in these sad circumstances, of his promise, and your duty." His lips tightened. "Do you follow me?"

"Oh Christ aye, I can follow you all right." Mary slapped the top of the mantelpiece in emphasis. "Mind you, before Billy died, I wouldn't have been much good at talking up to men come to see me. But I've had a couple of right specimens in here in the last lot of days, I'm telling you. And you're number three. And between you you've helped me one hell of a lot to follow things."

The priest shot a glance at Hugh, scribbling industriously, and Lizzie, whose head only could be seen, bent over the saucepans.

"I would think you'll likely be the last of the men. There couldn't be any more left in the world like yez. Before the first one called the only man that I could tackle was oul Johnny Millar next door, but he was aisy. All he wanted was to watch me going to the yard. But now? Now, there's no man can frighten me. None."

Mary turned her head towards the scullery: "Lizzie?"

The girl came into the kitchen. She was flushed from the heat of the stove. The black ringlets at her forehead were moist. She was an inch taller than her mother, with the full figure of a grown woman, and the candid eyes of early youth. "Yes, mammy?"

"Tell us again what they did on ye in the mill the day."

The girl gave a resigned smile: "They made me stand in front of the Queen's picture and sing God Save our Noble Queen."

"Did they ill-treat you, girl?" The priest's voice was sharp. Lizzie had come close to Mary. Her mother put an arm around her. "You let me worry about that," she said.

"It's the times we're living in, Missus Condit."

"And just who do you think makes the times, then?"

"I'm not sure I know what you mean."

"Four days ago I had an Orangeman in here telling me it was my duty to rear Hugh as a Protestant. It seems to me that, as far as my family's concerned, it's you and that Orangeman's making the times we're living in."

The priest stood up and walked to the dresser by the door. He felt better on his feet. He stared levelly down at the woman. "My duty is clear. I am here to see that your husband's promise to the Church is kept. It's as straightforward as that. Indeed, I'm surprised that I should have to repeat it, considering the circumstances of Mister Condit's passing."

Mary motioned the priest to the front step. Closing the kitchen door behind her, she jabbed a finger in his chest. His eyes narrowed angrily. "Look you, priest," Mary said, "my man made no promises to any church. The promise was between him and me. We said that we'd keep to our own churches, and that our childer would share in that. You've nothing to do with it."

"Does Hugh stay in the Church?" The priest's eyes were almost closed.

"He does, but only because my man wanted it. And I'll tell you something else we promised. They can either stay in their churches or change churches or give up their churches altogether, now that they're both over twelve it's up to them. It's not up to you or any bloody Orangeman."

The priest nodded. "It's an odd way to bring up children, but my work's done for the present. Good day to you. God be good in your trouble." He walked up the street, tucking the long strands of his hair under the brim of his little, flat priest's hat.

Over at her door, Beeny Mills chuckled, and hitched at her bosom. "One way and the other, you're having the time of it. I seen the time you couldn't have found a word for them big men."

"As you said the other day, it's doing me good," Mary said, closing the kitchen door.

The family sat around the table. The broth things had been

pushed to the one side. Hugh sat where his father had sat.

"Well, wee uns, we'll have to go and live with the Catholics." Mary sipped tea from a thick mug. She looked relaxed. She smiled at the two young ones.

"It'll be a relief going to some other school," Hugh said. "I'm fed up the way everybody looks at me."

"You tell me who's annoying you," Lizzie said, making a fist. "I'll hit them a dig on the gub, so I will."

"What about you and the mill?" Mary said.

"Well, I don't mind singing God Save the Queen," Lizzie said.

"Unless the mill has changed its way of going," Mary said, drily, "you'll be getting the sack if you're up before the Queen's picture any more."

Hugh was trying to keep a straight face: "Do you know what we call the priest in school?"

"No, what?" The two women had drawn together.

"Sure you won't hit me?"

"No, go on."

"Well, we call him oul empty trousers." Hugh's laughter burst out of him, the women squealed their appreciation, and rude, hearty laughter was heard in the house for the first time since the passing of Billy Condit.

"Hugh here'll have to look after us, when we go to live there," Lizzie added, giggling.

Hugh held a fist up: "You tell me who's annoying you and I'll hit them a dig on the gub," he said.

And outside the bolted door, all up and down the street, the red, white and blue bunting, caught in a sudden breeze, danced and chattered and whispered spitefully, as the young, strong city made ready for religious riot and commotion.

The Good Dead In The Green Hills

Bryan MacMahon

Every night it was our custom in Friary Lane to gather into Tommyo's to talk over the many little happenings of the day, piling tiny incident on incident until even such a commonplace thing as a man's crossing from one side of the road to the other could assume an immoderate importance. Tommyo himself was as old as an eagle. He was stone-blind into the bargain. He was also as cross as the bees, but we were inclined to overlook his crossness, especially from the time he bought the beautiful radio.

A wireless, we found, was a great background to our conversation, even if we never gave it the slightest heed. Before the radio arrived our only way of passing the nights was listening to Peadar Feeney telling stories of Ireland long ago. Peadar was old too, a proper crow in clothes he was, but he was a great warrant to eke out his tales - he made "The King of Ireland's Son" last for a full fortnight of nights. I don't know how on earth such a comparison can be relevant, but that tale always made me think of Ireland as a bright, tattered, patched shirt. Three other stories of his I can partly recall: "The Loaf in the Mare's Ear", "The Earl of Banemore" and the "Shower of Old Hags". Those were sound stories enough, with good blood and body to them, but they couldn't hold candlelight to "The King of Ireland's Son". His tales for the most part were reeking with anachronisms, but the skeletons had the authenticity of immemorial age.

We made him tell the stories over and over again, pressing him until such time as he could speak no more for want of spittle. In those days we were very proud of Peadar Feeney.

I'm behind a desk to-day with all the cleverness and the finality of printed papers to buttress me, but the time I'm speaking of, I was a poor perished creature, the blades of my naked shins honeycombed with ABCs, my two knees like two fingers of a mowing machine, my hair cut to the honest glib, and the two brown eyes deep in my skull draining my body of its vitality. Time and again I find myself thinking of Peadar Feeney. He was the man who stuffed my brain with fantasies. Even in this prosaic office I am occasionally horrified to find myself flattening hills and mountains with Iron Buttocks and draining rivers with Denis of the Drought. Those were the characters in the stories we heard from Peadar Feeney in Tommyo's thatched cottage long ago.

But the radio and the story-teller made sorry bedmates. I remember the night the man came to instal the set. I well remember the instant the machine or set or contrivance - we scarcely knew what to call it - leaped to light and life under his deft fingers. Old Peadar listened in stupefaction for a minute or two, then without speaking he rose and went out the door. At the doorpost he looked back at the ring of bewitched neighbours. A strange assortment of ingredients went to the making of the final glance - malevolence and dignity and fierceness and bewilderment and sorrow and enmity and pride. Small as I was on my stool under the cavernous chimney-piece. I had the good grace to appreciate that I had been witness to the end of an epoch.

After that, Peadar never came near Tommyo's any more. God's Gospel - but we didn't miss the man - hadn't we our wonderful versatile radio? At first blind Tommyo was inclined to chafe at Peadar's non-arrival, for the two men were distantly related. Once indeed Tommyo's conscience pricked him to the extent of sending me back to the Lane to Feeney's to invite the old story-teller to come down to listen to the radio. It was dark when I went into Peadar's house. The thatched roof was held up by a series of props, and the place was shrouded in the biting smoke of wet turf, so that I had great difficulty in seeing who was in the kitchen at all. Then, as fortune would have it, the fire yielded a sudden blink of flame, and in the brief moment allowed me I discerned Peadar squatting over the fire - I also saw his queer sister in the corner. She was down on her hands and knees and she was quietly attacking the wall. In common with everyone in the Lane I knew what she was at; she was clawing her way out through the mud wall, striving to break through to the neighbour's fireplace. Each bit of mud she scraped from the wall she placed in her mouth, chewed it until it was thoroughly moistened, then kneaded it with her fingers as children in the kinder-garten knead Plasticine. When she had made a substantial pellet she presently threw it away. In the few steps I walked across the mud floor, my bare soles broke numbers of these marbles.

Into the murk went my message. "Peadar," I said, "Tommyo says to have you come down to listen to the radio." His sister stayed at her scraping, but Peadar's head revolved upon his unmoving body until his face was resting squarely on his shoulder. Over this face was the mockery of a wide-awake hat.

"Spell Constantinople," he asked me.

"I couldn't, man," I said.

"There you are, see! There you are!" I did not break the puzzling silence which followed.

"Who's right, of course," said I, "but what'll I tell Tommyo?"

"First tell him that if the messenger is cold the answer is cold, and secondly tell him that under the watchful eye of the Sweet Man Above" (here Peadar raised his hat) "the Good Dead are alive in the Green Hills. Will you remember that?" he asked.

"I will indeed!" Then he made me repeat the message.

I went back to Tommyo's. "What did he say?" asked Tommyo.

"He said that if the messenger is cold the answer is cold, and that under the watchful eye of the Sweet Man Above the Good Dead are alive in the Green Hills."

Tommyo took the strange message with considerable gravity.

He raised his eyes and said, "A bed in Heaven to them that are gone before us all, and let Him who made us ummake us." He sent for Peadar no more.

In the running of time Peadar's queer sister died and Peadar himself was removed to the County Home which was in a town about twenty-five miles away from us. The poor man was whipped away almost before we knew it; he hadn't made any ins or outs on us for a considerable time previous, and for our part of it we were too much taken up with our beautiful radio to be bothered with him. But after his departure the memory of Peadar gradually achieved the proportions of a legend. An odd night, if our consciences happend to be extra-sensitive, or if the programme on the radio were not to our liking, we'd turn off the knob altogether and sit there by the fire with our two arms as long as one another, for we had lost the fine art of chaffing and conversation. Then, as naturally as anything, in the resultant silence, each person's thoughts would turn on Peadar and we were restless until such time as the blind man mentioned his name. After that it was Peadar this, Peadar that and Peadar the other thing, until we grew astonished at the immensity of his stature in our affection and pride. We began to regret the belatedness of our appreciation and made curious restitution by agreeing that in his day he had been a source of great glory to Friary Lane.

I was sitting at the fire in Tommyo's on the night that we heard that Peadar was dead in the County Home. It was early on a winter's night, about half-past six or so, and there were four or five of us around the great turf fire. Now and again the thunder of workmen's boots went west the Lane. The radio was turned off out of respect for poor dead Peadar, and now and again the dark man raised his hat (the old people always wore their hats inside or out) and spoke softly through the wintry rosebud lips in his beard, "The light of Heaven's candles be on you, Peadar Feeney," and we all chimed in with the Amen. Suddenly the blind man laughed harshly and said, "D'ye remember his message to me? The Good Dead are alive in the Green Hills!" Then all those present began to speak wryly and proudly of Peadar. For once I made bold enough to tell that he had asked me to spell Constantinople. This drew a short laugh from the men which the blind man killed at once. "He was a noted speller," said Tommyo with pride.

Then in ones and two the men of the Lane began to drop in, and the conversation was all about Peadar Feeney. About seven o'clock Big Jim Bruadar pushed his head in across the half-door. He stared at us all for a fierce moment until he was certain that he had the full attention of the gathering. Then, "God's curse on you, Friary Lane," said Big Jim, "to let poor Peadar lie on the slab of the dead-house for three days without a sinner's soul belonging to him to claim his four bones!"

"Is that true for you?" shouted the blind man. "The Relieving Officer will tell you whether I'm a liar or no."

"And do you tell me he's not buried yet?"

"He'll be buried to-morrow unless someone claims him and buries him in his own ground." Here Big Jim swore horribly and added, "And if it's a thing he's not buried at home may God's bitter curse fall on you, Friary Lane."

The blind man stood up. Oh, but it's a dreadful thing to see a blind man and he in his anger. "While I have a red penny," he roared,"I'll see that the man is buried in his own ground."

They sent down town for a hackney driver to arrange about bringing the body home. The hackney driver's father was a native of Friary Lane who had improved himself and gone down into the big street to better himself and his family. The driver himself had inherited the violence and the aggression of the Lane. He strode among the people in the kitchen like a minor king, but I gathered that by inversion he was secretly proud of his connection with the place. Moreover, that he was pleased that by the mere fact of asking him for his car, the people of the Lane had acknowledged the kinship. We all knew that his haggling over the price was perfunctory. When the ritual was at an end it was agreed that Big Jim Bruadar and Jack the Turkey should travel in the car to coffin the corpse and tie it on to the roof of the motor. Big Jim and Jack put on their Sunday coats and went off down town with the driver. Before they went the blind man spoke to them. "Pass up the chapel," said he, "and bring him west the Lane for the last time before ye put him in the deadhouse." That was about half-past seven. When they were gone we began to estimate how long it would take them to get there and back. We reckoned they should be back for ten o'clock - a good hour to go, a half-hour to coffin him and get a few drinks, and an hour to return. The kitchen was well crowded by this time but the conversation was very poor indeed. You see, we had learned to rely on the radio for topics to discuss, and in its absence we felt wholly lost. After a time we began to speak on pigeons - why pigeons I do not know, but that was what we discussed. Then the blind man suddenly remembered the parish clerk (the pigeons in the church belfry must have reminded him), so he sent me down to warn him to leave the dead-house open till ten o'clock or so and to be ready to receive the corpse. The clerk's name was Robby D'Arcy, and he was a man who was easily terrified. "Tck-tck-tck!" he said when I delivered my message, "Such an hour of the night!"

It was fully half-past ten before the coffin arrived. Every motor-car that went east or west the Lane before that brought the younger people among us spilling to the doors in excitement. At last we saw the lamplight gleam in straight lines on the coffin which was tied to the top of the motor-car. We all tumbled out into the street. Immediately it had passed the big three-storeyed houses of Bank Place the vehicle ground down to second gear, and then it purred reverently up the Lane. People began to emerge from all the houses right back along the length of the Lane, men adjusting their old smokey hats and caps and women hurriedly donning their black shawls. As the coffin passed slowly west each person made the Sign of the Cross and threw the dead man a prayer.

As was only natural, the car stopped in mid-road outside Tommyo's and waited for the dark man to come out. When he did so he was bareheaded. His head was cocked up for height and his beard was a proud jut under the street lights. We ringed the car, closing in around the dark man. He groped forward to the motor, then ran trembling fingers up along the polished bodywork until they reached the coffin. One by one the men took off their hats. Tommyo faltered around the car, his fingers all the while flickering on the coffin. That was the loneliness for you. A blind man's fingers on a coffin and a bareheaded ring of poor people underneath the lamplight.

Then Tommyo raised his voice loudly and protestingly, "The

disrespect of it! His coffin to have no mountings!"

The circle of people repeated the work "mountings" as if it had magic and terror in it. Indeed, that was the very first thing we had noticed about the coffin - its nakedness - but no one had dared to put the common thought into words until the dark man had given us a lead. We had chosen the pretence that everything was satisfactory. But the blind man was the wrong man to shield a disgrace. "Take it back to Harrington's," he said, "and tell him put mountings on poor Peadar's coffin."

The car drove up a lane-way off the lane; the ropes on the coffin were loosened and the coffin itself borne in and placed on the carpenter's bench. Old Harrington worked by candlelight. He drove the mountings in without raising the lid. As he worked he kept repeating, "Poor wood! Poor wood! Poor wood!" The crowd stood dumbly about him in the half-light, and whenever they moved, their boots brought up and stored smells of the shavings. The rest of the men and women were out on the passage-way leading to the workshop. Afterwards the men shouldered the coffin down to the dead-house. There was no further need for the motor-car, yet it purred after the people out of respect so as not to leave the little funeral bare and naked in the eyes of the townspeople. The town itself was half asleep as we passed through, and since it was long past the hour for funerals, we must have made a ghostly procession. People out late stopped to cross and gape at our passing. "There's a Laner dead," they said as they recognized the mourners.

The chapel itself was closed, but the dead-house was still open. The parish clerk lived at the chapel gate; he rushed out and lighted the candles as soon as he heard the crunch of the people's boots. He handled the coffin and placed it properly on the trestles. Then he gave out a decade of the Rosary which we all answered. The tiles under my knees were snow-cold. While the prayers were going on I read the legend which ran around the walls. It was difficult to read as it was painted in an old churchy lettering, and its sense was broken by the hiatuses of the windows.

After the funeral, as by common instinct, we mustered into Tommyo's. Since Jack the Turkey and Big Jim had brought back the body they were given places of honour at the fireside. They were urged and lured to tell all about their journey, and despite the fact that they had some drink taken, they narrated every little incident with a thoroughness that was, and still is, a characteristic of the people of the Lane. What the sister-in-charge had said to them; where the coffin had shifted slightly on the roof of the car; the crossroads where the people had lifted their caps to the passing coffin and the cross-roads where the unlettered boors had ignored it; the condition of the porter in the various public-houses they had visited, and so on and so on.

Suddenly the blind man leaned forward and asked them: "What kind of corpse did he make?" This we all knew was a very important question, since families take an especial pride in the appearance of their dead. We were surprised the blind man hadn't asked it long before. At once we noted fumbling on the part of Big Jim, who looked across at Jack the Turkey, but Jack the Turkey made no move towards answering. Big Jim spoke himself when the silence had grown oppressive. "We didn't see him at all. He was coffined when we got there. They went within the black o' your nail o' burying him."

"Bad messengers! Bad messengers!" said the blind man. "You should have asked to see his face."

Jack the Turkey was porter-valiant. "Admitting' we didn't see him - an' what did that signify?"

Up blazed the ready anger of the blind man. "What did that signify? In God's name are ye stumps of fools? How do we know that it isn't an old fisherman from the west ye brought home to us instead of our own Peadar Feeney?"

"Oh?" said all the men in the kitchen, and recovering themselves quickly they tore in like dogs on Big Jim and Jack the Turkey.

"Aye, or an old army pensioner with tattoos on his chest and hands and feet."

"Or maybe a rotten rope of a horse-coper."

"Or a tinker-man after his dirty years in the ditches."

Big Jim and Jack puffed down into a solemn contemplative silence. They would have rebelled, but it was never given down in the story of the Lane that there had ever been a rebellion against the blind man.

The sightless face swung around us pouring scorn on the

messengers. "Before God. I'm blind." he said, "but these here are blinder!"

Nobody spoke for a while. Then, "It isn't too late yet," said Tommyo. "I'll tell you what we'll do. We'll rap up Robby D'Arcy and we'll ask him to open the dead-house and give us one look at the face of the corpse." The way the dark man said it, it seemed the most natural thing in the world.

The blind man had his hand on my shoulder as we trooped through the sleeping streets. He never had need of a stick or a dog while there was a boy to be whistled for in Friary Lane. We came out into the open area before the chapel. There was the spire reaching up into the moonlit sky. Glancing over my shoulder now and again I could see Tommyo's face and chest. For all the world it looked like the figurehead of a ship. The men were clumping steadily behind him.

Robert D'Arcy was long time coming to the door. When he saw who was there, his white face hadn't the courage of saying "Tck-tck!" He looked out of his hallway at the cluster of faces.

He was in his shirt and pants and his feet were bare. The knocking must have dragged him out of bed. Robby was an early riser because he had to ring the Angelus in the morning.

"In the name of the Good God, what is it ye want now?"

Tommyo was stern. "It's the way we want to look at the face of the corpse," he said.

"Tck-tck-tck! Such a thing! And why so should ye want to look at the face of the corpse?"

The dark man spoke. "We're not sure but that it isn't an old fisherman out of the west we have."

"Aye, or maybe an army pensioner."

"Or maybe a rotten horse-coper."

"Or a dirty tinker-man."

Robby D'Arcy was whimpering. "D'ye know what hour of the night ye have at all? What would the new dean say if he heard it?"

"Get the keys of the dead-house," ordered the blind man.

"If 'twas th' ould dean maybe he'd understand ye. D'ye know who ye're dealing with? This is a man out of a college. I don't understand him myself, I tell ye. I'd advise ye to go home with ye'erselves."

"Get the keys of the dead-house, I tell you," said the blind man.

"If 'tis a thing he finds out about it e'll rip ye asunder off the altar a' Sunday. Aye, an' maybe he'll strip the soutane down off my own back."

The glass cross-door behind Robby D'Arcy opened and his wife appeared. She was a woman as tall as the sky. She had an old over-coat thrown across her night things. Her mother was a Sheehy woman from Friary Lane. The wife must have been listening to the conversation through the door, for she said to her husband:

"Get the keys for the respectable men at once." Up cocked the blind man's face towards the woman. Tommyo lifted his hat and said, "A bed in Heaven to you, Martha Sheehy."

"Amen to that," said the tall woman, answering the prayer for her own mother's soul.

Robby D'Arcy sighed and lighted a lantern. We moved down the alley by the side of the chapel between the grey towering walls. We grew terribly lonely even though there was a crowd of us there together. The moonlight came over our shoulders, pierced the iron gate of the dead-house, and tweaked a reflection out of our grand silvery mountings.

The parish clerk placed the lantern on the little altar and opened its window to let the light splay out. Through the back of the lantern the light came through a round window of red glass and made a circle of red on the white marble altar.

We were a long time unscrewing the coffin-screws. Someone had the wit to bring a timber key, and he made fair progress while the others were fumbling with their fingers. When the lid finally came away we were all at pins and points with one another as each side wanted to give the lid to the other side so as to obtain the first view of the corpse. The dark man's side prevailed on the other side, as his many helpers disdained to take the cofffin lid. The parish clerk brought the lantern to the open coffin and then removed the kype from the face of the corpse.

Yes. it was Peadar all right. At first we were doubtful enough about it, but whatever way it was the light shifted it gave him his old face. Not a wisp of doubt about it then; Peadar all right, poor

Peadar who now had the terrible astringency of death and the authentic aristocracy of the corpse. The death-rust was on his lips and in his nostrils. The smell of earth came up and filled the dead-house.

The blind man's fingers were on the dead man's face, recognizing it. Then the satisfied fingers moved down to the habit and rustled it with increasing disdain. "Habit, how are you?" scorned Tommyo. "You could shoot straws in and out through it," Now the angry fingers were on the breast, "No holy picture either," he said, "No tassels!" The light fell on Tommyo's indignant lustreless face. His left hand was on the lining of the coffin. "Ho! Sixpenny cotton and sawdust! God help the poor, the rich can beg!" Then with an intensity as the fingers of the right hand probed deeper into the habit, "Nothing next the corpse's skin. God again help the poor!"

"Tck-tck!" said the parish clerk. "Can't ye be satisfied now that it's Peadar? Can't ye put on the lid and go away for ye'erselves? Ye'll never stop till ye get us all into trouble. It 'twas th' ould dean now...."

Old Tommyo groped backwards and seated himself on a long stool running along the wall. The mouth of the lantern followed him, and since his hat was now removed he was like an apostle. He came to a sudden decision, "One of ye will go up to Martin Meehan's and get underclothes and a decent habit, onc with tassels and a picture on the breast. Also a pair of good brown socks. My work is good for more than that."

Robby D'Arcy was on the brink of crying with exasperation.

"This is too much of a thing altogether. I let ye in on condition that...."

"I'll give out the Rosary while the messenger is gone," said the blind man, groping down on the cold floor and beginning to intone the Creed. One by one men blundered awkwardly down.

When the messenger came back the men took the corpse out of the coffin and placed it on the stool. Someone brought the lantern closer. One thing we saw and we were glad to see it - the corpse had been washed as clean as a dog's tooth and the scapular was round the shoulder. The men dressed old Peadar in the fine underclothing, and over it they drew the grand habit with the picture and the tassels. They put the good brown socks on his feet, and then at last, when Peadar had been replaced in his coffin, it was Tommyo who pulled the new rich kype down over the face and knotted the lifeless hands on his own large rosary.

The parish clerk wasn't sorry to see the last of us. The following day all the people of the Lane mustered to the funeral. One man had left off drawing manure; another had given up grading eggs; another had ceased cutting turf in the bog outside the town; another had stopped plucking chickens in the fowl-yard. Yet another had washed his bloodied hands in a butcher's porcelain trough as soon as he heard the dead-bell banging out from the steeple. The funeral was a good one, even though the clothes of some of the mourners were soiled with dung and feathers and blood. A hundred yards before us walked the priest, his white cypress catching all the light in the dull street. The blind man was directly in front of the coffin. I was in front of him, and again he had his hand on my shoulder. Behind us I could hear the men changing fours frequently and even jostling subduedly for places under the coffin. That, I knew, was the best possible sign of a good funeral. The blind man ignored the halts, with the result that we were soon fifty or sixty yards in the lead walking in mid-road. We found ourselves alone with all the towns-people gawking at us. At first I felt ashamed, then suddenly pride began to choke me when I realized that I was the leader of all those beautiful people.

Author's Biographies

AUGUSTINE MARTIN

Currently Professor of Anglo-Irish Literature and Drama at University College Dublin, Augustine Martin is the author of many books including 'Anglo Irish Literature: A History' and 'The Genius of Irish Prose'. He is an internationally respected authority on both modern and contemporary Irish literature.

JOSEPH O'CONNOR

Joseph O'Connor was born in Dublin in September 1963. He attended UCD where he studied English Literature and History. He graduated in 1986 with a first class honours MA on the work of the Irish Poet Charles Donnelly. He has written for Magill Magazine, The Magill Book of Irish Politics, The Sunday Tribune, Labour Left, City Limits and various other publications. In 1985 he visited Nicaragua for four months, and reported from there for the Tribune and Magill. Thereafter he attended University College Oxford for a time and worked as a fundraiser for the British Nicaragua Solidarity Campaign. 'Last of the Mohicans' is his first work of fiction.

MARY COSTELLO

Mary Costello, was born near Menlough in East Galway in 1963. She graduated from St. Patrick's College, Drumcondra in 1983 and now teaches in Tallaght. She is married and living in Dublin. 'Disappearance' is her first published work.

AISLING MAGUIRE

Aisling Maguire was born in Dublin in 1958. She teaches adults in Community Education Projects. Other stories by her have been included in 'Raven Introductions 4' and 'The Blackstaff Book of Short Stories'.

DERMOT BOLGER

Dermot Bolger was born in 1959. He has published two novels, 'Night Shift' and 'The Woman's Daughter', which have received the AE Memorial Prize, The Macualay Fellowship and other awards. His fourth collection of poetry, 'Internal Exiles' was published in 1986 and he has received the Abbey Theatre's Playwright's Bursary. His play, 'Blinded By The Light', will be performed in Dublin in late 1989.

SEBASTIAN BARRY

Sebastian Barry was born in Dublin in 1955. He read Latin and English at Trinity College, Dublin. He has lived in France, Greece, Switzerland, America and England, and now lives in Dublin.

Books include 'The Water Colourist', (poems) 1983; 'Elsewhere', (children's novel), 1985; 'The Engine of Owl-Light, (novel) 1987; Boss Grady's Boys, (play) 1989. And due in September 1989, 'Fanny Hawke Goes to the Mainland Forever', (poems). Short stories have been published by Stand Magazine, London Magazine, and The Literary Review. Recent poems have appeared in The London Magazine, Stand, Antaeus (New York), Iowa Review, Ironwood (Tucson), and The London Review of Books.

Plays include 'Boss Grady's Boys' at the Abbey Theatre, August 1988, Irish Tour, Spring 1989; revived at the Peacock, Summer, 1989.

Awards include - Arts Council Bursary, 1982; Iowa International Writing Fellowship, 1984; Hawthornden Fellowships, 1985 and 1988;

Irish Exchange Playright, New Dramatists, New York, 1987; Irish Representative at Liege International Biennale of Poetry, 1988;

Elected to Aosdana, 1989; First BBC Stewart Parker Award, 1989.

GABRIEL BYRNE

Gabriel Byrne was born in Dublin in 1952. As an actor he has starred in 16 films including 'Defence of the Realm', 'A Soldier's Tale' and 'Miller's Crossing'. As a writer his stories have been broadcast on BBC and RTE. In 1988 he wrote a regular column for Magill.

AIDAN MATTHEWS

Aidan Carl Matthews was born in Dublin in 1952 and educated at Gonzaga College, University College Dublin and Trinity College; he gained the Teaching Fellowship of Creative Literature at Stanford University, California. At present he is a Radio Producer for Radio Telefis Eireann. His plays include 'The Diamond Body' produced at the Project Theatre, Dublin, 1984, and Exit Entrance, produced at the Abbey Theatre, 1988 and toured to London. His poetry collections include Windfalls, Dolmen: Dublin 1977, and 'Minding Ruth', Gallery Press: Dublin, 1983. His first collection of short stories, 'The Bathyscape', Secker and Warburg 1988 will be followed by 'Muesli at Midnight', planned for 1989.

HUGO HAMILTON

Hugo Hamilton was born in Dublin in 1953. His father was Irish and his mother German. He became involved in journalism and lived in Germany and Austria during the late seventies. He returned to Dublin where he now lives and had been working for some time in the recording business and in publishing. He has published numerous short stories three of which were included in the Faber First Fiction series 'Introduction 10'.

NEIL JORDAN

Neil Jordan was born in Sligo, Ireland in 1950. He is author of 'Night in Tunisia and Other Stories' 1976, (awarded Guardian Fiction Prize); 'The Past' (novel) 1979; and 'The Dream of a Beast' (novel) 1983. He is perhaps better known as a Film maker and director/writer of: 'Angel' (released in USA as 'Danny Boy') 1982: awards include - London Evening Standard Most promising Newcomer Award.

'Company of Wolves', 1984: awards include - London Critics' Circle, Best Film and Best Director.

'Mona Lisa', in 1986: awards include - Los Angeles Film Critics' Award, New York Film Critics' Award, London Critics'

Circle Award, Golden Globe Award, nomination for the screenplay from the Writers' Guild of America.

DESMOND HOGAN

Desmond Hogan was born in Ballinasloe, County Galway in 1951. He has written four novels including 'A Curious Street' (Picador), and 'A New Shirt' (Faber); and two books of short stories: 'The Mourning Thief' and 'Lebanon Lodge', both published by Faber. A collection of his stories 'A Link with the River' is published in America this spring. Hogan teaches creative writing at the American College in London and at the City Literary Institute.

ANNE DEVLIN

Anne Devlin was born in Belfast in 1951. She received a Hennessy Literary Award for short fiction in 1982 and her first collection 'The Way-Paver' was published by Faber in 1986.

She has written several plays for radio and television. Her first stage play 'Ourselves Alone' won several awards including the Susan Smith Blackburn Prize and the George Devine Award. She won the Samuel Beckett Award in 1984.

LINDA ANDERSON

Linda Anderson comes from Belfast and now lives in London. Her first novel, 'To Stay Alive', was shortlisted for the David Higham and Sinclair Prizes. Her second novel, 'Cuckoo', was published by Brandon in Ireland, and by Bodley Head in England. Her stories and poetry have been published in various collections and her first play, 'Charmed Lives', won a prize in the London Writers' Competition 1988. She has recently been Writer-in Residence at Trent Polytechnic, Nottingham.

BERNARD MACLAVERTY

Bernard MacLaverty was born in Belfast in 1943. Following work as a laboratory technician he changed direction to study at Queen's University. Having graduated in English Literature and gained a teaching qualification he and his family moved to the remote west coast of Scotland.

In 1977 his first collection of stories - Secrets and Other

Stories - was published and won the Scottish Arts Council Book Award. His first novel 'Lamb' (1980) won the same award, was runner up to the Guardian Fiction Award, and became a successful film. 'My Dear Palestrina', a 1980 short story was adapted for both tv and radio, winning the Pharic Maclaren Special BBC Award and runner up to the Pye Radio Award.

In 1982 'A Time to Dance and Other Short Stories' won the author a third Scottish Arts Council Book Award.

The novel 'Cal' was published to universal acclaim in 1983 and was made into a major film produced by David Puttnam, screenplay by Bernard MacLaverty. 'Cal' won The Evening Standard Award.

Bernard and Madeleine MacLaverty now live in Glasgow with their four children.

JOHN BANVILLE

John Banville was born in Wexford, Ireland, in 1945. His first book, 'Long Lankin', was published in 1970. His other books are 'Nightspawn'; 'Birchwood'; 'Doctor Copernicus', which won the James Tait Black Memorial Prize in 1976; 'Kelper' which was awarded the Guardian Fiction Prize in 1981; 'The Newton Letter', which was filmed for Channel 4; 'Mefisto' in 1986; and 'The Book of Evidence' in 1989. John Banville is literary editor of 'The Irish Times', and lives in Dublin with his wife and two sons.

EDNA O'BRIEN

Edna O'Brien's first novel, 'The Country Girls' was published in 1960 and since then she has written several novels and short stories including 'Night' and 'A Fanatic Heart'. Her plays include 'Pagan Place', and 'Virginia'. Her next collection of short stories 'Another Time' will be published in 1990.

EMMA COOKE

Emma Cooke was born in Portarlington, Co. Laois in 1934 and was educated at Alexandra College, Dublin. She began writing in the early 1970s and her work has appeared in magazines, newspapers and anthologies in Ireland, Europe, and America. It has also been featured on radio and in 1988 one of her stories was awarded second place in the Francis McManus Short Story Competition.

'Female Forms', a collection of her short stories was published in 1981, her first novel, 'A Single Situation' in 1982. In 1985 her second novel, 'Eve's Apple' was published by Blackstaff Press.

MAEVE KELLY

Born in 1930, Maeve Kelly has written a highly praised collection of short stories, 'A Life of Her Own', and two novels the first 'Necessary Treasons' and the second 'Florries Girls'. She is married, has two children and lives in Limerick.

JULIA O'FAOLAIN

Julia O'Faolain was born in London, brought up in Dublin, educated in Rome and Paris and married in Florence to an American Historian, Lauro Martines. After living for several years in Florence, interrupted by a spell in Oregon, Professor Martines took a job at UCLA, and they now commute between London and Los Angeles. Julia O'Faolain has worked as a teacher (of languages and interpreting) and as a translator. Her books include 'Women in the Wall', 1978; 'No Country For Young Men', 1980, which was shortlisted for the Booker McConnell Prize of that year; and 'The Obedient Wife', 1982.

LELAND BARDWELL

Leland Barwell was born in India in 1928 where her father was working on the Madras Southern and Midland Railways. She grew up in Leixlip County Kildare, and has since lived in London for many years and later in Dublin. She has published three novels, a collection of short stories, two books of poems and a number of plays (radio and stage). By and large her writing reflects the social/political climate of Ireland, especially the sectarian differences between Catholic and Protestant in the South. She was married and has six children. She now lives in Co. Monaghan.

VAL MULKERNS

Val Mulkerns was born Dublin 1926. Her recent books have included 'Antiquities' (1978), 'An Idle Woman' (1980), 'The

Summerhouse' (1984, winner of the Allied Irish Banks Prize for Literature) 'Very Like a Whale' (1986), and 'A Friend of Don Juan' (1988). She has worked as an associate editor, weekly columnist for an evening newspaper, broadcaster, reviewer and occasional lecturer at home and abroad. Between 1987-88 she was appointed Writer-in Residence at Mayo County Library in the West of Ireland where her work-in-progress included another novel.

WILLIAM TREVOR

William Trevor was born in Mitchelstown, Co. Cork. in 1928, he spent his childhood in provincial Ireland. He attended a number of Irish schools and later Trinity College, Dublin. He is a member of the Irish Academy of Letters.

Among his books are 'The Old Boys' (1964), 'The Boarding House' (1965), 'The Day We Got Drunk on Cake' (1967), 'Mrs Eckdorf in O'Neill's Hotel' (1969), 'Miss Gomez and the Brethren' (1971), 'The Ballroom of Romance' (1972), 'Elizabeth Anne' (1973), 'Angels at the Ritz' (1975; The Royal Society of Literature Award), 'The Children of Dynmouth' (1976; Whitbread Award), 'Lovers of Their Time' (1978) and 'The Distant Past' (1979). In 1976 Mr Trevor received the Allied Irish Bank's prize and in 1977 was awarded the CBE in recognition of his valuable services to literature. He has also written many plays for television, and for radio and the stage.

TERENCE DE VERE WHITE

Terence de Vere White, born 1912, is a graduate of Trinity College Dublin. He is a member of Aosdana, The Irish Academy of Letters, F.R.S.L. He resigned from legal practice to become Literary Editor of the Irish Times 1961 (retd.1977). Author of 26 books of which three are collections of short stories, and thirteen novels; he is Vice-Chairman of the National Gallery of Ireland.

BENEDICT KIELY

Benedict Kiely was born in Dromore, Co. Tyrone in 1919 and educated at Christian Brothers School, Omagh and the National University of Ireland. He worked as a journalist in Dublin, 1940-65.

Publications include:

Novels: 'Land Without Stars', 1946; 'In a Harbour Green', 1949; 'Call for a Miracle', 1950; 'Honey Seems Bitter', 1952; 'The Son of a Gambler; A Folktale', 1953; 'There was an Ancient House, 1955; 'The Captain With the Whiskers', 1960; 'Dogs Enjoy the Morning', 1968; 'Proxopera; a Novella', 1977; 'Nothing Happens in Carmincross', 1985.

Short Story Collections: 'A Journey to the Seven Streams', 1963; 'A Ball of Malt and Madame Butterfly', 1973; 'A Cow in the House', 1978; 'The State of Ireland; A Novella and Seventeen Stories', 1980; 'A Letter to Peachtree',1987.

Non-Fiction: 'Counties of Contention' a study of Irish Partition, 1945; 'Poor Scholar' a study of William Carlton, 1948;

'Modern Irish Fiction', 1950; 'All the Way to Bantry Bay', 1978; 'Ireland From the Air', 1985; 'Drink to the Bird' memoirs, (forthcoming).

Edited: 'Penguin Book of Short Stories', 1981; 'The Small Oxford Book of Dublin', 1983.

Awards: American Foundation Award, 1980; Irish Academy of Letters Award, 1980; Irish Independant Literary Award, 1985; D.Litt.(hon.causa), National University of Ireland, and of Queens University, Belfast.

SAM McAUGHTRY

Sam McAughtry, born in Belfast in 1921, came to the attention of the Irish public with his first book, 'The Sinking of the Kenbane Head' which had as its setting the disadvantaged Protestant background of pre-war Belfast. This book, published in 1976, was followed by three collections of short stories, and books on travel and World War II. He was for eight years a columnist in the Irish Times. His radio and TV broadcasts have made him well known on both sides of the Irish Border.

BRYAN MACMAHON

Bryan MacMahon, born Listowel, Co Kerry in 1909, has been by turn poet, balladeer, novelist, short story writer, schoolmaster and lecturer in the US and on the Continent. His pageants have graced national occasions in Ireland while his plays have been produced by the Abbey Theatre, Dublin. He has written for radio and TV and has also written stories for children. His short stories have appeared in most modern Irish anthologies. The National University of Ireland has conferred an honorary LL.D. on him for service to Irish Literature.

His publications include: 'The Red Petticoat and Other stories', 1955, 'The Lion Tamer and Other Stories', 1948, 'Children of the Rainbow', 1952, 'The Sound of Hooves', 1985. 'The Honey Spike', first published in 1967, is re-issued in paperback in 1989, and is also performed at the Abbey Theatre, Dublin.

Acknowledgements

INTRODUCTION © 1989 by Augustine Martin.

THE LAST OF THE MOHICANS © 1989 by Joseph O'Connor. Originally published in The Sunday Tribune. Published here by permission of the Author.

DISAPPEARANCE © 1989 by Mary Costello. Originally published in The Sunday Tribune. Published here by permission of the Author.

SWANS © 1989 by Aisling Maguire. Published here for the first time by permission of the Author.

DRIVING THE MINISTER © 1989 by Dermot Bolger. Originally published in The Sunday Tribune. Published here by permission of the Author.

REFLEX ACTION © 1982 by Sebastian Barry. Originally published in The Literary Review. Published here by permission of the Author.

THE QUIET MAN © 1989 by Gabriel Byrne. Originally published in Magill magazine. Published here by permission of the Author.

THE STRANGEST FEELING IN BERNARD'S BATHROOM © 1985 Aidan Matthews. Published here by permission of the Author.

GOODBYE TO THE HURT MIND © 1989 by Hugo Hamilton. Originally published in The Sunday Tribune. Published here by permission of the Author.

SKIN © 1976 by Neil Jordan. Published here by permission of the Author.

BROTHERS © 1972 by Desmond Hogan. Originally published in 'A Winter's Tale From Ireland', by Gill and Macmillan. Published here by permission of the Author.

THE HOUSE © 1981 by Anne Devlin. Originally published in Argo. Published by Faber & Faber 1986 in "The Way-Paver".